The Corporate Security Professional's Handbook on Terrorism

The Corporate Security Professional's Handbook on Terrorism

Edward Halibozek

Andy Jones

Gerald L. Kovacich

AMSTERDAM • BOSTON • HEIDELBERG • LONDON
NEW YORK • OXFORD • PARIS • SAN DIEGO
SAN FRANCISCO • SINGAPORE • SYDNEY • TOKYO

Butterworth-Heinemann is an imprint of Elsevier

ELSEVIER

Acquisitions Editor: Pamela Chester
Marketing Manager: Marissa Hederson
Project Manager: Jeff Freeland
Cover Designer: Eric DeCicco
Compositor: SPI Technologies India Pvt. Ltd.
Cover Printer: Phoenix Color Corp.
Text Printer/Binder: Sheridan Books

Butterworth-Heinemann is an imprint of Elsevier
30 Corporate Drive, Suite 400, Burlington, MA 01803, USA
Linacre House, Jordan Hill, Oxford OX2 8DP, UK

Library of Congress Cataloging-in-Publication Data
Halibozek, Edward P.
   The corporate security professional's handbook on terrorism/Edward Halibozek, Andy
Jones, Gerald L. Kovacich.
      p. cm.
   Includes bibliographical references and index.
   ISBN 978-0-7506-8257-2 (alk. paper)
1.   Corporations–Security measures–Management.   2.   Private security services–
Management. 3.   Terrorism–Prevention. I. Jones, Andy, 1952- II. Kovacich, Gerald L. III. Title.
   HV8290.H325 2007
   658.4'77–dc22

                                                                                    2007017123

British Library Cataloguing-in-Publication Data
A catalogue record for this book is available from the British Library.

ISBN: 978-0-7506-8257-2

For information on all Butterworth–Heinemann publications
visit our Web site at www.books.elsevier.com

Printed in the United States of America
07 08 09 10 11 12   10 9 8 7 6 5 4 3 2 1

Other Books by the Authors

Information Systems Security Officer's Guide: Establishing and Managing an Information Protection Program, Second Edition, by Dr. Gerald L. Kovacich; July 2003, ISBN: 0-7506-7656-6; published by Butterworth-Heinemann (First Edition: May 1998, ISBN: 0-7506-9896-9; Czech translation of First Edition also available).

I-Way Robbery: Crime on the Internet, coauthored by Dr. Gerald L. Kovacich and William C. Boni; May 1999, ISBN: 0-7506-7029-0; published by Butterworth-Heinemann; Japanese version published by T. Aoyagi Office Ltd, Japan: February 2001, ISBN: 4-89346-698-4.

High-Technology Crime Investigator's Handbook: Working in the Global Information Environment, Second Edition, coauthored by Dr. Andy Jones and Dr. Gerald L. Kovacich; June 2006, ISBN-10: 0-7506-7929-8; ISBN-13: 978-0-7506-7929-9; published by Butterworth-Heinemann (First Edition coauthored by Dr. Gerald L. Kovacich and William C. Boni, September 1999, ISBN: 0-7506-7086-X).

Netspionage: The Global Threat to Information, coauthored by Dr. Gerald L. Kovacich and William C. Boni; September 2000, ISBN: 0-7506-7257-9; published by Butterworth-Heinemann.

Information Assurance: Surviving in the Information Environment, Second Edition, coauthored by Dr. Gerald L. Kovacich and Dr. Andrew J. C. Blyth; published by Springer-Verlag Ltd (London); ISBN: 1-84628-266-7, March 2006.

Global Information Warfare: How Businesses, Governments, and Others Achieve Global Objectives and Attain Competitive Advantages, coauthored by Dr. Andy Jones, Dr. Gerald L. Kovacich, and Perry Luzwick; June 2002, ISBN: 0-84931-114-4; published by Auerbach Publishers/CRC Press.

The Manager's Handbook for Corporate Security: Establishing and Managing a Successful Assets Protection Program, coauthored by Dr. Gerald L. Kovacich and Edward P. Halibozek; April 2003, ISBN: 0-7506-7487-3; published by Butterworth-Heinemann. The book's Instructor's Manual is also available from Butterworth-Heinemann.

Mergers & Acquisitions Security: Corporate Restructuring and Security Management, coauthored by Dr. Gerald L. Kovacich and Edward P. Halibozek; April 2005, ISBN: 0-7506-7805-4; published by Butterworth-Heinemann.

Security Metrics Management: How to Manage the Costs of an Assets Protection Program, coauthored by Dr. Gerald L. Kovacich and Edward P. Halibozek; November 2005, ISBN: 0-7506-7899-2; published by Butterworth-Heinemann.

Risk Management for Computer Security: Protecting Your Network and Information Assets, coauthored by Dr. Andy Jones and Debi Ashenden; 2005, ISBN: 0-7506-7795-3; published by Butterworth-Heinemann.

Dedication

This book is dedicated to all those security, intelligence, law enforcement, and especially military professionals around the world who 24/7 fight those who would take away our freedoms and dictate how we should live our lives.

Contents

Preface

There are those who believe that terrorism is directed solely at governments and those who are to defend against terrorism are government agencies and their military and/or law enforcement personnel. This is a misconception, and one just has to look at the 9/11 attacks, where terrorists went through the airports operated by corporations and through their nongovernmental security systems, boarded commercial aircraft, and crashed them into corporately owned buildings housing corporate employees. Over the years, the kidnappings and killings of numerous personnel throughout the world were company employees, and other company assets were and still are targets for terrorists. They are the "soft targets," unlike fortified military bases and government buildings.

In this book we clarify the difference between terrorism against corporations and their assets and terrorist attacks against government assets. We show that government agencies never have and never will ever have the resources to protect all corporations from terrorists. It is up to the corporations themselves to harden themselves against terrorists—essentially, harden the corporate target. Government agencies work to protect the common infrastructure and the general welfare of the country. *Government agencies also can provide intelligence information—which they must learn to share more openly with corporations than they do now!* But they rely on businesses to help themselves. We address this issue with some proposals for correcting the problem. Furthermore, except for intelligence collectors, government agencies are mostly in a reactive mode. That is, they react *after* an attack occurs. However, since the event of September 11, 2001, this is slowly changing, with government agencies working more proactively and working to partner with the commercial and industrial communities.

Many corporations struggle with balancing the need for expanding into new, global markets with the increased terrorist risks that the expansion brings to some parts of the world. Security professionals are regularly faced with seeking ways to protect people and other assets in potentially hostile environments. From the collective experience of the authors, we know that there are few places where a security professional can go to for help. Having a security tool such as this book, we hope, will be a valuable asset and a trusted tool for security professionals.

In the post–September 11, 2001, world, the reality of terrorism continues to loom heavily over nations, citizens, and corporations. The world is still very much a dangerous place.

As the United States and its allies work to advance democracy around the world, confronting dictators and autocratic regimes, those regimes lacking conventional means to retaliate sometimes do so in unconventional ways. Sponsoring and engaging in terrorism is one of those unconventional ways. Moreover, as Western Civilization expands its influence into areas of the world with a tradition of Islam, resentment often develops among more radical practitioners (extremists) of Islam, generating strife, conflict, and unconventional retaliation through the use of terrorism.

The situation in Iraq, though changing, is likely to remain volatile for years to come. The struggle to transform Iraq into a democratic society could backfire; because the masses are free to make their own decisions, they could move toward a theocracy-based government established on Islamic law. Furthermore, there is still much uncertainty in most of the Middle East and parts of Africa.

Other areas of the world are becoming more volatile as they challenge Western intervention and influence. The expanding influence of radical Islam in Southeast Asia continues to generate conflict. In Central Asia, Iran's quest for a "peaceful" nuclear program threatens Western interests, which may ultimately lead to military action against yet another "Islamic state."

In a more fundamental way, tensions continue to grow between the developed and undeveloped worlds. The growing disparity between rich and poor nations (those who have and those who have not) is likely to spawn pockets of resistance, rebellion, and retribution, manifesting in acts of terror against the developed world and its interests.

International corporations represent, in a highly visible way, the interest of Western Civilization and the wealth of highly developed countries. This makes them potential targets for acts of terror. As corporations continue to expand their business interests, they must reach into areas of the world that offer new markets as well as greater threats.

Furthermore, with the advance of high technology and the proliferation of weapons of mass destruction, the targeting of nation-states that sponsor terror, while necessary, do not address the new targets—the powerful terrorists as individuals, not as part of a nation but as part of a small group or acting alone, such as the Oklahoma City bombing and the recurring attacks by lone bombers. Corporate security personnel are in a better position to address these types of attacks because their focus has always been on defending the corporate assets against individuals or small groups. Therefore, the philosophy is already in place, whereas government agencies usually think in terms of mass armies against which to defend. That bureaucratic mindset, which is necessary to fight terrorism, will take a long time to change, if it ever does.

We also address the growing business of outsourcing some aspects of defending against terrorist threats, such as providing security teams who under corporate contract will extract corporate employees from dangerous environments. This growing business is seldom discussed when the issue of defending against terrorism comes up.

The intent of this book is to provide security professionals and business executives with a better understanding of the threat of global terrorism against corporations and how that may impact them in their roles as executives or the protectors of corporate assets.

Our intent is to offer a book that will help prepare the company executives and the security professionals for operating in the increasingly hostile global business world. We wish to provide them with information that will assist them in the effort to protect corporate assets and people, react to and recover from an inflicted act of terror, and help them better understand what they may expect in the future. We also intend to address the many existing misconceptions regarding how terrorism does or does not affect corporations. All too often security professionals and business executives downplay the threat of terrorism, thereby not properly preparing for such an event, or they overreact and thereby expend unnecessarily resources that could be better utilized elsewhere.

The 14 chapters of this text are grouped into three sections.

- Section I provides an explanation of what terrorism is: its history, who engages in it, and why.
- Section II focuses on helping the security professional develop and implement an effective antiterrorism program in order to better protect the employees and assets of the corporation.
- Section III discusses the future world as it relates to working in a global environment and talks about potential future terrorist group and tactics as well as what the security professional must do to prepare for defending against terrorism.

The primary group this book is aimed at comprises the corporate security professional community and business executives with responsibility for protecting corporate and company facilities, people, and other assets within the global business environment.

The secondary group this book targets comprises the corporate managers who want to know more about this subject, business professors who teach international business courses, and researchers and students interested in the impact of terrorism on doing business in a global environment.

Many books have been written about terrorism and many about corporate security. Few books have been written about protecting corporations from terrorism. Most books written about terrorism and its affects on corporations focus solely on physical security or personal security. A few also focus exclusively on emergency response. None attempt to explain terrorism and its causes and relate that to an understanding of how to develop and implement a holistic, corporate antiterrorism program using the threat assessment model, where the threat agent is the terrorists. Furthermore, few if any books include actual case studies involving acts of terror perpetrated against corporate interests in such a way as to serve as a learning tool for security mangers and business executives. We provide such examples and describe what you should learn from the experiences of others.

Closing Comments

We believe that this book, in the described format and with the identified topics, provides an exceptional foundation for security professionals and business executives involved in developing and implementing a corporate antiterrorism protection program. The material contained in this book was taken from public sources, and under no circumstances was any information obtained or used that fell under the rules of national security of classified information.

This book was developed primarily from the knowledge and actual experience of the authors and their professional friends and associates. Together the authors have a long and experienced record of developing protective measures to help prevent acts of terror along with preparing response and recovery capabilities in the event an act of terror is perpetrated against a corporate interest.

Our intent is to provide the reader with a practitioner's guide (a "how-to" book), augmented by a historical assessment of terrorism and its impact on corporations that should enable them immediately to put in place useful security processes and methods to protect their corporate interests against potential acts of terror while operating in a global environment.

We hope the book meets your expectations. Please let us know if it has helped you and what we can do to make it better in future editions by contacting us through our publisher.

Edward P. Halibozek   *Dr. Andy Jones, PhD*   *Dr. Gerald L. Kovacich*
Los Angeles, California   *Woodbridge, Suffolk*   *Whidbey Island, Washington*
U.S.A.   *United Kingdom*   *U.S.A.*

Acknowledgments

These acknowledgments are the authors' way of saying thanks in writing to all those who assisted and supported us during this project. This section of the book is usually glossed over by readers. However, as authors we believe it is always important to recognize those who have willingly given of their time and expertise to help complete a project successfully. It is no small task to write a book, and one such as this requires the input of others who also are working "in the field" of the security professional, "crime fighter," and antiterrorism expert. Their perspective has been invaluable and we thank them all.

We send special thanks to the following:

- Motomu Akashi, mentor, great friend, and one of the best of the corporate security professionals ever to have protected a corporate asset.
- William C. Boni, Vice President and CISO, Motorola Corporation, one of today's leading 21st-century security professionals.
- Don Evans, InfoSec Manager, United Space Alliance; who is always there to lend a hand, provide advice to the security "rookies," and support a security conference anywhere, anytime.
- Bryan Littlefair, Head of Security Research at the BT Security Research Centre, who has provided friendship and support.
- Debi Ashenden, for the help and sanity on those occasions when it was required.
- George Stephens, retired security analyst and friend.
- Mitchell Zahnow, contingency planner and security professional.

To the staff and project team at Butterworth-Heinemann, Pam Chester, Misty Bergeron, and Jennifer Soucy—the very best of professionals—thanks again for providing great support for another one of our book projects and for having the confidence in us once again to sign us to a book contract.

To those other professionals in the book publishing world of Elsevier's Butterworth-Heinemann who helped make this book a successful and professional product we offer thanks for their help and professionalism. We are grateful to all of them, not only for their support on this project, but also for supporting our other projects over the years.

We of course thank our wives—Phillis Halibozek, Kath Jones, and Hsiao-yun Kovacich—for their continued patience, support, and understanding. They more than deserve our thanks and appreciation for the many years of giving us the "space" to write and the patience for putting up with us.

We also thank you, the readers, who have supported us over the years by attending our lectures and purchasing our books. We hope that our books have added to your body of knowledge and have helped you to be successful in leading the assets protection efforts of your company or government agency.

Introduction

In thinking about security, the need to protect against acts of terror is a relatively new phenomenon. It was not long ago when security professionals did not view the threat of terror as a real and present danger to their corporate assets and interests. As corporations become more global and Western Civilization and business practices enter areas of the world with customs, values, and religious practices vastly different from their own, tension and conflict develops. For corporations or businesspersons with a goal of expanding their markets, conflict is not good, yet it is inevitable.

For the most part, the world is truly a very large marketplace. Operating in that marketplace can be rewarding, economically and culturally, as well as fraught with danger. For security professionals, protecting company assets, in particular, against the threat of terror, the challenges faced could not be greater. Operating outside their host country, sometimes in strange and remote places of the world, security professionals must understand different threats and develop protective measures to mitigate those threats. Often working with limited resources and information, the security professional must find ways to protect corporate assets in high-risk environments.

In this book we hope to provide the security professional and other business executives with fundamental information that will assist them in mitigating the threat against their corporate assets. We have attempted to put together information and methods based on experience and research that will help those charged with the mission to protect us to accomplish that mission in a cost-effective way.

The Global World of Terrorism

This section addresses the background to terrorism and covers what the security professional and the business executive need to know about terrorism. This includes what terrorism is, a short history, a review of significant groups, and attack case histories.

Chapter 1: What Is Terrorism?

This chapter looks at what terrorism is. Terrorism takes many forms, and defining terrorism is influenced by the perspective and situations of the parties involved. In this chapter, acts and methods of terror are discussed, as are reasons for terror. Moreover, the difference between the soldier, the freedom fighter, and the terrorist are addressed. Regardless of how it is defined, in today's world terrorism is real and present. This chapter is meant to assist the security professional and executive management, who ultimately have responsibility for protecting assets, to know and understand their "new" adversary.

Chapter 2: A Short History of Terrorism

This chapter addresses the fact that terrorism is not a new phenomenon. Acts of terror have been committed throughout human history. In this chapter we explore that history, beginning with the earliest uses of terror, up to today's news headlines. Common causes, methods, and purposes are discussed.

Chapter 3: Old and New Groups

This chapter examines the fact that although terrorism can be and has been committed by individuals, it is more often carried out (and most dangerous) when effected by organizations. It explores some of the most active, effective, and dangerous terrorist groups and looks at the how and why of what they do vis-à-vis businesses. This is not intended to be a comprehensive treatise on terrorism—that is not the purpose of this book. The aim of this chapter is to examine some of the more significant and relevant groups.

Chapter 4: Case Studies of Terrorist Attacks

In this chapter, significant acts of terror are examined and the causes and effects of each are discussed. Any pre-event indicators are identified and discussed in the context of better predicting incidents of terror.

▢▢▢
▢▢▢ **1**
▢▢▢

What Is Terrorism?

In these matters the only certainty is that nothing is certain.
—Pliny the Elder (23–79 AD)

Terrorism takes many forms, and defining it is influenced by the perspective and situations of the parties involved. In this chapter, acts and methods of terror are discussed as are reasons for terror. Moreover, the difference between the soldier, the freedom fighter, and the terrorist are addressed. Regardless of how it is defined, in today's world terrorism is real and present. This chapter is meant to assist the security professional and executive management, who ultimately have responsibility for protection of assets, to know and understand their "new" adversary.

Introduction to the Term *Terrorism*

The word *terrorism* originates from the old 18th-century French word *terrorisme* and was used at the time of the French Revolution, during "The Terror" (also known as the "reign of terror"), to describe the state's use of terrorism. The term commonly refers to the calculated use of violence or the threat of violence against a civilian population, with the aim of producing fear, usually for some political end.

Unfortunately, things are rarely that clear. In many cases, terrorist groups will finance their activities through criminal activities such as robbery, fraud, extortion, and illicit drug business. While the aim of these crimes is the furtherance of the "cause" and are carried out by terrorists, they are not in themselves terrorist acts.

A second problem with this concept is that not all terrorism is politically motivated in the conventional sense. Fundamentalist terrorism such as we have seen recently with Islamic fundamentalism is aimed against a culture and a way of life and is targeted not against a single state, although the United States is seen as the epitome of what is identified by them as "evil." The targets of recent fundamentalist attacks have included states led by monarchies, democratic governments, dictatorships, communist states, and even Muslim-dominated nations.

While the term *terrorism* is described in a number of ways, it is commonly held that the characteristic that distinguishes the nature of terrorism is the deliberate and specific selection of the civilian population as the target. The choice of the civilian populace as the target is designed to gain news headlines and to cause public fear, shock, and outrage. The perpetrators believe that this type of activity will gain them the leverage and pressure for the political or religious changes they desire.

3

We've come to this moment through patience and resolve and focused action. And that is our strategy moving forward. The war on terror is a different kind of war, waged capture by capture, cell by cell, and victory by victory. Our security is assured by our perseverance and by our sure belief in the success of liberty. And the United States of America will not relent until the war is won.[1]

Definitions

There is no commonly accepted definition of terrorism, and, though many international organizations and countries have definitions with a lot in common, there are some significant variations. The definitions given next are intended to provide an indication of the range of interpretations with which an international corporation may have to deal.

The first definition, from a 1999 United Nations resolution, states that (the UN):

1. Strongly condemns *all acts, methods, and practices of terrorism as criminal and unjustifiable, wherever and by whomsoever committed;*
2. Reiterates *that criminal acts intended or calculated to provoke a state of terror in the general public, a group of persons, or particular persons for political purposes are in any circumstance unjustifiable, whatever the considerations of a political, philosophical, ideological, racial, ethnic, religious, or other nature that may be invoked to justify them. (GA Res. 51/210, Measures to eliminate international terrorism)*

The following definitions provide a range of national views.

From the United States

It is easy to take the view that terrorism is just that—terrorism, but to do so may be rather naïve. We exist, these days, in a global environment, and many large corporations operate in a number of countries on several continents. In the Western world, we have largely tended to adopt, in the main, a single view of what it is that constitutes terrorism, but this view is not, necessarily the same one that is adopted in other parts of the world, by other nations or cultures.

In the United States, while there is no single, universally accepted definition of terrorism,[2] most of those in use have a common theme. The definition most widely accepted in the United States is the one contained in Title 22 of the *United States Code*, Section 2656f(d):

> *The term* terrorism *means premeditated, politically motivated violence perpetrated against noncombatant targets by subnational groups or clandestine agents, usually intended to influence an audience.*
>
> *The term* international terrorism *means terrorism involving citizens or the territory of more than one country.*
>
> *The term* terrorist group *means any group practicing, or that has significant subgroups that practice, international terrorism.*

The U.S. government has employed this definition of terrorism for statistical and analytical purposes since 1983.

Domestic terrorism is probably a more widespread phenomenon than international terrorism. Because international terrorism has a direct impact on U.S. interests, it is the primary focus of this report. However, the report also describes, but does not provide statistics on, significant developments in domestic terrorism.

Other Definitions of Terrorism Used in the United States

Other definitions of terrorism used in the United States include:

- Terrorism is the unlawful use of force or violence against persons or property to intimidate or coerce a government, the civilian population, or any segment thereof, in furtherance of political or social objectives.—FBI
- International terrorism is a terrorism conducted with the support of foreign governments or organization and/or directed against foreign nations, institutions, or governments.—CIA
- Terrorism is "premeditated, politically motivated violence perpetrated against a noncombatant target by subnational groups or clandestine state agents, usually intended to influence an audience. International terrorism is terrorism involving the citizens or territory of more than one country.—Departments of State and Defense.

Even within the U.S. Army, a 2003 report identified more than 100 definitions in use. Some of these follow:

- In the U.S. Code of Federal Regulations it is defined as "the unlawful use of force and violence against persons or property to intimidate or coerce a government, the civilian population, or any segment thereof, in furtherance of political or social objectives" (28 C.F.R. Section 0.85).
- In the current U.S. national security strategy: "premeditated, politically motivated violence against innocents."
- According to the U.S. Department of Defense: it is the "calculated use of unlawful violence to inculcate fear; intended to coerce or intimidate governments or societies in pursuit of goals that are generally political, religious, or ideological."

Europe

The definitions used within Europe are, in the main, very similar in meaning, which can be seen from the following selected definitions.

In Germany, the definition used is from the Office for the Protection of the Constitution of the Federal Republic of Germany:

> *Terrorism is the enduringly conducted struggle for political goals, which ... [is] intended to be achieved by means of assaults on the life and property of other persons, especially by means of severe crimes as detailed in art. 129a, sec. 1 of the penal law book (above all: murder, homicide, extortionist kidnapping, arson, setting off a blast by explosives) or by means of other acts of violence, which serve as preparation of such criminal acts.*

In Britain, one legal definition states that terrorism is "the use of violence for political ends, and includes any use of violence for the purpose of putting the public or any section of the public in fear."

Australia

The Australian definition of terrorism is taken from the Criminal Code Act 1995, which states:

> *A terrorist act means an action or threat of action where the action causes certain defined forms of harm or interference and the action is done or the threat is made with the intention of advancing a political, religious, or ideological cause.*

Further, the act states that

> *The action is done or the threat is made with the intention of:*
> 1. *Coordinating or influencing by intimidation, the government of the Commonwealth or a State, Territory or foreign country, or part of a State, Territory or foreign country; or*
> 2. *Intimidating the public or a section of the public; and where the action*
>   a. *causes serious harm that is physical harm to a person; or*
>   b. *causes serious damage to property; or*
>   c. *causes a person's death; or*
>   d. *endangers a person's life, other than the life of the person taking the action; or*
>   e. *creates a serious risk to the health or safety of the public or a section of the public; or*
>   f. *seriously interferes with, seriously disrupts, or destroys an electronic system including, but not limited to: (i) an information system; or (ii) a telecommunications system; or (iii) a financial system; or (iv) a system used for the delivery of essential government services; or (v) a system used for, or by, an essential public utility; or (vi) a system used for, or by, a transport system.*

The penalty for other terrorism-related offenses just outlined ranges from 10 years to life imprisonment.

Russia

Following are two Russian views of terrorism, one old and one more recent. When considering these, it is worth keeping in mind the history of Russia during the last century, when it changed from a monarchy, to communist republic, to the center of the Soviet Union, to a single nation state that is moving toward a capitalist economy.

The old view: "Terrorism is politics and practice of terror—frightening of political opponents, in a form of physical violence." (S. I. Ozhegov)

One of the more modern Russian definitions:

> *Terrorism is a tactic of political fighting, which is characterized by the systematic employment of ideologically motivated violence. This violence may take the form of murders, diversions, sabotages, kidnappings, and the other actions creating a threat to life and security of people. (E. Kozhushko)*

A Libyan View

The Libyan leader Colonel Muammar al-Gaddafi, during the period when the country was politically isolated and considered to be a "terrorist state," stated that the term *terrorism* should be reserved for acts such as the 1986 punitive U.S. raid on Libya and that the Rome and Vienna attacks were more properly described as actions of revolutionary violence, armed struggle, or fighting for freedom.

An Egyptian View

A member of the Egyptian Military, General Ahmed Galal Ezeldin, described it in the following way:

> *Terrorism, when translated into Arabic as irhab, is technically incorrect, because the fear of murder, injury, kidnapping, destruction—typical terrorist actions—does not evoke awe toward perpetrators. It is no more than a material fear that can be expressed by the word terror and not awe. Therefore, the correct translation in Arabic for terrorism should be iraab, not irhab.*

Common Features

There are three common features in the definitions just quoted:

1. the use of violence;
2. political objectives, and
3. the intention of sowing fear in a target population.

Academic Research

Two Dutch researchers, Alex Schmid and Albert Jongman, from the University of Leiden conducted research on the subject of terrorism and collected 109 academic and official definitions of terrorism. They discovered that the term *violence* was included in 83.5 percent of the definitions, *political goals* in 65 percent, and some aspect of inflicting fear and terror in 51 percent. The research also showed that only 21 percent of the definitions referred to the indiscriminate nature of the targeting and only 17.5 percent included the victimization of civilians, noncombatants, neutrals or outsiders.

This list may seem exhaustive and repetitive, but it is worth bearing in mind that it is a very small sample of the range of definitions currently in use.

The next section examines a number of the nuances that complicate the matter even further. The first of these is the issue of guerrilla warfare.

Causes of Terrorism

There are a number of reasons why individuals and groups undertake terrorism, some of which are terrorism within the normal definitions and some, which are acts that may cause terror, that do not. The underlying reasons that individuals and groups initiate terrorist activity may be based on any one or more of the following:

- Oppression
- Religious beliefs
- Cultural suppression
- Tribalism
- Hatred
- Retribution or revenge
- Desperation
- Injustice
- Fear
- Poverty
- Enforced political settlements
- Lack of autonomy
- Defending/securing economic status/wealth

Types of Terrorism

Terrorist organizations can be broadly grouped into eight main categories, although the distinction between these groups is not always precise and may also change over time. In addition, terrorism, by its nature, will be either domestic or international. The main categories of terrorism are:

- state terrorism
- nationalist terrorism
- religious terrorism
- left-wing terrorism
- right-wing terrorism
- anarchist terrorism
- pressure group terrorism (eco and animal rights, etc.)
- tribal terrorism

State Terrorism

There are two opposing points of view on this topic, one holding that governments are, by definition, incapable of carrying out acts of terrorism and the other holding that they are. There are two types of state-led terrorism: action by the state against another state and action against its own citizens.

State Use of Terrorism Against Another State

The most common form of aggression by one state against another is that of conventional warfare. This will normally take the form of a clash between conventionally organized and equipped standing armed forces. However, in one case it is the way these "conventional" forces act against the civilian population that will determine whether they are a source of terrorism. Also, during periods of conflict between nations, there may be periods where, in addition to or in place of the conventional full armed conflict, asymmetric or low-intensity tactics are used, which may include guerrilla warfare or terrorism.

Also, within the conventional armed forces of most nations are special forces teams, the role of which is to operate behind "enemy lines" and disrupt the infrastructure through espionage, sabotage, assassinations, and the demoralizing of the populace. These acts may be considered terrorism by the nation on which they are inflicted.

There are also concepts such as the "ethnic cleansing" of sections of a population that has been seen in a number of regions, where it has taken the forms, at one extreme, of the displacement of people from the region to, at the other extreme, the wholesale genocide of a section of the population. An example of ethnic cleansing can be found in the actions of the warring factions in the former Yugoslavia. While the Serbians are accused of the most excessive actions, the Croats also, subsequently, expelled Serbs from Croatia. It is estimated that ethnic cleansing created more than 2 million refugees and displaced persons in the former Yugoslavia during the war in Bosnia and that more than 200,000 were killed in Croatia and Bosnia. More than 10 years after the war, the Red Cross still has records of over 14,000 individuals who are unaccounted for. Actions of this type are carried out with the sole purpose of killing and terrorizing all or a part of the civilian population.

State Use of Terrorism Against Its Own Citizens

State terrorism against its own citizens is normally conducted under the banner of national security and initiated as a short-term measure during a period of instability. It will also normally be supported by state-funded propaganda. Terrorism by the state against its own citizens normally takes the form of the clandestine use of illegal violence designed to intimidate and terrorize either all or one or more groups of citizens, with the intention of preventing them from opposing the state government. The state use of terrorism may involve a wide range of activities at a number of levels and, for example, can come about if the populace believes that due process of law is not being followed or that it is not being equally applied or through one favored group holding undue influence without apparent consequence for their actions.

States widely classed as having carried out terrorism against their own citizens include:

- The Russian Stalinist regime (1934–38)
- Nazi Germany(1933–45)
- Cambodia under Pol Pot (1975–79)
- Serbia under Slobodan Milosevic (1992–99)
- Chile under Augusto Pinochet (1973–90)
- Iraq under Saddam Hussein (1979–2003)
- Romania during the Ceausescu regime (1965–89).

Case Study

The Khmer Rouge communist movement, under the leadership of Pol Pot, overthrew the Cambodian government in 1975. After widespread atrocities against the civilian population, including the systematic extermination of between 1 million and 4 million of the Western-influenced educated and middle classes, the regime was deposed in 1979 following a Vietnamese invasion.

Nationalist Terrorism

The category includes those groups that exist within a country that seek to form a separate state for their own group and try to draw attention to their fight for "national liberation."

Examples of nationalist terrorist groups include:

- Irish Republican Army (IRA)
- Basque Fatherland and Liberty—Euzkadi Ta Askatasuna (ETA)
- Chechen separatists
- Kurdistan Workers Party (PKK)
- Palestine Liberation Organization (PLO)

Religious Terrorism

Religious terrorists use violence to further what they see as some divine purpose. It is worth remembering that religion has played a significant role in a large number of the major conflicts that have taken place in the last 2,000 years. This includes the Crusades, the Holy Wars, Northern Ireland, Israel/Palestine, the conflict in the former Yugoslavia, and, most recently, the Muslim fundamentalist terrorism.

Examples of religious terrorist groups include:

- Al Qaeda, global
- Abu Sayyaf Group (aka Al Harakat Al Islamiyya), Muslim separatists, Philippines
- Egyptian Islamic Jihad, Egypt
- Harakat al-Muqawama al-Islamiya (Hamas) (the Islamic resistance movement), Palestine
- Hezbollah (Party of God), Islamic fundamentalist, Lebanon
- Jemaah Islamiyah (JI), Islamic separatist movement, Indonesia
- Kach (Kahane Chai), radical Jewish organization, Israel
- Moro Islamic Liberation Front (MILF), Islamic movement, Philippines
- Palestinian Islamic Jihad, Islamic militant group, Gaza Strip
- Silent Brotherhood (aka the Bruders Schweigen or The Order), anti-Semitic, United States of America

Left-Wing Terrorism

Terrorist groups that seek to undermine or destroy capitalism or right-wing dictatorships and replace them with communism or socialism are normally referred to as left-wing terrorists.

Examples of left-wing terrorist groups include:

- Baader Meinhof (aka Red Army Faction), Germany
- Red Brigade, Italy
- Red Army, Japan
- November 17, Greece
- Sendero Luminoso, Peru
- Weathermen (aka the Weather Underground Organization), United States
- Revolutionary Armed Forces of Colombia (Fuerzas Armadas Revolucionarios de Colombia), military wing of Colombian Communist Party, Colombia

Right-Wing Terrorism

Right-wing, or neo-Fascist, terrorists aim to destroy liberal democratic governments and replace them with authoritarian regimes. They often claim nationalistic aims and frequently are both racist and xenophobic. In many cases, right-wing terrorists identify with neo-Nazi groups.

Examples of right-wing terrorist groups include:

- Grey Wolves, Turkish exile group based mainly in West Germany
- Ojo Pok Ojo (An Eye for an Eye), Guatemala
- Combat 18, UK
- Aryan Nations (AN), right-wing militant group, United States

Anarchist Terrorism

Anarchists hold the view that all states are founded on violence. Anarchist terrorism was most prevalent in the period from the 1870s to the 1920s. The justification for acts of anarchist terrorism was that such acts would gain publicity for the concept of anarchism (their cause). Present-day anarchists are regularly seen participating with the more violent elements of demonstrations, such as those against the G8, the World Trade Organization (WTO), and the International Monetary Fund (IMF) summit conferences during the last two decades. It should be noted that many mainstream anarchists do not support the use of violence.

Examples of anarchist terrorist groups are:

- The Informal Anarchist Federation, Italy
- The Black Block, widespread
- Freie Arbeiter Innen Union (FAU), Germany
- International Solidarity (Solidarieta Internazionale), southern Europe

Pressure Group Terrorism (Ecological [eco] and Animal Rights, Antiabortion, etc.)

Pressure groups such as the eco-terrorists and animal rights activists have been observed to move to increasingly violent methods to achieve their aims and have also started to target individuals and organizations that are not the direct target. An example of this in the UK is where animal rights activists are now targeting building companies, telephone companies, finance houses, and shareholders in an attempt to prevent the creation of a medical research facility at Oxford University.

Examples of pressure groups that have utilized terrorist tactics include:

- Animal Liberation Front (ALF), animal rights
- Earth Liberation Front (ELF), ecological issues
- Stop Huntingdon Animal Cruelty (SHAC), animal rights
- Operation Rescue, antiabortion
- "Army of God," antiabortion

Tribal Terrorism

While this may be considered a strange grouping in the modern, high-technology world, it still occurs, particularly in a number of regions of Africa.

Examples of Tribal Groups that have used terrorism include:

- Lendu and Hema tribes, Congo
- Tutsis and Hutus, Rwanda
- "Highlanders" (primarily the Tigray and Amhara) and the Anuak and Nuer peoples, Gambella region of Ethiopia

- The Guji ethnic group and the Borena, Ethiopia
- The Sudanese government and Arab Janjaweed gangs and the ethnic Fur, Masalit, and Zaghawa groups, Sudan

Narcoterrorism

The term *narcoterrorism* refers to terrorist acts carried out by groups directly or indirectly involved in the business of illicit drugs. This can include the cultivation, manufacture, transportation, or distribution of illicit drugs. The term is most often applied to groups that use the money from the drug trade to fund terrorism, but it has also been used to refer to those powerful drug lords who are motivated by simple criminal profit and who develop close ties with terrorist groups. This is particularly relevant to terrorist groups such as FARC in Colombia and other, similar groups in Afghanistan and Syria.

Guerrilla Warfare

Guerrilla warfare or revolutions are not normally, in their own right, considered acts of terrorism, unless the civilian population is specifically targeted by the guerrillas or revolutionaries for acts of violence in the pursuit of their political or religious ends. The motive for guerrilla warfare is one of the classifications identified earlier in this chapter. There have been numerous examples of guerrilla warfare in which the citizen has been targeted in order to gain control over the civilian population. One example can be found in the 1980s from a left-wing terrorist group, when the Peruvian terrorist group Sendero Luminoso (Shining Path) became one of the most ruthless guerrilla groups. During this period, approximately 30,000 persons died and the group was reported to have killed or maimed villagers for offenses such as voting in national elections. They also carried out indiscriminate bombing campaigns and selective assassinations. The stated goal of the Sendero Luminoso was to destroy the existing Peruvian institutions and replace them with a communist peasant revolutionary regime. The group was still in existence as recently as 2003, and reports of the number of members of the group vary between 400 and 2,500.

Another example can be found in the case of the terrorist acts carried out by terrorists in Chechnya, who have carried out a number of attacks against Russian civilians. The Chechen separatists have fought for independence from Russia since the collapse of the Soviet Union in 1991. Among the attacks that have been attributed to the Chechen terrorists are:

- The hijacking of a Turkish ferry in January 1996.
- A 1999 spate of apartment block bombings in Moscow and two other Russian cities that resulted in the deaths of nearly 300 people.
- A group that took approximately 700 hostages at a Moscow theater in October 2002. In the ensuing raid by Russian forces to release the hostages, more than 110 of the hostages and most of the terrorists were killed.
- The holding of hostages and the subsequent massacre of over 300 people, mostly children, by 32 Chechen terrorists at a school in the town of Beslan in September 2004.

Freedom Fighters

It should always be remembered that a terrorist in one country or religious or cultural grouping may well be considered a freedom fighter in another. As such, the terms should be considered as interchangeable. History has shown that it is the victor that writes the history books and that, as a result, will define how groups are eventually categorized.

International Terrorism

As discussed earlier, terrorism may be national or international in nature and will fall into one of the classifications defined earlier in this chapter. The majority of the examples given here have been nation-based terrorism; however, the international aspects of terrorism deserve some discussion. Until the end of the 20th century, most of the terrorism that took place was against a nation-state. There was certainly collaboration and resource sharing between terrorist groups in different countries, such as the Irish Republican Army (IRA) in the United Kingdom and the Palestine Liberation Organization (PLO) in the Middle East. There was also overt support of these groups from counties such as Libya and Syria. What has come to prominence in the latter part of the 20th century and the start of the 21st is the rise of international terrorism, where the target of the terrorism is not a country but a belief system and where the perpetrators will attack the holders of the opposing belief system wherever they find a target of opportunity. This is currently manifested in the Muslim religious fundamentalist attacks on the West. While these attacks are carried out in the name of the religion, it is interesting to note that they are conducted in total contradiction of the teaching of the religion.

Summary

In this chapter, the meaning of terrorism has been discussed and a range of definitions examined. The causes of terrorism and the targets of it have been reviewed and a number of case studies have been used. The range in motivation to conduct terrorist acts and the scope of potential targets show that it is possible to be affected by it at almost any time and in any location.

Endnotes

[1] President George Bush, following the capture of Saddam Hussein.
[2] John Pynchon Holms with Tom Burke, *Terrorism: The Complete Book of Terrorist Groups, Their Deadly Weapons, Their Innocent Targets, and Their Terrible Crimes* (New York: Windsor, 1994).

2

A Short History of Terrorism

History is a vast early warning system.
—Norman Cousins

Terrorism is not new. Acts of terror have been committed throughout human history. In this chapter we explore that history, beginning with the earliest uses of terror, up to today's news headlines. Common causes, methods, and purposes are discussed.

Introduction to the Use of Terror

Why use terror methods? Maybe that's because those who employ this tactic find no other way to meet their objectives. A number of groups have been observed resorting to terrorism when they believe that all of the other "normal" avenues, including the use of economics, protest, public appeal, and organized warfare, are unlikely to succeed.

Terrorism may also be used in order to gain or maintain power either by creating fear in the population to be controlled or to demoralize an enemy. The rationale for the use of terrorism will vary depending on the group that is perpetrating it, and may over time also migrate from one of the reasons detailed earlier to another and as circumstances change.

An act of terrorism is, in addition to the reasons just detailed, intended to create maximum publicity for the group involved, for terrorist attacks are both horrific and shocking and are almost guaranteed to gain wide media coverage, both broadcast and print. When more than one terrorist group is acting in an area, it is not uncommon for the responsibility for a terrorist attack to be "claimed" by a number of these groups.

Terrorist Methods

Because of the broad scope of environments and the differing motivations and sizes of the groups involved, a range of methods has been seen in use over time. It is imperative for the security professional who must protect corporate assets against terrorist attacks to understand not only the history and mindset of the terrorists but also the methods they employ. This is important because in establishing an antiterrorist program for your corporation, you must provide defenses that would mitigate the threats and the methods that the terrorists will use against your corporate assets: people, facilities, and information.

The terrorists' methods vary from the relatively crude to the much more complex, including:

- Bombing of civil events or locations
- Suicide bombing and plane or ship hijacking
- Car bombs
- Intimidation
- Assassination, particularly of political leaders
- Letter-bombing campaigns
- Genocide
- Hostage taking
- The use of weapons of mass destruction
- Cyberattacks

Motivation

The motives of terrorists vary, depending on the aspirations of the group. Groups will adopt terrorist tactics if they

- are attempting to attack a government that has an overwhelming superiority in forces.
- feel a sense of injustice.
- exist in an environment of violence created by the government.
- lack the numbers to achieve the level of attention they seek.
- seek to impose a set of values alien to the populace.

Individual groups normally develop a "modus operandi" that will have identifiable characteristics; however, this may change over time as the situation develops or as one technique is found to be more or less effective. This holds true generally, but with increased communications and the sharing of knowledge between terrorist groups, there is increasing commonality in the methods used. Terrorist groups do learn from others and from their own experience, adjusting their techniques and tactics to improve their "modus operandi."

Early Terrorism

It should always be borne in mind that in conflict, history is written by the victor and that, as such, historic accounts of political and military struggles will always be influenced by the outcome.

As explained in the previous chapter, the word *terror* comes from the French Reign of Terror that followed the Revolution of the late 18th century (the term was reportedly coined by the infamous Robespierre). It was reported that during the Reign of Terror, more than 40,000 people died as a result of being sent to the guillotine.

One of the earliest records of terrorism was of a group known as the Zealots, a Jewish group reported to have carried out attacks on members of the Roman and Greek authorities in an attempt to get them to leave.

Another early group that operated the Middle East in the 11th century was the Assassins (from whom the word *assassin* has been taken). This was a group of fanatical Muslims that would murder anyone who deviated from the strict Muslim law.

The Spanish Inquisition

Most people associate the Inquisition with Spain (hence the "Spanish Inquisition"). However, the roots of the Inquisition are in Rome, and the Inquisition was a Roman Catholic tribunal for the discovery and punishment of heretics. The Inquisition was instituted by Pope Innocent III and in 1233 was established by Pope Gregory IX to combat the heresy of a French religious sect, the Abilgenses. Within 20 years it had spread throughout both central and western Europe.

The range of punishments for those found guilty of heresy included the confiscation of property, imprisonment, physical abuse, torture, banishment, and death through being burned at the stake. For those that did not confess, the burning at the stake was without strangulation, while those who did confess were strangled first.

At the start of the Inquisition, it only dealt with Christian heretics. However, by 1242 those of the Jewish faith were being harassed and copies of the Talmud were being burned in large numbers. By 1288, Jews were reported being burned at the stake in France.

The Inquisition in Spain started in 1481 and is reported to have surpassed the medieval Inquisition in both scope and intensity. Tomas de Torquemada became the inquisitor-general for the majority of Spain, together with two Dominican monks, Miguel de Morillo and Juan de San Martin. During the Spanish Inquisition more than 700 Jews were burned at the stake and a further 5,000 repented. In all, more than 13,000 Jews were put on trial during the first 12 years of the Spanish Inquisition, before Spanish Jews were expelled in 1492.

Around 1531, the next phase of the Inquisition began, when the Inquisition was extended to Portugal and affected thousands of the Jews that had fled Spain during the 1492 expulsions. The Inquisition continued in Spain until the late 18th century.

Terrorism in India

In India between the 16th century and approximately 1837, a cult known as the Thugees (aka Phansigars) was thought to be responsible for tens of thousands of deaths. This group was reported to operate by kidnapping travelers to sacrifice them to the Hindu goddess of death and destruction, known as Kali. The group was not thought to have any other motive. The British hanged nearly 4,000 Thugees in the period 1831–37, and the cult was thought to have been destroyed.

The Concept of Modern Terrorism

The beginnings of modern terrorism are thought to be based in the mid-19th century when an Italian revolutionary, Carlo Pisacane, is reported to have theorized that terrorism could deliver a message to an audience and draw attention to and support for a cause. The terrorist of today seeks to achieve exactly the same effects.

Four waves of modern terrorism are described by David C. Rapoport.[1] He calls the first wave the "anarchist wave," which started in the 1880s and continued for around 40 years. The second wave he calls the "anticolonial wave," beginning in the 1920s and lasting until the 1960s. The third wave, called the "new left wave," began in the late 1960s and lasted until the 1990s, with just a few groups remaining in areas such as

Sri Lanka, Spain, France, Peru, and Colombia. The fourth wave, the "religious wave," began in 1979 and, according to Rapoport, is likely to continue for 20–25 years if it follows the pattern of its predecessors.

Examples of terrorist groups from the "first wave" include the Ku Klux Klan, which was created to try to dissuade Reconstructionists after the Civil War, and the Young Bosnians, which assassinated Archduke Franz Ferdinand in Sarajevo in 1914, leading directly to the outbreak of World War I. While it is possible to argue that the Bolshevik revolution in Russia was a first second-wave event, the outcome was that in 1917, an extreme communist state was created and a reign of terror followed in which the Cheka (the secret police) arrested, tortured, and killed all opponents and the tsar and his family were executed.

Examples of terrorist groups from the "second wave" can be found in the Jewish terrorist offensive against British rule between 1945 and 1946, through the bombing of railways, oil refineries, and offices of the British government in Palestine. Other examples include the fight against French rule in Algeria, between 1954 and 1962, insurgency against the French colonial government in Indochina during 1954, and the Palestinians, who, in the 1960s, began to commit terrorist acts of resistance against the Jewish rule of Israel and China, where insurgent forces conducted campaigns against the Kuomintang (Chinese Nationalist Party) regime.

Other regions where anticolonial terrorism took place against British interests were Kenya, Malaysia, and Cyprus. In Indonesia, the Free Aceh Movement (GAM) has fought to establish an independent Islamic kingdom in the province of Aceh, which is located on the northern tip of the island of Sumatra.

Examples of terrorist groups from the "third wave" include groups such as the Red Army Faction and the Baeder-Meinhof gang in Germany, Action Directe in France, the Red Brigades in Italy, the Weather Underground and the Symbionese Liberation Army in the United States, the Red Army of Japan, and the Peruvian Shining Path (Topac Amaru) group.

Most of these groups were actually quite small. For example, it is estimated that the Red Army Faction consisted of only 20–30 hard-core members and approximately 200 sympathizers.

The western European country that had the highest number of deaths during this period was Italy, with nearly 200 deaths between 1973 and 1980. In a concerted effort to control the terrorism, the Italian government had imprisoned around 1,300 left-wing and 240 right-wing terrorists by the mid-1980s. One of the most publicized terrorist incidents during this period was the 1972 murder of 11 Israeli athletes at the Munich Olympics by the Abu Nidal terrorist group, a splinter group of the Palestinian Liberation Organization.

Examples of terrorist groups from the "fourth wave" (religious wave) include the revolution to depose the Shah of Iran, which was considered to be an example of Muslims returning to the fundamentalist teachings of the Koran and resisting Western influence in the Middle East.

In 1984, a group of Israeli religious fanatics was convicted of plotting to bomb the Dome of the Rock in Jerusalem, the third-holiest shrine in the Islamic religion. This attempt was thought to have been carried out to provoke a holy war between Jews and Muslims.

Another example can be found in the United States in 1987, when 14 American white supremacists were indicted for plotting to engage in the indiscriminate poisoning of municipal water supplies in two major American cities.

Sri Lanka, formerly known as Ceylon, is another example. There, the people are Tamil-speaking Hindus who continue to fight for an independent state from the Sinhalese-speaking Buddhist majority.

In Africa, the Sudan has been a war zone almost continuously since it gained independence from Britain in 1954. The north of the country is populated, mainly, with Arabic-speaking Muslims, while the south of the country is populated by black African Christians and Animists. The current government, which is predominantly Muslim (the National Islamic Front), aims to become the first African all-Islamic state and uses Islamic Law and the Jihad to persecute and oppress other religions.

While the four waves of terrorism described earlier show a cycle of development in terrorism, they do not represent the first time that any of the various types have been observed. However, they do show the history of terrorism in the recent past.

In the following sections, terrorism is looked at from regional perspectives. Although this may seem repetitive, it is worth remembering that different religions and types of government in different parts of the world have provided different environments and motivations for terrorism.

European Terrorists

From 1960 onward, European leftists and communists, supported in part by the Soviet Union and Cuba, were the "global terrorists." Subsequently, the Palestinian and Middle Eastern terrorists, which had once played a small part, expanded as the others declined. As with everything in this world, it seems there are cycles, both good and bad.

At a secret terrorist meeting in Lebanon's Baddawi refugee camp in about 1970, a Palestinian terrorist leader was alleged to have said, "Palestine has joined the European Revolution; we have forged organic links with the revolution in the whole world." It is reported that those present at the meeting included:

- The IRA
- The Spanish Basques' ETA
- The German Red Army Faction
- The Italian Red Brigade
- The Iranian National Front
- The Turkish People's Liberation Army
- The Japanese Red Army
- Tupamaros

The Cuban ambassador to Lebanon was also rumored to be present.

The term *terrorism* was defined in Chapter 1; however, let's revisit that term, because we all know that it means different things to different people. As many people have said (including Ronald Reagan), "One person's terrorist is another's freedom fighter."

Terrorism in Ireland

Great Britain claimed the lands of Ireland in 1172 AD. Between then and the middle of 1916, Great Britain ruled the whole of the Island of Ireland. In April 1916, in what became known as the Easter Rising, a small group of revolutionaries, led by Padraig Pearse and James Connolly, captured key sections of Dublin and proclaimed Irish independence. Despite the fact that the uprising was not generally popular among the population and the fact that the revolt was defeated, the actions taken by the British in executing the leaders of the uprising turned the tide of acceptance, and by 1918 a political party known as Sinn Fein had won a majority of the seats in the election.

This political party formed an independent parliament in Ireland and declared independence for the Irish. The military wing of this party, the Irish Republican Army (IRA), then fought a guerrilla action against the British, known as the Anglo-Irish war, which lasted from 1919 to 1921. In 1921, a truce was called that resulted in the Anglo-Irish treaty. This allowed for the creation of the Free Irish State, covering approximately three-quarters of the island, but also allowed for the existence of the province of Northern Ireland, which was to remain a part of the United Kingdom. The retention of this part of the island by Great Britain was a result of a desire by the largely Protestant population of this region to remain within the United Kingdom. In 1949, the Free Irish State formally declared itself the Republic of Ireland and left the British Commonwealth.

The population of Northern Ireland is made up of two main groups, the Unionists and Nationalists. The Unionists, who have historically represented the major part of the population, are primarily Protestants and wish for Northern Ireland to remain a part of the United Kingdom. The Nationalists are mainly Catholics and desire a United Ireland, free from British interference. With the majority of the population being Unionists, most of the government and local government posts were occupied by them, whereas the Nationalist (Catholic) population felt they were being discriminated against.

The Irish Republican Army (IRA) and other groups that splintered from the original IRA started the struggle for the reunification of the island and their independence from Britain in earnest in the late 1960s. A cease-fire that has held to this date was declared by the Provisional IRA (PIRA) in July 1997.

In the period between the late 1960s and the current cease-fire, the paramilitary organizations on both sides of the conflict in Northern Ireland are reported to have killed between 3,000 and 4,000 people, of which the majority were civilians.

There is increasing evidence that despite the declaration of the cease-fire, there has been continuing activity by the PIRA from that cease-fire to the current date. This activity has included punishment beatings, bank robberies, and murders.

Some Notable Atrocities from This Period

Some of the most notable atrocities carried out during this period are:

- **1971:** Northern Ireland. A Catholic mother of 10, Jean McConville, was kidnapped and killed by the PIRA for supposedly giving information to Britain.
- **1972:** Belfast, Northern Ireland. Twenty-two bombs were planted by PIRA at a number of locations around the city. Despite the defusing of a number of the devices, the explosion resulted in the deaths of 9 and injury to a further 130.
- **1974:** Guilford, England. The Guilford Pub Bombing killed five people, four soldiers, and a civilian and left more than 100 injured.
- **1974:** Woolwich, England. A pub in Woolwich was bombed, killing two.
- **1974:** Birmingham. The bombing of two pubs (the Mulberry Bush and the Tavern in the Town) resulted in the deaths of 19 and injuries to more than an additional 180 persons.

- **1981:** London. Two bombs, claimed by the PIRA, killed three and injured a further 39.
- **1982:** Hyde Park, London. A bombing killed two soldiers and seven horses. In Regents Park the same day, seven members of the Royal Green Jackets military band were killed in a separate bombing incident.
- **1984:** Brighton, England. A Hotel bombing killed five in a failed attempt to assassinate the British prime minister at the time, Margaret Thatcher.
- **1987:** Enniskillen, Northern Ireland. The PIRA bombing of a Remembrance Day parade killed 11 people and injured another 60.
- **1989:** Kent, England. Ten Royal Marine Band members were killed and 22 more were wounded in a bombing at their base.
- **1991:** London. The bombing of Victoria Railway Station in London killed one person and injured a further 38. Two members of the PIRA active service unit were also killed when their bomb detonated prematurely.
- **1992:** London, London Bridge Railway Station. A bomb exploded, injuring 29.
- **1992:** London, The Baltic Exchange, a bomb exploded, killing 3 and injured 91.
- **1992:** Omagh, Northern Ireland. Eight builders going to work at a military installation were killed by a PIRA bomb.
- **1993:** Warrington, England. A PIRA bomb exploded, killing two children.
- **1993:** London, England. A truck bomb exploded, causing two deaths and approximately half a billion dollars in damage.
- **1998:** Omagh, Northern Ireland. A bomb exploded in the town center, killing 28 and injuring a further 220.

This list of events is extensive but shows only a fraction of those incidents that were recorded during the 27-year period that is covered. They have been shown here to give the reader some idea of the length of time involved and the damage that occurred over that period.

Middle Eastern Terrorism

While we tend to think of Middle Eastern terrorism as fairly recent phenomena, it is perhaps worth a brief foray into the history books. A paper by Joshua London[2] reported on a meeting in London in 1786 between Thomas Jefferson, John Adams, and Sidi Haji Abdul Rahman Adja, the Tripolitan ambassador to Britain. Jefferson and Adams, the American ambassadors to France and Britain, respectively, met with Ambassador Adja in order to negotiate a peace treaty that would protect the United States from the threat of Barbary piracy. These American ambassadors, both of whom would become president of the United States, asked the ambassador why his government was so hostile to the new American republic. The Ambassador replied, "that it was founded on the Laws of their Prophet, that it was written in their Koran, that all nations who should not have acknowledged their authority were sinners, that it was their right and duty to make war upon them wherever they could be found, and to make slaves of all they could take as prisoners, and that every Musselman who should be slain in Battle was sure to go to Paradise."

As shown in the earlier section dealing with "anticolonial" terrorism, the Middle East has been subject to waves of terrorism since the end of the Second World War and the creation of the state of Israel. Initially, it was by the Jews against the British colonial rule and then later by the Palestinians against the Israeli state. Middle East politics and terrorism itself saw a significant change at the end of the 1960s, when Palestinian groups achieved a number of significant hijackings of aircraft (skyjackings). One of the most infamous terrorist incidents of that time period was the "Munich massacre," which occurred during the 1972 Summer Olympics in Munich, when Palestine terrorists took 11 Israeli athletes hostage. Both the hostages and the terrorists were killed during a rescue attempt. In more recent times, there were more than 70 bomb attacks by Palestinians aimed at Israeli targets since the present conflict erupted in September 2000.

Terrorism in the United States

When we think of terrorism, we do not normally think of it occurring in the United States. However, the United States has experienced terrorism throughout its history and is increasingly the target for terrorist attacks from external groups.

Terrorism occurs as a result of a range of motivations, and though the current emphasis is on fundamentalist-based attacks, in the past America has experienced attacks that were motivated by diverse reasons, from animal rights activism by groups such as the Animal Liberation Front (ALF) to eco-terrorism by groups such as Earth Liberation Front (ELF) to antiabortionism and fundamentalism.

Attacks by groups such as the ELF and the ALF have followed campaigns of civil disobedience, sit-ins, and acts such as individuals and groups chaining themselves to trees and being prepared to use violence and massive destruction to convey their beliefs and principles. This escalation of activity is typical of the background to attacks from most of the groups that undertake terrorist activity.

Between 1973 and 1975, members of the American paramilitary group known as the Symbionese Liberation Army were accused and convicted of carrying out acts of violence, murders, and bank robberies. The group was always very small and is thought never to have had more than 13 members. The most notorious of their acts was the kidnapping of the wealthy media heiress Patty Hearst.

In February 1993, a bomb attack that left a crater 200 by 100 feet wide and five stories deep was carried out on the World Trade Center in New York. The attack resulted in the deaths of five people and thousands of injuries.

Between March and July 1994, there were a number of attacks on logging company equipment in the areas of Snoqualmie Pass and Olympia in Washington State that were claimed by ELF and another group, Earth First.

On April 19, 1995, a large bomb exploded that resulted in significant damage to the Oklahoma City federal building and the death of hundreds of federal employees and a large number of children in the on-site day-care center. The blast occurred on the anniversary date of the Waco massacre and was carried out by Timothy McVeigh.

In July 1996, there was a bomb attack at the AT&T Global Village stage in the Olympic Centennial Park in Atlanta, Georgia, that resulted in at least 100 people being injured.

In October 1996, in Detroit, Oregon, a government truck was set on fire. The attack was claimed by the Earth Liberation Front. In addition, antilogging graffiti were sprayed on U.S. Forest Service buildings and vehicles at the Detroit District Ranger Station.

In January 1997, a Reproductive Services Clinic in Tulsa, Oklahoma, was bombed. The same clinic was also attacked with Molotov cocktails at the start of the year.

In January 1997, a building in Atlanta that houses an abortion clinic was badly damaged by an explosion.

In March 1997, a night watchman interrupted a group of terrorists who had doused the outside of a building belonging to Montgomery Furs of Ogden, Utah, with gasoline. The Coalition to Abolish the Fur Trade claimed credit for the incident on behalf of the Animal Liberation Front.

In 1997, a group of masked Earth First terrorists laid siege to Californian Congressman Riggs' office and threatened his staff. They caused several thousand dollars worth of damage to the facility.

During 1997, there were a number of pipe bombs attacks carried out on federal employees and a waste disposal company in California. The bombs were reported to carry stamps depicting flowers.

One day earlier, on January 25, 1997, children in Vallejo, California, found a back-pack stuffed with 30 sticks of dynamite leaning against a section of the county library that houses police evidence. That bomb, safely dismantled, helped lead investigators to one suspect, police said.

In November 1997, a series of eight letter bomb attacks in the United States were thought to have been carried out by Muslim fundamentalists.

Though not on the U.S. mainland, the October 12, 2000, terrorist attack on the *U.S.S. Cole,* a destroyer ship that was moored offshore while refueling in Aden Harbor, Yemen, was a clear attack on the people of America. Seventeen people died and 39 were injured.

This list covers a period of 27 years, the same as for the IRA in the UK. It shows that terrorist attacks were the result of a range of motivations. Again, the list is far from complete, but it has been included to show that terrorism is not a new phenomenon in the United States.

Recent Events

No account of the history of terrorism could be written without including the events of September 11, 2001. The details are recent and well known, so no attempt will be made here to reiterate them. What was significant in these attacks was that:

- This attack was the largest and most horrific that has been seen to date.
- It was specifically aimed to cause the maximum level of civilian casualties, causing more than 2,630 deaths.
- It was an attack on cultural values rather than directly against a government.
- It was the first time in the West that a large group of suicide bombers had been seen to operate together (although since then, particularly in Iraq, as many as 12 suicide bombers a day have been observed).
- It was well planned over a period of time

Shortly after the events of September 11, there was a second wave of terrorist attacks on the United States. This second wave used the fear of biological agents, including a particularly powerful agent, anthrax. The attacks started with the finding on October 4 of a case of the intentional release of anthrax *(B. anthracitis)* in Florida. By the end of November of that year, 23 cases had been reported (19 confirmed and 4 suspected); most of them could be linked to three anthrax-infected letters sent at some time earlier.

The prevention and control of terrorism have always been almost impossible for any government to achieve, even when the people carrying out the acts valued their own lives. The rise of Muslim fundamentalism, and with it the increase in the number of individuals willing to commit suicide in the name of their cause, has made the problem almost unsolvable. The number of terrorist incidents that actually occur is largely controlled by the use of good intelligence and the vigilance of the authorities.

Countries that Sponsor Terrorism

A small number of governments are considered to be supportive of terrorism and are thought to harbor terrorists. A recent list of these, published by the U.S. State Department,[3] includes the following countries: Cuba, Iran, North Korea, Syria, and the Sudan. A number of other governments, such as Iraq (prior to the overthrow of Saddam Hussein's regime), Pakistan, Libya, and Yemen have also, in the past, been accused of promoting or protecting certain terrorist groups.

Summary

In this chapter the history and the development of terrorism over time has been examined. The motivation of terrorists has been investigated, and the four waves of terrorism that were observed during the 20th century have been reviewed. Terrorism has also been looked at from a regional perspective, examining the different groups and the types of incidents that have occurred. This chapter was intended to give the reader some perspective on terrorism and to indicate the breadth and range of groups and the fact that terrorist attacks can occur anytime and anywhere. That statement is not meant to be alarmist, just to act as a reminder that all organizations can be affected and should ensure that they have considered how they might deal with such an event.

Endnotes

[1] David C. Rapoport, "The Four Waves of Rebel Terror and September 11," *Anthropoetics 8*(1) (spring/summer 2002).

[2] Joshua E. London, "Lessons from America's First War Against Islamic Terror," *NRO 16* (Dec. 2005).

[3] U.S. Department of State, *Country Report on Terrorism, 2004.*

3

Old and New Groups

Throughout history, it has been the inaction of those who could have acted, the indifference of those who should have known better, the silence of the voice of justice when it mattered most that has made it possible for evil to triumph.
—Haile Selassie

This chapter examines the fact that although terrorism can be and has been committed by individuals, it is more often carried out (and most dangerous) when effected by organizations. It explores some of the most active, effective, and dangerous terrorist groups and looks at the how and why of what they do vis-à-vis businesses. This is not intended to be a comprehensive treatise on terrorism—that is not the purpose of this book. The aim of this chapter is to examine some of the more significant and relevant groups.

Old Terrorist Groups

This may seem an interesting title for a section, but it refers to groups that used to exist (and in many cases may still exist) that operated via techniques that are conventionally understood. Some of the more significant domestic and overseas terrorist groups of the 20th century are described next.

Domestic Terrorism—Within North America

Most people believe that until the events of 9/11, there had been very little terrorism within North America. While such incidents have been fairly widely spaced, there has actually been a fairly unbroken string of them over many years. A discussion of the main domestic terrorist groups follows.

Ku Klux Klan

The Ku Klux Klan was established in May 1866, and most of the early leaders were former members of the Confederate Army. An early objective of this white supremacist organization was to prevent black people from voting and to maintain their subjugation, which was achieved through torture and murder. By the early 1870s, the objectives of the group had mostly been achieved and the organization practically disappeared. It resurfaced in 1915 and by the end of the First World War had extended to include all foreigners and in particular Jews, socialists, and communists. The power of the group grew; by the mid-1920s the membership was estimated to be around 4 million and it had achieved considerable political influence, until it was found to be corrupt, which led to its being disbanded in the mid-1940s.

It resurfaced in the mid-1950s to counter the emergence of the civil rights movement, and in the 1960s in the Deep South the lynching of black citizens was still taking place. The campaign of terror during the mid-1960s included, in 1964, the murder of three men, the firebombing of 30 black homes and 37 black churches, and the beating of over 80 of the volunteers of "Freedom Schools." A random lynching took place in 1981 after a jury was unable to reach a verdict in the trial of an African American charged with the murder of a white policeman.

Black Panther Party

The Black Panther Party was initially known as the Black Panther Party for Self-Defense. The group was formed in 1966 and supported Black Nationalism in the United States. The group, which had a left-wing political philosophy, criticized the United States as a racist, capitalist state and believed that the U.S. government and economic structure were oppressing black people. The group developed a list of "Ten Points," which outlined the beliefs and objectives of the group. The list also demanded freedom for all imprisoned blacks, the exemption of black people from military service, and full employment of the black population.

The Black Panther group initially only advocated the use of self-defense tactics. But following the 1968 assassination of Martin Luther King, Jr., the group became increasingly militant and began to offer military training and equip their members with weapons. In 1970, the group was thought to be approximately 2,000 members strong. But as a result of numerous run-ins with police and organization member infighting, the group was no longer operational.

The group was involved in a series of incidents with the police that resulted in the deaths of both police and Black Panther members. These incidents and severe infighting incapacitated the group, and in the late 1960s and early 1970s the leadership either fled the country or went into hiding within the United States. Incidents that the group was involved in included a number of high-profile airline hijackings, during which they forced planes to fly to Cuba, Algeria, and North Korea, where they then requested political asylum. With the collapse of the group, it is thought that some of the Black Panther members went on to join terrorist organizations such as the Black Liberation Army. (*Note*: The New Black Panther group that was formed in the 1990s has no relationship with the Black Panther Party of the 1960s–70s.)

The Weathermen

Created in 1970 by a splinter group of the Students for a Democratic Society, the Weathermen group was initially centered at the University of Chicago and was based on a mix of the philosophies of Karl Marx, Che Guevara, and Ho Chi Minh and had the stated aim of "bringing the [Vietnam] war home." The group was responsible for the bombing of a National Guard headquarters in Ohio, the New York City police headquarters, the U.S. Capitol building, the Queens Courthouse in New York, and a Harvard international-studies center. They are thought to have been responsible for up to another 20 bombings between 1970 and 1975.

In March 1970, an improvised explosive device (IED) that was intended for a military noncommissioned officers' (NCOs) ball at Fort Dix, New Jersey, detonated prematurely at a Weathermen hideout in Greenwich Village, killing three members of the group and injuring two others. One of the final acts attributed to the Weathermen was in 1980, when one of the leaders, Kathy Boudin, was involved with three heavily armed members of the Black Liberation Army in a holdup of a Brinks Security van in New York that resulted in the death of one security guard and significant injuries to another. In their escape from the scene they also ran over and killed two police officers.

Foreign Terrorist Groups—Outside of North America

The groups that are detailed next have affected countries and regions outside of North America, but in many cases the target has been either the citizens or the interests of the United States. Primary targets of U.S. interests have been embassies, military bases, and oil interests. As stated in preceding chapters, groups are considered to be "terrorist" in one area of the world may be considered "freedom fighters" in another. One of the most obvious cases is the one detailed later: the IRA. This group was a designated terrorist group in a country that has been the main ally of the United States for a very long time, yet it received significant American funding and political support during the whole of its active period. This is despite the group's having known and active links to organizations such as the PLO, FARC in Colombia, and countries such as Libya.

Even worse, this was a "religious"-based territorial dispute in a region of a Western nation. How can we possibly start to understand the best way to deal with disputes that are rooted in other cultures and regions? Actions by U.S. agencies and corporations that were supported and encouraged during the Cold War are now proving to be counterproductive in the changed environment where terrorism is no longer regional but truly global.

Provisional Irish Republican Army (IRA)

The Provisional Irish Republican Army (IRA) is thought to have been formed in 1919 and is associated with the partition of Ireland and the creation of Northern Ireland. It has been revived a number of times since then, with the latest period of activity started in 1969. In this latest revival, the main aims of the organization were the restoration of a united Ireland and the removal of the British forces from Northern Ireland. The IRA was the clandestine armed wing of the Sinn Fein political group and operated like a conventional terrorist cell organization. The IRA is thought to have an active membership of several hundred supported by several thousand sympathizers.

The modus operandi of the group was bombing of commercial targets, including the City of London and the center of the City of Manchester. They carried out regular bombings of Belfast city center and a number of locations. They also targeted members of the British Army and prominent political figures. Other activities included assassinations, kidnappings, extortion, smuggling, and robberies. The IRA maintained dominance in the areas of the Catholic population that they claimed to represent by a brutal campaign of intimidation, shootings, punishment beatings, and "kneecappings." The IRA carried out attacks until it agreed to a cease-fire in 1997. As a result of the cease-fire, a measurable decrease in the level of sectarian violence was achieved, although it did not end completely. According to police sources, even with the cease-fire, the paramilitary groups in Northern Ireland were responsible for nearly 80 bombings, 22 deaths, and more than 250 shootings during 1997.

The IRA is known to have had links with Libya, which supplied arms and training. It also received funds, arms, and other terrorist-related materiel from sympathizers residing in the United States. Other links included relationships with ETA in Spain and the FARC in Colombia, where three IRA members were arrested in 2002.

The 1998 peace accord that resulted from the 1997 cease-fire was not universally supported by the IRA; as a result, two radical splinter groups were created: the Continuity IRA (CIRA) and the Real IRA (RIRA).

The IRA is thought to have retained the capability to mount armed operations, and the group was implicated in at least two significant robberies during 2004, one of which involved nearly $50 million.

☐ ☐ ☐ ▬▬▬▬▬▬▬▬▬▬▬▬▬▬▬▬▬▬▬▬▬▬▬▬▬▬▬▬▬▬▬▬▬

"Republican movement" is a euphemism to cloak the illegality of all those proscribed IRA organizations which come under that umbrella term, such as Na Fianna Eireann, the IRA, and Cumann na mBann (the women's grouping). It is not unlawful to be a republican or to express the republican aspiration that Ireland should be unified. Therefore members of those organizations which are illegal use the term "republican movement" to mask their true affiliations.
—*Martin Dillon*

▬▬▬▬▬▬▬▬▬▬▬▬▬▬▬▬▬▬▬▬▬▬▬▬▬▬▬▬▬▬▬▬▬ ☐ ☐ ☐

Euzkadi Ta Askatasuna (ETA)

The Spanish Euzkadi Ta Askatasuna (ETA) was founded in 1959 to establish an independent homeland encompassing the Spanish Basque provinces of Alava, Guipuzcoa, and Vizcaya and the autonomous region of Navarra, in addition to the bordering French Departments of Labourd, Basse-Navarra, and Soule. The political wing of the group, Batasuna, is based on Marxist principles.

The primary activity of the group included the bombings and assassinations of Spanish government officials, politicians, members of the security forces, and members of the judiciary but has also targeted journalists and the tourist industry through bombs in tourist areas.

The group, the membership of which is numbered in the hundreds, has killed nearly 900 people and injured hundreds of others since it started operations in the 1960s. This group does not normally operate outside Spain and France; however, in the past it has operated and some of its members have been arrested in Belgium, Germany, and The Netherlands. The group is supported financially primarily through extortion and robbery and is thought to have received training in the past in Libya, Lebanon, and Nicaragua.

German Red Army Faction

The German Red Army Faction (also known as the Baader-Meinhof Gang) was founded 1967, based on a communist philosophy, and utilized violence to gain attention and support for their cause. In the early 1970s two of the founders of the group, Baader and

Meinhof, attended a terrorist training camp run by the Popular Front for the Liberation of Palestine (PFLP). Following this there was ongoing contact and support with the PFLP. Once the two founders returned from the training camp, they started a violent terrorist campaign of bombings, abductions, and gun attacks. Despite the capture of Baader, Meinhof, and Ensslin in 1972, the group continued to operate, until 1977. And even following the death in jail of all three in 1976, the group continued to operate, until 1998.

Italian Red Brigades

The Italian Red Brigades was formed in 1969 and founded on a Marxist-Leninist philosophy. The group, which advocated violence to achieve its aims, targeted businesspeople and politicians and was a significant terrorist threat during the 1970s and early 1980s. The group eventually lost support as a result of its increasingly brutal attacks, effectively ceasing operations in 1984 when the imprisoned leadership disavowed violence. However, two splinter groups formed: the New Red Brigades/Communist Combatant Party (BR/PCC) and the Red Brigades/Union of Combatant Communists (BR/UCC). The former has specifically stated that it will continue to follow the doctrine and tactics of the Red Brigades.

Hamas

Hamas was a splinter group of the Palestinian branch of the Muslim Brotherhood and was created as a separate organization in 1987. The aim of the group is the establishment of an Islamic Palestinian state within Israel. The group has used both violent and nonviolent means to pursue its goals. Hamas is a loose coalition of groups, with some operating openly through mosques and social service institutions to provide aid to the population, recruit, raise funds and support, and distribute propaganda to others operating as terrorists.

The group, which has an unknown number of activists but tens of thousands of supporters, is based primarily in the Gaza Strip and the West Bank territories. It is supported chiefly by financial donations from Palestinian expatriates around the world and individuals in the Arab states, although it also receives funding from Iran. Additional fund-raising and propaganda activity takes place in Europe and North America.

Palestine Liberation Organization (PLO)

The Palestine Liberation Organization (PLO) was originally formed by the Arab League in 1964 and controlled by the founding Arab states. However, following the six-day war in 1967, Yasser Arafat, a member of the Al Fatah terrorist group, eventually took control. The group officially ceased all violence and terrorism in 1993 with the signing of the Oslo Peace Accord, although one of the groups that existed under the umbrella of the PLO, the Popular Front for the Liberation of Palestine (PFLP), separated from it in protest against the cease-fire agreement and has continued a sporadic campaign of violence. The PLO was a Palestinian umbrella organization dedicated to creating an independent Palestinian nation-state and had an early aim of the destruction of Israel. This view was later modified to one of mutual coexistence, in that the PLO now recognizes Israel's right to exist, but only if an independent Palestinian state also exists on part of the "historic lands of Palestine." Some of the groups that were a part of the PLO included al-Fatah, the Palestine Liberation Front (PLF), the PFLP, and Force 17.

Popular Front for the Liberation of Palestine (PFLP)

The PFLP, one of the groups that formed the PLO, was based on Marxist-Leninist, Palestinian secular nationalist philosophy. The PFLP was founded in 1967 after the defeat of the Arabs by the Israelis in the 1967 Arab–Israeli War. Habash, the founder of the PFLP, saw the Palestinian nationalist movement as part of a broader movement to transform the Arab world along Marxist-Leninist lines. The PFLP became part of the PLO in 1968 and formed a significant faction, with only Al Fatah being larger. Though the PFLP is committed to destroying Israel, it also opposes conservative Arab regimes, seeking to replace them with Marxist-Leninist states.

The PFLP was responsible for a large number of terrorist attacks, including multiple aircraft hijackings, such as the 1970 hijacking of four commercial aircraft that they forced to fly to Jordan, where they landed and eventually blew up the planes after evacuating the hostages. This particular incident led to the "Black September" of 1970, in which King Hussein expelled all Palestinian organizations from Jordan.

The PFLP had connections to the German Baader-Meinhof gang, and in 1976 they jointly hijacked Air France flight 139, which was en route to Paris from Tel Aviv and which they eventually forced to land at Entebbe, Uganda. The raid was a disaster, and the Israeli Special Forces mounted a successful rescue.

It is thought that the decreasing levels of support the group received from the Soviet Union in the late 1970s and early 1980s severely weakened the organization.

The PFLP is still strongly opposed to the peace process with Israel. However, in 1999 the PFLP leadership reconciled with Arafat and his Fatah group in an attempt to increase the group's role and visibility in the Palestinian cause. The PFLP has continued to carry out small-scale operations against Israel, including the assassination of Israel's tourism minister in 2001.

Black September

Black September was a Palestinian organization founded in 1970 after the expulsion of Arab terrorist groups from Jordan. The group had links with the Al Fatah and the PFLP groups and was suspected of being under the control of Yasser Arafat. One of the first acts of the group was the attempted assassination of Wasfi Tel, the Jordanian prime minister. The terrorist act for which the group is most remembered is the massacre of Israeli athletes at the 1972 Munich Summer Olympics.

The group was also responsible for an assassination attempt on the Jordanian ambassador in London in 1971 and the sabotage of a West German power installation and a Dutch gas facility in February 1972. Other actions attributed to the group are the hijacking of a Belgian airliner en route from Vienna to Tel Aviv in May 1972 and the 1973 attack on the Saudi Arabian embassy in Khartoum, which resulted in the deaths of two Americans and one Belgian.

Black September appears to have ceased operations after the March 1973 attack, probably as a result of the changing political pressures in the Middle East. However, it is thought that the Abu Nidal group and the PFLP may have claimed to be "Black September" during a number of incidents in 1974.

Abu Nidal

Abu Nidal, also known as the Fatah Revolutionary Council (a different organization than the Palestinian Al Fatah group) was created when the group split from the PLO in

1974. The aims of the group were the creation of a Palestinian state that would encompass the whole of Israel.

The group is thought to have carried out more than a hundred terrorist attacks on behalf of a number of governments, including Libya, Syria, and Iraq. The group was responsible for some of the bloodiest attacks before the rise of Al Qaeda, and Abu Nidal, the leader of the group, was considered to be "the world's most dangerous terrorist." The most significant attacks by the group included the 1982 attack on the Israeli ambassador to London, which led to Israel's invasion of Lebanon, and the abortive 1985 hijacking of an Egyptian aircraft in Malta, which ended with the plane's being stormed and the killing of the four hijackers. This latter incident resulted in the deaths of 60 of the passengers.

Other significant incidents included the December 1985 attacks on El-Al airline ticket desks in Rome and Athens airports, which resulted in 18 people being killed and a further 120 being injured, and the 1988 attack on the City of Poros cruise ship, which resulted in the deaths of 9 people and injuries to an additional 98.

The group is thought to have been badly affected by internal disputes, and as many as 150 members of the group may have died as the result of these internal conflicts.

Hezbollah

Hezbollah, also known as the Party of God and the Islamic Jihad, was formed in 1982 in response to an Israeli invasion of Lebanon. The group, which is based in Lebanon, is a radical Shia Muslim group and bases its ideology on the Iranian revolution and the teachings of the late Ayatollah Khomeini. The aims of the group are the liberation of Jerusalem and destruction of the state of Israel.

The group has been involved in numerous anti-United States and anti-Israel terrorist attacks that have included the suicide truck bombings of the U.S. Embassy and U.S. Marine barracks in Beirut in 1983 and the U.S. Embassy annex in Beirut in 1984 and the 1985 hijacking of TWA flight 847. They were also responsible for attacks on the Israeli embassy in Argentina in 1992 and the Israeli cultural center in Buenos Aires in 1994.

More recently, members of the group have captured Israeli soldiers, the latest incident being the kidnapping of two soldiers in 2006, which resulted in an Israeli invasion of southern Lebanon and the deployment of a UN peacekeeping force.

The group has its main area of operations in the Bekaa Valley, the southern suburbs of Beirut, and southern Lebanon, but it is know to have cells in a number of countries in Europe, Africa, North America, South America, and Asia. It is thought to have a few hundred active members and several thousand supporters and also has relationships with a number of Palestinian extremist groups, for which it provides guidance and financial and operational support.

The group receives the majority of its financial support, training, weapons, and explosives from Iran and gets additional support from Syria. In addition, Hezbollah obtains further funding from charitable donations and business interests.

Egyptian Islamic Jihad

The Egyptian Islamic Jihad, also known as the *Islamic Jihad,* is an Egyptian Islamic group formed in the late 1970s. Its aims were the replacement of the Egyptian government with an Islamic state and attacks on the interests of the United States and Israel, both in Egypt and abroad. The group's activities have been inhibited by the arrests of a number of its members, most recently in Lebanon and Yemen.

The primary activity of the group has been armed attacks against high-level Egyptian government personnel, including cabinet ministers, and car bombings against Egyptian government and U.S. facilities. In 1981, the group was responsible for the assassination of the Egyptian President Anwar Sadat and in 1993 for the attempted assassinations of Interior Minister Hassan al-Alfi and Prime Minister Atef Sedky. The group has not operated inside Egypt since 1993, although it has carried out or attempted bombings against Egyptian and U.S. embassies in Pakistan and Albania.

The group's main area of operations was Cairo, but it is thought to have had contacts and supporters in Pakistan, Afghanistan, Yemen, Sudan, Lebanon, and the United Kingdom. It is thought to have received financial support from Iran and Al Qaeda and their own front organizations and criminal activities.

Chechen Terrorist Groups

Chechen terrorist groups, such as the *Special-Purpose Islamic Regiment (SPIR)*, came into being around 1994, following the invasion of Chechnya by Russian troops, who were charged with the task of preventing the secession of the Chechnyan Republic. The main aim of the terrorists is the removal of Russian troops and the establishment of an independent Chechnya, and they mainly consider themselves to be irregular forces. SPIR is currently thought to have about 400 activists.

The types of tactics the Chechens have adopted have been, in the main, both brutal and large in scale. Examples of the type of incident for which they have been responsible include the 1994 invasion of a hospital in the southern Russian town of Budyonnovsk, when rebels herded hundreds of civilians into the hospital that resulted in the deaths of over 100 people during the initial rebel assault and ensuing botched Russian commando rescue mission. In 1995, Chechen rebels seized a ferry with more than 200 people aboard; in 2001 pro-Chechen gunmen hijacked a plane en route from Istanbul to Medina. Both incidents ended without major loss of life. In 2002, Chechen terrorists took more than 700 people hostage in a Moscow theater, resulting in the deaths of nearly 130 hostages and more than 40 rebels.

The most significant and memorable attack to date took place with the invasion of a school in the southern Russian town of North Ossetia, where the rebels eventually detonated explosive charges they had set around the school, resulting in the deaths of more than 330 people. A noticeable trend in the latter attacks was the wearing of explosive harnesses by the terrorists and a clear indication that the terrorists were prepared to turn themselves into human bombs. The targets of the Chechens have been almost totally indiscriminate, with attacks on theaters, rock concerts, trains, subways, and aircraft.

Chechen terrorists are believed to have strong links with Al Qaeda and the Jemaah Islamiyah group.

Shining Path (SL)

Shining Path (Sendero Luminoso [SL]), formed by Abimael Guzman in Peru in the late 1960s, was based on a militant Maoist doctrine. By the 1980s, the group had become one of the most ruthless terrorist groups in the Western Hemisphere, and it has caused the deaths of approximately 30,000 people since it started armed operations. After losing ground to government forces in the 1990s, it has more recently been involved in narcotrafficking and kidnapping for ransom, a possible indication of a resurgence.

The aims of the group are the destruction of the Peruvian infrastructure and its replacement with a communist peasant revolutionary regime and opposition to any foreign government influence or interference. It is believed to comprise about 300 armed militants, whose modus operandi has been indiscriminate bombing campaigns and assassinations in Peru, mainly in rural areas.

Tupac Amaru Revolutionary Movement

The Tupac Amaru Revolutionary Movement is another Peruvian group, formed in 1983. Its aim is the establishment of a Marxist regime in Peru.

The most notable attack by this group was the December 1996 attack on the Japanese ambassador's residence in Lima, as a result of which 72 hostages were held for a period of four months until Peruvian forces stormed the residence in April 1997.

The current aim of the group, which has suffered a number of setbacks, including the imprisonment or deaths of a number of its senior leaders, government counterterrorist operations, and a loss of communist sponsorship, is the release of its imprisoned members. It is estimated that the current strength of the organization is approximately 100 members.

Aum Shinrikyo

Aum Shinrikyo is a religious doomsday cult established in 1987 by Shoko Asahara, with the purpose of taking over Japan and, subsequently, the world. The cult believes in the imminent end of the world and also that the United States will initiate the Armageddon by starting a war against Japan. In January 2000, the group changed its name to Aleph and attempted to distance itself from the violent and apocalyptic teachings of its founder. However, in July 2001 some Russian followers of the group, who had planned to set off bombs near the Imperial Palace in Tokyo as part of an operation to free Asahara from jail, were arrested by Russian authorities. The group operates in Japan but has approximately 300 followers in Russia.

The group, which is currently thought to be in decline with a membership of approximately 1,600, is remembered for the 1995 attack on several Tokyo subway trains, when it released the chemical nerve agent sarin, killing 12 people and injuring up to 1,500, and a number of other unsuccessful biological and chemical attacks.

Tamil Tigers

This group is more properly known as the Liberation Tigers of Tamil Eelam (LTTE). The group was formed in 1976, with the aim of establishing an independent Tamil state in Sri Lanka. The group currently holds control over most of the northern and eastern coastal regions of Sri Lanka, where the population is made up predominantly of the Tamil people, as opposed to the rest of the country, where the Buddhist Sinhalese people are the majority ethnic group. The group is thought to have strength of 8,000–10,000 combatants.

The group started to carry out terrorist attacks, including suicide bombings, on government targets in 1983, and in 1984 the Sea Tigers, the naval wing of the Tamil Tigers, was formed. In 1983, in what was seen as the first battle of the civil war in Sri Lanka, they ambushed a military patrol and killed 13 people. Sixteen years later, in 1999, it was estimated that the struggle for independence had claimed as many as 60,000 lives.

The most recent incident this group has been involved in resulted in the deaths of 19 Sri Lankan Navy personnel, who were ambushed in a May 2006 incident.

The type of activities the Tamil Tigers have undertaken has included assassinations, bombings, and a range of other terrorist tactics. The group targets people who do not support their (Tamil Tigers') aspiration for an independent Tamil state and includes police officers and politicians. A cease-fire was negotiated in 2002 and was reconfirmed by both parties in 2006. However, there has been a recent escalation of bombings, and, considering the May 2006 naval incident, it is now believed that there is little likelihood of a long-term peace.

Khmer Rouge

The Khmer Rouge (the party of Democratic Kampuchea), under the leadership of Pol Pot, was responsible for the genocide that killed more than 1 million people during the four-year period in the late 1970s in which it was in power in Cambodia. The group is currently engaged in low-level insurgency activity designed to destabilize the Cambodian government.

Although the main targets of the group's activities are the indigenous villagers, the group has occasionally been responsible for the kidnapping and murder of foreigners traveling in the more remote rural areas. Currently the group is thought to have about 8,000 active members, and its main area of operations is in rural Cambodia, particularly along the border with Thailand.

Japanese Red Army (JRA)

The Japanese Red Army (JRA) was created in or around 1970 by a splinter group of the Japanese Communist League–Red Army Faction. The stated goals of the organization are the overthrow of the Japanese infrastructure, including the government and the monarchy. The group is thought to have links with the Anti-Imperialist International Brigade (AIIB) and the Antiwar Democratic Front. The group also has links with Palestinian terrorist groups, from which it receives most of its support. It is probable that the organization may have cells in other Asian cities, such as Manila and Singapore.

The JRA carried out a series of violent attacks, including the 1972 massacre of passengers at Lod airport in Israel and the hijacking of two Japanese airliners in 1973 and 1977. The group has carried out a number of attacks on American interests, including the attempted takeover of the U.S. Embassy in Kuala Lumpur in 1975. In April 1988, a member of the JRA was arrested while carrying explosives on the U.S. mainland. At the same time another member of the JRA bombed a USO club in Naples, which resulted in the deaths of five people. The group is thought to consist of around 30 active members and an undetermined number of sympathizers.

New Terrorist and Extremist Groups

This section of the chapter examines the new and emerging organizations and considers who they are and how they operate.

Al Qaeda

Al Qaeda was established by Osama Bin Laden in 1988, together with other Arabs who fought in Afghanistan against the former Soviet Union. Bin Laden is a Saudi Arabian citizen from a wealthy family. One of the stated aims of the organization is to unite Muslims against the United States as part of the fight to defeat Israel. Another of its aims is the overthrow of what it considers to be non-Islamic regimes and the expulsion of Westerners and all non-Muslims from what it considers to be Muslim countries. The group's long-term aim is to establish a pan-Islamic caliphate across the world. The group serves as an umbrella organization for many Sunni Islamic extremist groups, including some members of Gama'a al-Islamiyya, the Islamic Movement of Uzbekistan, and the Harakat ul-Mujahidin. The group merged with the Egyptian Islamic Jihad in June 2001 and with the Iraqi Abu Mus'ab al-Zarqawi's organization in late 2004.

The group rose to prominence as a result of the 9/11 attacks on the World Trade Center in 2001 and introduced a new aspect to terrorism in the West—mass suicide bombings. In 2004, the group was responsible for at least 11 attacks that killed over 60 people and wounded more than 225 in Saudi Arabia.

The strength of the group is extremely difficult to determine. They probably have several thousand extremists and associates around the world that support their ideology.

The group is financed through its own moneymaking front businesses and by "donations" from supporters and the siphoning of funds from donations to Muslim charitable organizations. In recent years, international efforts to block funding for the organization are thought to have reduced the group's ability to obtain funds. The groups is based in Saudi Arabia and was based in Afghanistan until coalition forces removed the Taliban from power in late 2001, but it is supported by Sunni Muslim extremist groups around the world. Al Qaeda is now thought to have dispersed into small groups across South Asia, Southeast Asia, the Middle East, and Africa.

The group has been notable for the spectacular and indiscriminate nature of the attacks it has carried out or planned. The types of attacks have included vehicle bombs, infantry assaults, kidnappings, targeted shootings, bombings, and beheadings in the Middle East. Overseas, the attacks have included bombings of aircraft, embassies, hotels and restaurants, military centers, and high-population impact targets as well as high-profile assassinations.

Stop Huntingdon Animal Cruelty (SHAC)

Stop Huntingdon Animal Cruelty (SHAC) was formed around November 1999, with the objective of closing down the UK Huntingdon Life Sciences (HLS) animal-testing laboratory. With a high degree of success the group has employed a wide variety of tactics against HLS and a large number of the companies and individuals that have been supporting them. The tactics have evolved over time and have included fire bombing, physical violence, large-scale vandalism, both verbal and physical intimidation, extortion, theft and burglary, mail fraud, and even identity theft. Examples of the tactics employed by SHAC include the persecution and intimidation of employees of companies that provide supplies or services to HLS.

The aim of these attacks was straightforward intimidation of the supply and finance companies' staffs and their families, who have no direct connection, allegiance, or loyalty to HLS and who are more likely to value a normal life, free of intimidation, than any benefit their employer trading with HLS is likely to provide. SHAC has demonstrated that they are very willing to take extreme measures against anyone who may be able to influence any organization that has or may have dealings with HLS.

One example of this was in January 2000, when SHAC obtained a list of the major shareholders in HLS and mounted a campaign of intimidation against both the organizations (mostly pension funds) and individuals, to put pressure on the shareholders to sell their shares. The method of intimidation they employed was to threaten to publish the names and addresses of all of the shareholders that did not sell their shares and inform the group by a prespecified date, with the implicit threat that, once their names were published, they would become the target of extremists, who would then know who they were and where they lived. SHAC claimed that as a result of their campaign, the share price for Huntingdon Life Science had fallen significantly. The group also targeted the High Street banks and their staffs in the UK to intimidate them into not acting on behalf of HLS. As a result of these intimidation tactics, the Bank of England was forced to step in and act as the bank for the company, a role it does not perform for other companies. Why is this in the domestic terrorism section? The group is active in mainland United States and has taken actions against U.S. domestic organizations to pressure U.S. organizations not to support or deal with HLS.

Another example occurred in 2003, when the third-largest drug company in the United States was firebombed by militant animal rights activists and employees' homes were threatened. A number of pipe bombs were set off outside the headquarters of Chiron Corp. pharmaceutical company. Damage was limited to a few broken windows. The attack was claimed by the "Animal Liberation Brigade," which is believed to be a cell of the Animal Liberation Front. In a communiqué issued to other animal rights organizations, it was stated that Chiron Corp. was targeted because of its ties to drug tester Huntingdon Life Sciences (HLS). The communiqué contained a warning for Chiron that "this is the endgame for the animal killers and if you choose to stand with them [HLS] you will be dealt with accordingly. There will be no quarter given, no more half measures taken. You might be able to protect your buildings, but can you protect the homes of every employee?"

From the start of 2003, SHAC has encouraged activists to take action against Chiron Corp. as part of its anti-HLS campaign. Prior to the attack just detailed, a number of Chiron employees had been repeatedly harassed by militant animal rights activists, including one of the company's vice presidents who had the graffiti "Puppy Killer" scrawled on his car, and another employee who had a number of stuffed dogs painted red left on her front porch.

Animal Liberation Front (ALF)

The Animal Liberation Front (ALF) campaigns for the rights of animals and is described by the North American Animal Liberation Press Office (NAALPO), its legitimate public face, as follows:

> *The men and women of the Animal Liberation Movement pattern themselves after the freedom fighters in Nazi Germany who liberated war prisoners and Holocaust victims and destroyed equipment—such as weapons, railways, and gas ovens—that the Nazis used to torture and kill their victims. Other comparisons would include the Apartheid movement, led by Nelson Mandela, who used and supported violence in the fight for liberation in South Africa, and the current struggle by Palestinians against their Israeli oppressors.*

The aims of the organization are to free animals from enslavement by man. The stated tactics are that "ALF activists will pursue two different types of tactics against animal exploiters. First, they use sabotage or property destruction to strike at their economic heart and make it less profitable or impossible to use animals. Second, in direct and immediate acts of liberation, the ALF breaks into prison compounds to release or rescue animals from their cages."

The ALF and the Earth Liberation Front (ELF) have extremely strong links in the United States, and individuals are often members of both organizations or move between them. The ALF also has strong links with SHAC.

The types of incident that have been attributed to the ALF include the March 2003 arson attack on three Albuquerque, New Mexico, fast-food restaurants. In these attacks, the outlets were firebombed. In the same month the group was also suspected of two arson attacks at California McDonald's outlets. In both of the California incidents, graffiti was found on the building after the incident containing the words "liberation" and "ALF."

Another incident was the February 2003 ALF attack on the trucks of seafood distributors in Chicago. The group issued a communiqué claiming the sabotage attack in which 48 refrigerated delivery trucks were vandalized.

A further example is the August 2002 raid by the ALF on a small Iowa farm, in which between 2,000 and 3,000 domesticated mink were released and abandoned. In a statement after the attack ALF said that they would continue "until every animal confinement operation is empty and every slaughterhouse is burned to the ground" and that "in the fight for the freedom of these animals, all is justified."

Counterterrorism

The activity and investment that have taken place with regard to countering terrorism increased massively around the world in the wake of the events of 9/11. The "war on terrorism" has resulted in new alliances between countries that were previously culturally and philosophically incompatible and has received almost universal political support around the world. The unfortunate aspect of this is that, in some countries, the "war on terrorism" has been used to justify ongoing human rights abuses. Unfortunately, the United States, due to its policy with regard to the prisoners in Guantanamo Bay, has effectively given up any right it may have had to the higher moral ground and to influence over less developed countries. The range of counterterrorist actions that have now been implemented around the world has demonstrated one common theme: a huge increase in the level of international cooperation in the war on terror.

Forecasting Terrorism

With the increase in the level of international cooperation, the level of intelligence that is available to government agencies has increased significantly. As a result, there has been a significant improvement in the ability of governments to track terrorist activity and, as a result, to predict forthcoming attacks. This unfortunately does not flow down easily to corporations, and, other than improved assessments and advice from government, the changes have not significantly enhanced the ability of organizations to predict terrorist attacks that might affect their interests.

Summary

This chapter has examined a number of the most significant terrorist groups, both domestic and overseas. It has looked at the type of activities these groups have undertaken and tried to determine the reason for the existence of each group and its aspirations. The themes that have evolved are that terrorism has become increasingly globalized and that a group that seeks to put pressure on a government in one region of the world may take action many thousands of miles away. The trends have been for terrorist acts to be increasingly more spectacular and violent and also, because we have experienced an upsurge of Muslim fundamentalism over the last decade or so, a propensity for suicide bombings, where the bomber who delivers the payload to the target is also willing to die.

Useful Terrorism Resources

The following list of resources is intended for guidance only and makes no pretense at being comprehensive. It is in no particular order.

- Center for Defense Information, http://www.cdi.org/terrorism/terrorist.cfm
- Naval Postgraduate School, http://library.nps.navy.mil/home/tgp/tgpndx.htm
- Patterns of Global Terrorism Report, http://www.state.gov/s/ct/rls/pgtrpt/
- Wikipedia—list of terrorist organizations, http://en.wikipedia.org/wiki/Terrorist_group
- Council on Foreign Relations, http://www.cfr.org/publication/
- Terrorism Research Center, Inc, http://www.terrorism.com/modules.php?op=modload&name=TGroups&file=index
- Memorial Institute for the Prevention of Terrorism (MIPT) Terrorism Knowledge Base, http://www.tkb.org/Group.jsp?groupID=183
- Federation of American Scientists, http://www.fas.org/irp/world/para/index.html
- MILNET: terrorist group profiles, http://www.milnet.com/tgp/tgpndx2.htm
- UK Home Office, http://www.homeoffice.gov.uk/security/terrorism-and-the-law/terrorism-act/proscribed-groups?version=1
- South Asia Terrorism Portal, http://www.satp.org/
- Simply Tah-Chee website, http://www.simplytaty.com/broadenpages/terroristgroups.htm
- The Rand Organization, http://www.rand.org/pubs/monograph_reports/MR1782/MR1782.pdf

Case Studies of Terrorist Attacks

Prosperity is a great teacher; adversity a greater.
—William Hazlitt

In this chapter, significant acts of terror are examined. The causes and effects of each are discussed. Any pre-event indicators are identified and discussed in the context of better predicting incidents of terror.

A report from the RAND organization[1] identified a number of trends that have become apparent:

1. Terrorism has become bloodier.
2. Terrorists have developed new financial resources, so they are less dependent on state sponsors.
3. Terrorists have evolved new models of organization.
4. Terrorists can now wage global campaigns.
5. Terrorists have effectively exploited new communications technologies.
6. Some terrorists have moved beyond tactics to strategy, although none of them have achieved their stated long-range goals.

Some of these observations are highlighted in the incidents that are detailed in what follows.

Attacks Against Nations

Terrorist attacks have occurred internationally.

United States

The first three items discussed next were attacks on the United States and its personnel and interests, but they took place in the Middle East and Europe.

In April 1983, a large vehicle packed with high explosives was driven into the U.S. embassy compound in Beirut, where it exploded, killing 63 people. Six months later, in October 1983, a truck loaded with approximately 2,500 pounds of TNT was driven through the main gate of the U.S. Marine Corps headquarters in Beirut and exploded, resulting in the deaths of 241 and injuries to 60 U.S. service personnel. At almost the same time a second attack took place on the French headquarters, causing the deaths of 58 French service personnel and one civilian and injury to 15 other service people. These two attacks were claimed by a number of radical Shiite Muslim groups, including the Free Islamic Revolutionary Movement; however, U.S. sources believe the attacks were probably by the terrorist group Hezbollah.

In August 1985, a VW loaded with explosives was driven into the main gates of the U.S. Air Force Base at Rhein am Main, Germany, resulting in the deaths of 22 people.

On October 7, 1985, the cruise ship *Achille Lauro* was hijacked by a group of four men claiming to be members of the Palestinian Liberation Front, who singled out and executed an American passenger in a wheelchair, Leon Klinghoffer.

The motivation for the hijacking was as part of a "negotiation" for the release of Palestinian prisoners from Israeli prisons. (*Note*: The suspected leader of the hijackers escaped capture but was convicted "in absentia" and finally captured in Iraq in 2003.)

On April 19, 1995, the terrorist bombing of the Alfred P. Murrah federal building in Oklahoma City took place. The building was a U.S. government office complex in the downtown area of Oklahoma City, Oklahoma, and the bomb caused massive damage to the building and the deaths of 168 people. The attack was attributed to two U.S. citizens, Timothy McVeigh and his friend Terry Nichols, and has been classified as the deadliest domestic terrorist attack in the history of the United States. Until 9/11, it was also the deadliest act of terrorism to take place within the borders of the United States. The two men arrested and convicted for the attack had sympathies with an antigovernment militia movement, and one of the men, Timothy McVeigh, later claimed that the attack was in revenge for the actions taken by federal officers at the siege at Waco, Texas.

On September 11, 2001 (9/11), a series of coordinated terrorist attacks took place on predominantly civilian targets in New York City. Nineteen terrorists, who belonged to the Al Qaeda terrorist group, hijacked four commercial passenger airliners, and the four planes were then crashed into their respective targets: Two planes crashed into the twin towers of the World Trade Center in New York City (one into each tower), causing both towers to collapse. The third plane crashed into the Pentagon in Arlington County, Virginia. On the fourth plane, the passengers and members of the flight crew attempted to regain control of the plane. As a consequence of this action, it subsequently crashed into a field in Somerset County, Pennsylvania. As a result of the attacks, nearly 3,000 people died, including the 246 passengers on the four planes, 2,605 people in the twin towers of the World Trade Center and on the ground around it in New York City, and 125 at the Pentagon.

Al Qaeda claimed responsibility for the attack, as an attack on the interests of the United States and the West. In a statement from Osama bin Laden, the leader of Al Qaeda, which was contained in a video, he claimed that "terrorism against America deserves to be praised because it was a response to injustice, aimed at forcing America to stop its support for Israel, which kills our people."

In February 2006, three Muslim men from the Middle East were charged with plotting terrorist attacks against U.S. and coalition troops in Iraq and other countries. One of the men, 26-year-old Mohammad Zaki Amawi, was a citizen of both the United States and Jordan and was also accused of threatening to kill or injure President Bush and distributing information about making and using bombs. The other two were named as Marwan Othman El-Hindi, 42, a U.S. citizen born in Jordan, and Wassim I. Mazloum, 24, who came to the United States from Lebanon in 2000. All three had lived in Toledo,

Ohio, and were charged with conspiracy to kill, kidnap, maim, or injure people or to damage property in a foreign country. They were also charged with conspiracy to kill Americans and harboring or concealing terrorists.

According to the indictment, two of the men had discussed plans to practice setting off explosives on the 4th of July in 2005, and the group had also traveled together to a shooting range to practice and had studied how to make explosives. The indictment further alleged that at least one of the men researched and tried to obtain government grants and private funding for the training.

In a related action, the U.S. government also ordered a freeze on the assets of KindHearts, a Toledo-based group suspected of funneling money to the militant organization Hamas.

In August 2006, a Maryland man, Mahmud Faruq Brent of Gwynn Oak, was arrested on charges of conspiring to support the Lashkar-e-Taiba terrorist group between 2001 and May 2005 by attending a terrorist training camp run by the group in Pakistan. He was further charged with receiving martial arts training from a Tarik Shah, who was also under indictment in New York on similar charges.

United Kingdom

On October 5, 1974, two bombs exploded in Guildford, England. One bomb exploded at the Horse and Groom pub on North Street, which killed five people, four of them soldiers and one civilian, and injured an additional 44. The other bomb exploded at the Seven Stars pub but failed to kill or injure anybody, for the establishment had been evacuated after the explosion of the first bomb. This attack was claimed by the Provisional Irish Republican Army (IRA).

On November 21, 1974, two bombs exploded in Birmingham, England, one at the Tavern in the Town pub and the other at the Mulberry Bush pub, killing 21 people (11 at the Tavern in the Town and 10 at the Mulberry Bush) and injuring more than 180. A third device, left outside a bank, failed to explode. This attack was attributed to the Provisional IRA but was subsequently denied by them two days later.

On April 24, 1993, a massive IRA bomb caused significant damage to the City of London, the financial center of London, killing one person and injuring more than 40. The explosion damaged a large number of buildings and caused the collapse of St. Ethelburga's, a medieval church. A second church and the Liverpool Street subway station were also wrecked. The cost of repairing the damage was estimated at more than £1 billion.

On August 15, 1998, a car bomb exploded at the junction of Market Street and the Dublin Road in the center of Omagh, County Tyrone, Northern Ireland, killing 29 people and injuring approximately 220 others. A splinter group of the Irish Republican Army known as the "real" IRA eventually claimed responsibility for the attack. The attack followed the normal pattern for IRA attacks, and a warning had been telephoned to a news agency in Belfast approximately 40 minutes before the explosion. In a statement from the Royal Ulster Constabulary (RUC) it was revealed that the warning had referred to the Omagh Courthouse, which is located approximately 400 meters from where the bomb actually exploded. A large number of those killed and injured in the bombing had been moved from the vicinity of the courthouse and into the area where the explosion occurred.

The motivation for these attacks was part of the ongoing attempts by the IRA, who represented the minority Catholic community, to gain independence for Northern Ireland from the United Kingdom. While there were no specific indicators of this type of attack, other than what may have been gathered by intelligence agencies, these were two in a series of massive bomb attacks that formed part of the IRA campaign. The timing of the attacks may have been indicated by the political dialogue and progress in the preceding months. IRA bombings were typically targeted against Belfast and the major cities in England, such as London, Manchester, and Birmingham. Other targets were places such as pubs where British soldiers were known to congregate.

On July 7, 2005, a series of coordinated suicide bombs exploded on London's transportation system during the morning rush hour. At approximately 08:50 a.m. three separate bombs exploded within less than a minute on three separate London subway trains. Nearly an hour later, a fourth device exploded on a number 30 bus in Tavistock Square. As a result of the attacks, 52 people died and a further 700 were injured. The attacks took place during the first full day of the 31st G8 summit, which was being hosted by the UK, and a day after London had learned that it had been chosen to host the 2012 Summer Olympics. The bombings led to a severe, daylong disruption of the city's transportation and mobile telecommunications infrastructure.

Two weeks later, on July 21, 2005, a second series of four bombs were discovered on the London subway and a London bus. The bombs had failed to explode properly (although the detonators of all four bombs exploded, none of the main explosive charges had detonated). Because of this, there were no casualties. The individuals suspected of being the bombers from these failed attacks all escaped from the scenes but were arrested later.

These bombings are attributed to Al Qaeda and form a part of that organization's ongoing campaign against the United States and Western interests. There had been no preincident indicators and no warnings of these attacks.

In January and February 2007, a series of seven letter bombs exploded at a number of locations around the United Kingdom. The targets of the attacks appeared to be related to companies and vehicle-related government agencies. No group or individual has claimed responsibility for the attacks.

Continental Europe

On August 2, 1980, terrorists exploded a bomb in the Central Station of Bologna, Italy. As a result, 85 people were killed and 200 were wounded. The attack was attributed to a right-wing terrorist group called New Order (Ordine Nuevo). The bomb was left in an unattended suitcase in a waiting room. When it detonated, the resulting explosion caused significant damage to the main building and also damaged a train that was waiting at the first platform. The motives of those who carried out the attack remain unknown.

In June 2006, 25 people were convicted in France for their roles in preparing for a terrorist attack in France in support of Islamic fighters in Chechnya. It was thought that the proposed attack was to have involved the use of the chemical ricin. In December 2002, investigators searched two houses in the La Courneuve suburb of Paris and the nearby town of Romainville. During the searches they discovered gas canisters, fuses, chemicals, and a chemical-protection suit. More than a year later, in January 2004, investigators raided a house in Venissieux, again finding chemical products, including ricin. The group was thought to have been formed in Algeria in 1999, after eight members there had refused an Algerian government amnesty plan for Islamic insurgents in the

North African country. A number of members of the group moved to Spain, France, Italy, and the border region between Pakistan and Afghanistan; at the same time, a core group formed in the Paris region in late 2000 to create a support ring for Islamic militants in the war-ravaged Russian republic of Chechnya. The Benchellali family, who were at the heart of the group, were known to have occasionally used a makeshift mosque on the ground floor of a high-rise building in Lyon to collect funds for Islamic fighters in Chechnya.

In 1991, it is believed, the Red Army Faction (Baader-Meinhof Gang) was responsible for the assassination of Detlev Rohwedder, who headed the agency responsible for the privatization of state holdings of the former East Germany.

In 1993, the Red Army Faction carried out an operation in which they exploded a bomb of several hundred kilos of commercial explosives that destroyed a new prison. During the attack, one member of the German Security Service (GSG9) and one member of the Red Army Faction, Wolfgang Grams, were killed in an exchange of gunfire. (*Note*: The group disbanded on April 20, 1998.)

In October 2005, four Arab men, three Jordanians, and one Algerian, who had been accused of planning attacks on Jewish targets in Germany and belonging to a terrorist organization, were sentenced to jail terms of between five and eight years. Three members of the group were convicted of supporting the terrorist group al-Tawhid, which is led by Jordanian Abu Mus'ab al-Zarqawi. The Al-Tawhid group is said to have links to Al Qaeda.

In December 1973, Euzkadi Ta Askatasuna (ETA) used a bomb that had been placed in a sewer to assassinate Admiral Louis Carrero Blanco in Madrid, Spain. The admiral was President Franco's chosen successor and president of the government.

In 1995, an ETA car bombing attempt failed against Jose Maria Aznar, the leader of the opposition Partido Popular (PP). Shortly after the attack, Aznar was elected president of the government.

On July 10, 1997, Spanish Partido Popular council member Miguel Angel Blanco was kidnapped. He was subsequently killed in the city of Ermuas in the Basque region. The government had been threatened with his death unless it met ETA's demands.

On August 24, 2001, six suspected ETA members were arrested by Spanish police in the Barcelona suburb of Terrasa. At the time of the arrest police also seized more than 550 pounds of explosives, firearms, and electronic detonator components.

On March 24, 2006, ETA declared a permanent cease-fire.

On February 14, 2006, a car bomb exploded close to a discotheque in northern Spain, causing damage but no injuries, after police had cleared the area following a warning call in the name of the Basque separatist group ETA. The blast occurred four days after Spanish Prime Minister Jose Luis Rodriguez Zapatero said he thought they could be witnessing the "beginning of the end" of ETA.

On December 12, 2006, Spanish police arrested 11 suspected Islamic radicals linked to a cell of the terrorist Salafist Group for Call and Combat (GSPC) in the Spanish enclave of Ceuta on the north coast of Morocco. The individuals arrested were thought to be in the initial phase of plotting a terrorist attack and recruiting and indoctrinating for Islamic terrorist attacks. Those arrested were reported to have connections to terrorist groups in both Britain and Morocco. Two of the arrested were brothers of Abderrahaman Ahmed, a Ceuta-born Spanish citizen who had been held at the U.S. Guantanamo Naval Base but was repatriated to Spain, where he was convicted of membership in Al Qaeda but later acquitted by Spain's Supreme Court.

On December 30, 2006, a large car bomb demolished a five-story parking garage at Madrid's Barajas Airport terminal 4. Three warning calls were received from ETA in the hour preceding the blast, officials said. Two Ecuadorian men who had been asleep in their car in the garage were killed.

On February 5, 2007, in Bilbao, Spain, one or more bombs exploded at the railway station at Lutxana in the Basque country. No deaths or injuries were reported. The bomb was thought to be related to the arrest of 18 youth leaders linked to ETA. The ETA attacks were motivated by the struggle for independence by the Basque separatists and targeted against Spanish interests.

Middle East

On May 30, 1972, a three-man team belonging to the Japanese Red Army (JRA) arrived at Lod Airport in Tel Aviv, Israel. The group flew to the airport onboard Air France flight 132, dressed in business suits and carrying what appeared to be violin cases. As the three men passed through the terminal building they pulled automatic weapons from their violin cases and began to shoot indiscriminately into the crowd and threw hand grenades. Of the three attackers, one, Yasuyuki Yasuda, ran out of ammunition and was shot by his companions. A second, Tsuyoshi Okudaira, apparently committed suicide by pulling the pin on a grenade and detonating it against his body. The third, Kozo Okamoto, was captured while attempting to escape the terminal. The operation is thought to have been planned and supported by the Popular Front for the Liberation of Palestine (PFLP). As a result of the attack, 26 people were killed and 78 injured. Investigations later revealed that the JRA received considerable support in the form of training and funds from Iran, Libya, Syria, and the PFLP and other Palestinian factions.

In the period from 1997 to 2002, more than 1,700 people were kidnapped in Colombia. A report by Héctor Abad Faciolince held that terrorism acquires a distinct form according to the country or region in which it is taking place. In Colombia it has assumed the specific form of a battle weapon known as *miracle fishing,* which is intended to keep the population confined to their homes and concentrated in the cities. Of the kidnappings that took place in Colombia in 2002, 60 percent were attributed to armed groups and 35 percent to common criminals, according to the Fundación País Libre. (The remaining 5% was not attributed.) It is thought that the Colombian armed groups conduct kidnappings in order to finance their operations.

In 2001, a Scottish oil worker, Alistair Taylor, held hostage for almost two years by South American guerrillas was released. Mr. Taylor had been kidnapped in Colombia by the rebel National Liberation Army in August 1999, in the eastern town of Yopal, an oil center near the border with Venezuela. At the time of his capture he had been working for Weatherford International, a Texas-based oil company. It was reported that the terrorists demanded $3 million for his release, although it is not known if this ransom was paid.

In May 2002, it was reported that a cell phone detonated an explosive device that had been attached to the underside of a fuel tanker truck in the Israeli central fuel and gas depot, north of Tel Aviv. As a result of the explosion, the truck, which was being loaded with fuel at the time, caught fire. Fortunately, the fuel being loaded was of a low volatility, and the fire did not spread to the fuel storage drums. Had the attack succeeded in its aim, it would have caused a major catastrophe that would probably have led to a significant Israeli response that could, in turn, have changed the political landscape of the Middle East. This was again a part of the ongoing dispute between Israel and the Palestinians, and, although there are no specific precursors to this attack, it formed part of the ongoing campaign to put pressure on Israel in the treatment of Palestinians that has been ongoing since the 1970s.

In June 2002, it was reported that a group of Al Qaeda operatives had been arrested by the Moroccan government. The group was suspected of plotting raids on British and American tankers passing through the Strait of Gibraltar.

In October 2002, five members of Al Qaeda carried out an attack off the coast of Yemen that badly damaged the French supertanker *Limburg*. In the attack, the supertanker was rammed with a boat packed with explosives. As a result, one of the crew of 25 was killed and a fire was started onboard the supertanker, loaded with 400,000 barrels of Saudi Arabian crude oil.

In August 2004, five members of Al Qaeda were convicted of the attack on the *Limburg,* and another who was accused of planning with the other defendants to assassinate the U.S. ambassador to Sanaa, who was sentenced to death. The report stated that nine more Yemenis had received prison sentences of three to ten years for their part in the assassination conspiracy and also for plotting with the others to conduct attacks on the embassies of the United States, Britain, Germany, France, and Cuba.

On March 11, 2004, a number of trains were bombed in Madrid, Spain, part of a series of coordinated bombings on the commuter train system that killed 192 people and wounded approximately 2,050. Given the history of terrorism in Spain, the initial reaction was that this outrage had been perpetrated by the terrorist group Euzkadi Ta Askatasuna (ETA) (in the Basque language this means Basque Homeland and Freedom). The bombings took place three days before a scheduled general election in Spain. Although ETA had a history of mounting bomb attacks in Madrid and had previously attempted to attack trains, the March 11 attacks were on a far larger scale than anything previously attempted by a European militant organization. The following day a number of Moroccans were arrested for the attacks, and it was confirmed that the attacks came from an Islamic group. In the period since the attack the responsibility had been attributed to local Islamic extremist cells that had remote links to Al Qaeda rather than to GIA or the Islamic Group Combatant Moroccan. (*Comment*: Because this bombing took place a few days before an election, it may well have affected the outcome of that election. It is considered unlikely that this was one of the objectives of the attack, but it was an unintended side effect. The attack is thought to have been part of the ongoing campaign by Al Qaeda against Western interests.)

In an April 2005 report,[2] George Thomas stated that in the previous 12 months, Al Qaeda–linked groups had launched a series of attacks on a number of oil-rich countries, including Nigeria. The report went on to state that Nigeria was continuing to suffer from a rising Islamist threat and that Al Qaeda had developed training and recruiting bases in this country. A video message broadcast by Osama Bin Laden on the Arab television station Al-Jazeera singled out Nigeria, Africa's leading oil producer and a country with a population of 60 million Muslims, as a country worthy of jihad because of its close ties with the United States. For the Al Qaeda organization, any opportunity to attack the interests of Western nations is viewed as sufficient justification for an attack. In the case of Nigeria, with high U.S. interest and a high Muslim population, any action would be seen as beneficial.

On April 3, 2004, four Arab terrorists blew themselves up at Leganes, South Madrid, Spain. The explosion killed one of the special assault police and wounded 11 regular police officers. According to witnesses, between five and eight additional suspects escaped. No warning of these attacks had been given.

Asia

The Indian subcontinent has a modern history of bomb attacks on trains that dates back to the 1990s. On December 31, 1996, a bomb caused severe damage to an express train packed with holiday travelers in Guahati, in Assam, in eastern India. At least 26 of the passengers and crew were killed and an additional 42 were injured. The rebel Bodo tribesmen, who had waged a campaign for a separate homeland for more than 20 years, were suspected of carrying out the attack.

In July 1997, a bomb exploded on an express train in the state of Punjab in northern India. The blast occurred soon after the train left the station of Bhatinda, 125 miles north of New Delhi, killing at least 30 passengers and injuring 67 more.

Eight people were reported to have died in a bombing on June 6, 1997, the beginning of the Sikh "Genocide Week." This week marks the anniversary of June 6, 1984, when the raid took place on the Golden Temple in Amritsar to flush out Sikh militants engaged in an armed revolt for independence.

In June 1998, a time bomb exploded on the Karachi-to-Peshawar train as it approached Khairpur in the southern province of Sindh in Pakistan, killing 22 people and injuring at least 36. The bomb exploded in the early hours of the morning aboard a carriage where most of the passengers were asleep. According to the Pakistani authorities, the Research and Analysis Wing (RAW) of the Indian intelligence service was responsible for the attack.

In June 1999, a suitcase bomb at a rail station resulted in eight deaths and 59 injured. The explosion took place at the New Jalpaiguri station in North Bengal. Three of the dead were later identified as members of the Armed Forces traveling to Kargil, where the Indian army was fighting guerrilla infiltrators. The separatist group United Liberation Front of Assam claimed responsibility for the attack.

Indian authorities have been struggling with separatist uprisings in five of India's seven remote northeastern states. The rebel groups have often carried out attacks as part of their campaigns. The ongoing tension in the region is the main indicator of what will probably be a continuing campaign.

According to a BBC report of July 29, 2005,[3] an explosion took place on the Shramjivi Express in the northern state of Uttar Pradesh, resulting in the deaths of at least 10 people and injuries to more than 50 others. According to a police report, similar explosives had been used in a previous attack at Ayodhya, which was blamed on Muslim militants.

On July 11, 2006, eight separate bombs exploded on rush-hour trains in a coordinated attack in Mumbai, India. The attacks resulted in 207 deaths and more than 625 people were injured. The attacks were targeted against the first-class carriages of the trains. Lashkar-e-Qahhar, a little-known Islamic militant group, claimed responsibility for the bombings and warned that it was planning further attacks against government and historic sites in India.

Russia

On June 14, 1999, a suspected terrorist explosion occurred in an oil pipeline in the southern Russian republic of Dagestan, close to the Chechen border. The pipeline, which carries oil from Baku in Azerbaijan to Novorossiysk in Russia, was damaged; it took fire-fighters more than two hours to control the resultant blaze. Oil pipelines in the region are frequently attacked by armed gangs from Chechnya and individuals seeking to steal oil.

On October 23, 2002, a group of Chechen terrorists took control of a crowded Moscow theater and took over 900 hostages. The group claimed allegiance to the separatist movement in Chechnya and demanded the withdrawal of Russian forces from Chechnya. After a siege that lasted two and a half days, Russian Special Forces (Spetznaz) attacked the theater and retook it. All 42 of the terrorists and 130 of the hostages were killed, but there were no casualties among the attacking special forces. This was attributed to a gas that was used in the theater to subdue the terrorists.

On September 1, 2004, a group of approximately 32 terrorists held 1,181 people hostage in the school in Beslan, North Ossetia, Russia. Russian troops from the Federal Security Service kept the school under siege for three days, until medical workers the terrorists had agreed to allow to remove bodies from the school grounds moved in, when bombs exploded in the school and terrorists fired on hostages trying to escape from the school's gymnasium where they were being held. In all, 334 of the hostages and 31 of the terrorists died as a result of the incident. The last of the terrorists were captured.

The attack on the school at Beslan was the fourth terrorist attack in 10 days on Russian interests related to Chechnya. Other incidents included two passenger planes that crashed on August 24 following explosions, killing 89 people, and a suicide bomb attack that killed 10 people near a Moscow subway station. These attacks were motivated by the ongoing separatist campaign by the Chechen people against Russia.

Attacks Against Corporations

On June 14, 1999, a suspected terrorist explosion occurred in an oil pipeline in the southern Russian republic of Dagestan, close to the Chechen border. The pipeline, which carries oil from Baku in Azerbaijan to Novorossiysk in Russia, was damaged; it took firefighters more than two hours to control the resultant blaze. Oil pipelines in the region are frequently attacked by armed gangs from Chechnya and individuals seeking to steal oil.

In July 2001, according to a report from the BBC Worldwide Monitoring, The Free Aceh Movement (Gerakan Aceh Merdeka, or GAM) launched a number of attacks, including the bombing of barracks of the Indonesian Armed Forces (Tentera Nasional Indonesia, TNI) at South Hagu in Lhokseumawe, followed by a bomb attack at the rear of the Pertamina State Oil and Gas Company depot on the old Lhokseumawe jetty. It was also claimed that the GAM had detonated a bomb under a truck convoy at Alue Bade in Kuta Makmur, killing a number of TNI troops, and another under a truck at Aleule Mudik in Nisam, this time killing eight members of the TNI.

In March 2001, it was reported that increasing violence had forced the multinational oil giant Exxon Mobil to suspend operations at its natural gas plant in Aceh for more than a week following a number of security problems that had occurred over several months. The report indicated that the resumption of production was dependent on resolution of the security issues in the area.

A report by CNN in August 2001[4] stated that 31 people were killed in an attack by gunmen on the Bumi Flora palm-oil plantation in the Idi Rayeuk district in the strife-torn Indonesian province of Aceh.

In April 2004, terrorists attacked an oil refinery jointly owned by Exxon Mobil and the Saudi Arabian company SABIC in Yanbu, 550 miles west of Riyadh in north-western Saudi Arabia, killing at least three Americans, two Britons, an Australian, and a Saudi national. During the attack three of the attackers were also killed and a fourth was captured.

In November 2004, Russia's Federal Security Service (FSB) prevented a major terrorist attack against a gas distribution plant of strategic significance in the Astrakhan region of southern Russia. The FSB claimed that its forces killed the leader of the would-be attack, identified as Adam Sultanovich Magomadov, and had detained an accomplice, also known as Adam Salmanovich Magomadov. Chechen separatists were blamed for this attack and have also been blamed for other attacks against pipelines, electrical towers, and other infrastructure in Russia.

In February 2006, a report was published on a terrorist attack on a barge in the Delta area of Nigeria.[5] The report stated that rebel raiders, members of the Ijaw tribe, had attacked the barge and had seized nine foreign hostages. The group was demanding a greater share of the region's oil wealth. The vessel, which was attacked by a group of around 40 rebels, was the WB318 barge that was operating in the Forcados oil fields, Warri State, in the Niger Delta. As a result of the attack, a number of foreign nationals, consisting of one Briton (the head of security), three Americans, two Thais, two Egyptians, and a Filipino, were taken hostage. As they departed the scene, the rebels set fire to an onshore installation.

In June 2006, it was reported, five South Korean gas workers employed by Daewoo Engineering and Construction and Korea Gas were released in the Port Harcourt area by Nigerian rebels after being kidnapped during an attack on the Daewoo camp two days before. Dozens of heavily armed rebels from a number of groups, one of which was identified as the Movement for the Emancipation of the Niger Delta (MEND), had staged a bloody raid on the natural gas plant in the Niger Delta. The rebels had demanded the release of their jailed leader, Mujahid Dokubo-Asari, in exchange for the Koreans' freedom.

Attacks Against People

Christian girls beheaded in grisly Indonesian attack: Three teenage Christian girls were beheaded and a fourth was seriously wounded in a savage attack on Saturday by unidentified assailants in the Indonesian province of Central Sulawesi. The girls were among a group of students from a private Christian high school who were ambushed while walking through a cocoa plantation in Poso Kota subdistrict on their way to class.... "In the holy month of Ramadan, we are again shocked by a sadistic crime in Poso that claimed the lives of three school students," he [the mayor] told reporters at the airport as he prepared to fly to Sumatra Island.[6]

In January 1975, the Armenian Secret Army for the Liberation of Armenia (ASALA), a previously unknown group, claimed the bombing of the World Council of Churches (WCC) office in Beirut. As a result it came to prominence as both a Middle Eastern terrorist group and an International terrorist group. Between approximately 1975 and 1982 the activities of the ASALA militants were targeted against a number of Western and

Turkish installations and a significant number of Turkish diplomats. Although the group had only a small number of members, they managed to achieve the level of international publicity they desired on the issue of the Armenian genocide.

The origins of ASALA can be found in the frustration that arose as a result of the lack of interest in the Armenian genocide committed by the Turks in the course of World War I by the international community. The members of ASALA found common ground and drew strength from its links with other militant groups, including the Palestine Liberation Organization (PLO).

In December 1996, the Tupac Amaru Revolutionary Movement (MRTA) (shining path) assaulted and took over the Japanese ambassador's residence in Lima, Peru. The group had entered the compound dressed as waiters during a celebration of the Japanese emperor's birthday and took the estimated 600 guests hostage. Around 225 of the hostages were released soon after the takeover, and more were released throughout the month of December. The siege of the residence was brought to an end on April 22, 1997, when Peruvian soldiers stormed the residence and rescued the remaining 72 hostages. During the assault, one of the Japanese hostages, two soldiers, and all 14 of the Tupac Amaru hostage takers were killed. The motive for the attack on the residence was to gain the release of Tupac Amaru from jail.

On December 21, 1988, Pan Am flight 103 from Frankfurt to New York, via London, blew up over the town of Lockerbie in Scotland after a bomb exploded onboard. All 259 passengers and crew were killed, together with 11 residents of Lockerbie. Passengers on the flight were from 21 different countries. Two Libyan nationals were eventually convicted of carrying out the attack, and the motive is thought to have been retaliation by Libya for the bombing of Tripoli after an earlier bombing of a Berlin nightclub.

On May 12, 2003, a suicide bombing attack took place on three residential compounds in Riyadh, Saudi Arabia. The attacks, which were attributed to Al Qaeda, killed 26 people and injured more than 160.

In October 2004, a number of car and suicide bomb attacks, subsequently attributed to Al Qaeda, exploded at holiday resorts that were popular with Israeli tourists in the Sinai Peninsula of Egypt. The most devastating of the attacks was at the Taba Hilton, where a car laden with explosives crashed into the lobby and detonated, causing the collapse of a 10-story wing of the hotel. There were reports of two further explosions in the hotel compound, and further explosions occurred in the area of Ras Shitan, a popular camping area near the town of Nuweiba, to the south of Taba. As a result of the attacks, at least 27 people were killed and more than a 100 were injured, with some reports placing the figure as high as 160. No established groups claimed responsibility for the bombings, but at least three previously unknown groups separately claimed responsibility for the attacks.

On October 10, 2004, a powerful car bomb, which was hidden in a white Mitsubishi van, was detonated by remote control outside the Sari nightclub in Kuta Beach, Bali, Indonesia, causing the death of at least 202 people and injuries to a further 209. The detonation of the main bomb followed that of a smaller, crude device hidden in a backpack that severely damaged a local establishment, Paddy's Bar. The smaller device killed only the backpack owner, who was thought to be a suicide bomber. The people injured in the blast immediately fled into the street, where very shortly afterward the second, much more powerful device exploded. The majority of the dead and wounded were Australian nationals, but tourists from New Zealand, Indonesia, Germany, France,

Britain, and America were also among the casualties. The defense minister of Indonesia, Matori Abdul Djalil, blamed Al Qaeda and its extremist allies for the attack.

On November 8, 2005, police in Australia arrested 16 terror suspects in a series of raids, stating they had foiled a catastrophic terrorist attack. One of those arrested was shot and wounded by police when he opened fire as they were attempting to arrest him. In a statement, New South Wales Police Commissioner Ken Moroney said, "I'm satisfied that we have disrupted what I would regard as the final stages of a large-scale terrorist attack … here in Australia." Prosecutor Richard Maidment later said, "The members of the Sydney group have been gathering chemicals of a kind that were used in the London Underground bombings."

On November 26, 2005, four Westerners—one American, two Canadians, and one British citizen—were kidnapped from Baghdad by a group calling itself the Swords of Truth. The four had traveled to Iraq with the Canada-based international peace group Christian Peacemaker Teams (CPT) as a "gesture of solidarity" with the people. The group that had taken them hostage had threatened to kill the men if the U.S. and Iraqi authorities did not release all Iraqi prisoners. During their captivity, the American hostage was executed; the remaining three were rescued by the British SAS after 117 days in captivity.

On August 12, 2006, one of two kidnap victims was beheaded on Jolo Island, about 950 km south of Manila, by suspected Abu Sayyaf militants. Security forces have been battling the terrorist group that is thought to be associated with the Indonesian Jemaah Islamiya network.

Earlier, in June 2006, 41-year-old pharmacy owner Bren Vergara was released by his kidnappers, who were also suspected of being Abu Sayyaf, after more than two months in captivity. It is thought that the family had paid a ransom of more than 1 million pesos.

Prior to this, in August 2002, Abu Sayyaf terrorists had beheaded two male members of a Jehovah's Witness group two days after militants had kidnapped them and four women in Jolo.

Narcoterrorism

The connection between narcotics trafficking and terrorist groups is increasingly well documented. Terrorist groups have turned more and more to trafficking drugs as a source of revenue as the level of funding from state sponsorship has dropped and, in many cases, to further their cause.

In March 2002, U.S. State Department officials told a Senate panel, "Not only does it (the drug trade) provide funds; it also furthers the strategic objectives of the terrorists. Some terrorist groups believe that they can weaken their enemies by flooding their societies with addictive drugs."[7]

Francis Taylor, ambassador-at-large for counterterrorism, stated that "relations between drug traffickers and terrorists benefit both." He went on to state, "Drug traffickers benefit from the terrorists' military skills, weapons supply, and access to clandestine organizations. Terrorists gain a source of revenue and expertise in illicit transfer and laundering of proceeds from illicit transactions." He then went on to list terrorist groups with known links to drug trafficking around the world, from the South American nations of Colombia, Peru, Bolivia, and Paraguay to Afghanistan, which, he said, accounts for more than 70 percent of the world's supply of opiates.

The Lebanese Hezbollah group is increasingly involved in drug trafficking, he said, and terrorist organizations in Europe and Southeast Asia also are tied to illicit drugs. This has been mirrored by the motivation of the terrorism we are experiencing. During the Cold War, the primary driver for terrorism was communism—the "new left wave." And there was undoubtedly state sponsorship by both Soviet bloc countries and Western nations.

International pressure against Islamic terrorist and extremist groups in particular and the state sponsors of terrorism in general increased dramatically after the Al Qaeda–sponsored terrorist attacks against the World Trade Center and the Pentagon on September 11, 2001.

The traditional state sponsors of terrorism, such as Cuba, Iran, and Libya, have come under growing pressure to stop their sponsorship of terrorist groups. Some of these countries have responded, but their reasons have varied: Libya is seeking acceptance by the West and the removal of sanctions, while it is thought that with the collapse of the Soviet Union, Cuba has less motivation, support, and funding available.

As a result, there have been increasingly well-documented links between the drug trade and terrorism. As an example, in most cases the relationship between Colombian and Peruvian insurgent and paramilitary groups and drug-trafficking organizations or cartels is a mutually beneficial one that allows exchanges of drugs for weapons, use of the same smuggling routes, use of similar methods or resources for laundering money, use of the same corrupt government officials, and so forth. The major difference between the two types of organizations is that the cartels and the drug-trafficking terrorist and extremist groups have different goals: The cartels are motivated primarily by financial gain, while the terrorists and extremists are motivated by political or, in the case of the Islamic groups, religious goals.

It is reported that in the early 1990s, Osama bin Laden, the head of Al Qaeda, had sent Arabs from Afghanistan into Albania and then to Bosnia to fight for the Muslims in battles with the Serbian aggressors in the neighboring former Yugoslavian state. Many of these Arab Afghanistani mercenaries are thought to have subsequently gone on to fight in Kosovo.

According to Bodansky,[8] "The support and management echelons of the new Islamist networks operate in conjunction with organized crime." He went on to explain that Iranian intelligence agencies had first encouraged radical Islamic groups to participate in the drug trade. Since then, Islamic terrorist groups have expanded into a wide range of criminal activities that include money laundering, distribution of forged U.S. $100 notes, and prostitution rings that involve mainly Bosnian Muslim and North African women.

Bodansky also explains how Hezbollah's fatwa (religious edict), issued in the mid-1980s on the distribution of drugs, has provided a rationale for drug trafficking: "We are making these drugs for Satan—America and the Jews. If we cannot kill them with guns, then we will kill them with drugs."

Increasingly, terrorist organizations, rich with funds derived from the drug trade, have been establishing a presence in North America. According to a November 2001 report by the Royal Canadian Mounted Police (RCMP), drug shipments of up to 25 tons of cocaine are entering Canada from South America, worth as much as $50 million annually, and are a potential source of terrorist funds. The report in addition stated that the proceeds from shipments of the more than 100 tons of Asian hashish that are thought to be smuggled into Canada annually are also likely to end up in the hands of "terrorist elements in Afghanistan." The report went on to state that Afghan, Pakistani, East Indian, Tamil, Turkish, and Middle Eastern terrorist or extremist groups were "suspected of fund-raising in Canada by various means."

Narcoterrorist groups based in Europe are thought to include the Real Irish Republican Army (IRA), the Basque Fatherland and Liberty (Euzkadi Ta Azkatasuna—ETA) terrorist group from Spain's Basque region, and the Albanian Liberation Army (KLA). The KLA spin-off groups are well positioned to exploit what is known as "the Balkan Route," which links the Golden Crescent area of Afghanistan and Pakistan to the European drug markets. The Kurdistan Workers' Party (PKK) is also thought to have laundered money and taken part in drug trafficking and is suspected of "taxing" drug shipments and of protecting drug traffickers throughout the southeastern parts of Turkey.

In the Middle East, according to Beers and Taylor, Hezbollah has increasingly been thought to be involved in drug trafficking.[9] They are suspected of smuggling cocaine from Latin America to Europe and the Middle East and have in the past smuggled opiates out of Lebanon's Bekaa Valley. Analyst Frank Cillufo stated[10] that in 2000 Hezbollah was reportedly cooperating with the PKK to export narcotics into Europe.

In Central Asia, U.S. Drug Enforcement Agency (DEA) statistics indicate that in 2000, before the Taliban imposed a poppy-cultivation ban that greatly reduced the size of the 2001 harvest, Afghanistan was producing around 70 percent of the total global crop of opium poppies. Unfortunately, the ban had little effect on world drug markets, because the Islamic fundamentalist regime of Mullah Mohammed Omar had been stockpiling vast quantities of heroin, which it sold after the growing ban by the Taliban had driven up the world price for heroin.

Use of the Internet by Terrorists

An English-speaking hacker known as Irhabi ("Terrorist") 007, who was thought to be a key conduit for Al Qaeda after he had spread propaganda for Iraqi insurgents led by Abu Mus'ab al-Zarqawi and gave instructions to other online jihadists on how to use their computers for the cause, was arrested in November 2005 by London police. At the time of the arrest of the 22-year-old West London resident, Younis Tsouli, on suspicion of participation in an alleged bomb plot, his online identity was unknown.

The fortuitous arrest of Irhabi 007 happened at a time when such sympathizers of Al Qaeda are increasingly finding uses for the Internet. A large number of websites and forums now cater to such would-be jihadists. The individuals who congregate in those cybercommunities are rapidly becoming skilled in disciplines such as hacking and programming and carrying out online attacks.

It is interesting to note that during a raid on his house as a part of the investigation into Tsouli, police found stolen credit card information and that the cards had been used to pay American Internet providers on whose servers Tsouli had posted jihadi propaganda. It is believed that the websites and forums were used to disseminate weapons manuals, videos of acts such as beheadings, and other inflammatory material. On one occasion he is thought to have made a 20-page posting titled "Seminar on Hacking Websites" to the Ekhlas forum. This posting gave details on how to hack and listed a significant number of websites that were vulnerable.

According to a May 2006 report by J. L. Shreeve,[11] the terror attacks of 9/11 and 7/7 can be seen as just a forerunner to the devastation that could be created if terrorists were to turn their attention from the physical to the digital world. The report states that, according to Scott Borg, the director of the U.S. Cyber Consequences Unit (CCU), a Department of Homeland Security advisory group, attacks on computer networks are poised to escalate to full-scale disasters that could bring down companies and kill people. The report goes on to say that Borg also warns that intelligence "chatter" is increasingly pointing to possible criminal or terrorist plans to cause damage to or destroy elements of the physical infrastructure, such as power grids, and stresses that Al Qaeda is becoming increasingly capable of carrying out such attacks.

Most organizations seem not to have recognized or taken measures to prevent such actions or to mitigate their effects, with the majority of their attention focused on the day-to-day problems of hacking and malicious software. To date, hackers and criminals have targeted personal and sensitive corporate and financial information on the Internet.

A key target of a terrorist attack would probably be the supervisory control and data acquisition (SCADA) systems that many of the utility companies and manufacturing companies rely on. SCADA systems are computer systems that monitor and control physical processes. They are used remotely to open and shut the valves, monitor and regulate system pressures, and make or break electrical connections.

An example of the type of damage that can be caused when SCADA systems are tampered with can be seen in the 2000 case of Victor Boden, a disaffected consultant who had been refused full-time employment. He spent three months and made more than 45 attempts attacking the SCADA systems of Maroochy Water Services in Brisbane, Australia, causing the release of millions of gallons of sewage into waterways, canals, and the grounds of a hotel.

These concerns about a potential cyberattack are not confined to the United States and Europe. In Malaysia, Prime Minister Abdullah Ahmad Baddawi has announced the creation of a center to fight cyberterrorism. This new organization, called the International Multilateral Partnership Against Cyber-Terrorism (IMPACT), located at Cyberjaya, near Kuala Lumpur, will provide an emergency response capability for high-tech attacks around the world.

Prime Minister Baddawi[12] stated that the threat of cyberterrorism was too serious for governments to ignore. "The potential to wreak havoc and cause disruption to people, governments, and global systems has increased as the world becomes more globalized," he said. "The economic loss caused by a cyberattack can be truly severe, for example, a nationwide blackout, collapse of trading systems, or the crippling of a central bank's check-clearing system."

In 1995 in Japan, the Aum Shinrikyo sect was responsible for a sarin gas attack on the Tokyo subway. The adherents of the cult were later found to have been responsible for the installation of a significant number of information systems for the Japanese police and government and a number of major companies. The potential for this terrorist group to affect the software and hardware they installed in order to create a significant incident at a later time of their choosing cannot be discounted.

An August 2005 report from a London-based Islamist, Asharq al-Awsat, postulates that the Internet is Al Qaeda's new leader. While this may seem a strange proposition, according to Dr. Hani al-Siba'i, director of the Al-Maqrizi Studies Center, many of the "offspring" of "Al Qaeda" consider the Internet to be their sheikh, rather than Osama

Bin Laden or Ayman al-Zawahiri. He said, "The new generation of Al Qaeda organization in the West and East does not have a sheikh that it receives instructions or orders from. This 'generation's sheikh and leader is not Al-Zawahiri or Bin Laden but the jihadist instructions on the fundamentalists' websites and also the photos of the massacres in Afghanistan, Iraq, and Palestine."

Al-Siba'i believes there is no ideological connection between Al Qaeda's new generation in the various countries hit by the terrorist operations: Egypt, Britain, and Turkey. But "they share one concern and one idea, namely, that the West is insulting Islam and humiliating its sons."

One of the major issues that Al-Siba'i addresses is that the new generation of Al Qaeda goes beyond the previous Islamic fundamentalist organizations because the adherents were born in the West, are proficient in modern sciences such as chemistry and physics, speak several languages, and are extremely competent in the use of computers and the Internet.

There is now evidence that they know how to design websites to spread their ideas and also to show images and movie clips. He also observed that the new generation has never visited Afghanistan or Iraq and probably does not know how to use a gun. They are also, as the experience in the United States and the UK is showing, not known to the security services; as a result they pose a significant danger.

Summary

This chapter has looked at a number of significant acts of terrorism from around the world over more than two decades. The people who are the direct target of a terrorist attack will almost always be the public, but those the terrorists seek to influence and affect may be the government, corporations, or the entire populace of a country. It is clear that the underlying cause of terrorism has changed over time and continues to change. New causes continue to appear, some of which, such as Islamic fundamentalism, we have not experienced before and we will struggle to deal with. But at the same time, we continue to see the old causes, such as separatism and nationalism, but repeated in different places.

Héctor Abad Faciolince, in his comment that "terrorism acquires quite distinct forms according to the country in which it operates," captured part of the essence of the problem. There are indicators and warnings that terrorism is more likely to occur in certain regions or at certain times, and these tend to be well publicized, both by governments and by companies that specialize in threat management. Unfortunately, by the very nature of the problem, if terrorist activities can be predicted and interdicted, then that's what happens. The incidents that *do* occur are those that the respective agencies cannot prevent. The probability that any corporate organization has the intelligence resources or the local contacts to be able, separate from the relevant government resources, to predict or avoid a terrorist incident would appear to be remote.

Endnotes

[1] B. M. Jenkins, The New Age of Terrorism, RAND, www.rand.org
[2] George Thomas (CBN News senior producer), "Terror Havens: Al Qaeda's Growing Sanctuary in Nigeria," http://www.cbn.com/cbnnews/news/050430a.aspx

[3] Story from BBC News, July 25, 2005, http://news.bbc.co.uk/go/pr/fr/-/1/hi/world/south_asia/4726737.stm

[4] CNN, "Gunmen kill 31 in Aceh attack," August 10, 2001, CNN.Com/World.

[5] *South African Tribune*, February 26, 2006.

[6] "Indonesia is the world's most populous Muslim nation, but Central Sulawesi has a roughly equal number of Muslims and Christians. The province was the scene of a bloody religious war in 2001–2002 that killed around 1,000 people from both communities. At the time, beheadings, burnings, and other atrocities were common. A government-mediated truce succeeded in ending the conflict in early 2002, but there have since been a series of bomb attacks and assassinations of Christians. The Christian–Muslim conflict in Sulawesi was an extension of a wider sectarian war in the nearby Maluku archipelago in which up to 9,000 perished between 1999 and 2002. The Maluku conflict intensified soon after it began with the arrival of volunteers belonging to Laskar Jihad, a newly created militia from Indonesia's main island of Java that was supported by hard-line elements of the security forces. Analysts and diplomats accused senior army commanders of funding and training the militia, which was hurriedly disbanded following the terrorist attacks on the tourist island of Bali in 2002 which claimed 202 lives, including 88 Australians." See: http://www.smh.com.au/news/world/schoolgirls-beheaded-in-grisly-indonesian-attack/2005/10/29/1130400398091.html

[7] Testimony of Assistant Secretary of State for International Narcotics and Law Enforcement Affairs Rand Beers and Ambassador-at-Large for Counterterrorism Francis X. Taylor, Hearing of the Senate Judiciary Subcommittee on Technology, Terrorism, and Government Information, March 13, 2002.

[8] Yossef Bodansky, *Bin Laden: The Man Who Declared War on America* (New York: Prima/Random House), p. 322.

[9] The Library of Congress "A Global Overview of Narcotics-Funded Terrorists and Other Extremist Groups." May 2002, http://www.loc.gov/rr/frd/pdf-files/NarcsFundedTerrs_Extrems.pdf

[10] Frank Cillufo, "The Threat Posed from the Convergence of Organized Crime, Drug Trafficking, and Terrorism." Statement before the U.S. House Committee on the Judiciary, Subcommittee on Crime, December 13, 2000.

[11] J. L. Shreeve, "The new breed of cyberterrorist: Could a ruthless new breed of cyberterrorists cause meltdown at the click of a mouse?" May 31, 2006, http://news.independent.co.uk/world/science_technology/article622421.ece

[12] BakuToday.net, Malaysia to establish global centre against cyberterrorism: reports, May 09, 2005, http://www.bakutoday.net/view.php?d=20560

Establishing and Managing a Corporate Antiterrorist Program

This section addresses what must be done to develop and implement a corporate anti-terrorism program. Conducting a risk analysis, developing physical security controls, developing processes to protect people, developing emergency response and contingency plans, educating employees, and other security processes are discussed, with the intent of providing a solid protection framework on which the security professional or business executive can build.

Chapter 5: Determining the Corporate Risks to Terrorist Attacks

How does a global business determine if it is vulnerable to acts of terror? How can a security professional know if there is a credible terrorist threat against the corporation he/she is protecting? How can a security manager assess the likelihood that an act of terror will be committed against the company? There are many corporations in the world, and most are not the target of terrorists. Is it possible for a corporation to know they are a potential target prior to the occurrence of an act of terror? Is it cost effective and prudent to assume that the risk of terrorism against any particular business, particularly a global business, is low? Are some corporations more vulnerable than others? These and many other questions are addressed.

Chapter 6: Physically Securing Corporate Premises in Order to Mitigate Attacks

To what extent should every corporation prepare to mitigate an act of terror? Must a fortress be built? Or is it only necessary to be better protected than your neighbor? How can the corporate target be hardened?

Chapter 7: Protecting Employees from Terrorist Attacks

This chapter addresses ways a corporate security professional can develop and implement an effective security awareness training and education program that increases employees' awareness as to how they can contribute to their own protection against acts of terror by knowing and using basic, simple security and safety measures. Increased employee security situational awareness contributes to a more secure environment.

Since employees are more vulnerable when they leave the safe confines of a company facility, this chapter covers how to keep them safe when they venture into the often-dangerous world. Guidelines and recommendations are provided concerning basic measures that can, and in some cases must, be done to ensure the protection of employees operating under the following conditions:

- During travel—protecting the moving target
- On assignment—operating in a foreign and often-unfamiliar environment
- Expatriates—living and working on a long-term basis in a foreign environment to include the risk of "going native"

Chapter 8: Preparing for a Terrorist Attack: Emergency Planning and Implementation

This chapter covers the measures that must be taken to prepare a corporation to respond to an act of terror. If an act of terror is perpetrated against a corporation, what can and must be done in response? How does a company recover from such a tragedy? What is the impact on employees? Is terrorism like lightning, seldom striking the same place twice?

Chapter 9: Operational Security Methods for Mitigating Terrorist Attacks

This chapter addresses the operational security methods security professionals can use to help mitigate a terrorist attack against a business's or corporation's facility, product, information, employees, or any other assets. How operational security is part of the security-in-layers approach of using systems, controls, and processes designed to protect people, assets, and information are discussed and examined.

Chapter 10: Coordinating and Planning with Antiterrorist Agencies

Within the United States, the United Kingdom, Australia, and Canada, many local, state, and federal or national agencies have as their mission, in part or in total, the combating of terrorism. Some of these efforts are fully coordinated among agencies; other are more isolated and disconnected. Corporate security executives must understand how these government agencies operate and what support they can or will provide the company. Furthermore, the security professional should understand what is expected of them by these agencies in order to ensure an effective counterterrorism working partnership.

Determining the Corporate Risks to Terrorist Attacks

All that is necessary for the triumph of evil is that good men do nothing.
—Edmund Burke (1729–1797)

How does a corporation determine if it is vulnerable to acts of terror? How can a security professional know if there is a credible terrorist threat against the corporation he/she is protecting? How can a security executive assess the likelihood that an act of terror will be committed against the company? There are many corporations in the world, and most are not the target of terrorists. Is it possible for a corporation to know they are a potential target prior to the occurrence of an act of terror? Is it cost effective and prudent to assume that the risk of terrorism against any particular corporation is low? Are some corporations more vulnerable than others? These and many other questions are discussed.

By now it should be clear to the reader that terrorism is a real, present, and growing global threat. In its April 2005 report "A Chronology of Significant International Terrorism for 2004," the United States National Counterterrorism Center declared there had been a total of 651 significant international terrorist attacks in 2004. Of that number, 1,907 persons were killed, 6,704 persons were wounded, and 710 were held hostage.[1] Victims of terrorism were predominately from Europe, Eurasia, the Near East, and South Asia, although Africa and the Western Hemisphere were not untouched.

Many people believe terrorism is a government problem and not one for businesses to deal with. However, when you look at the government's responsibilities, aside from the military actions they take, you can quickly see that the government is in a reactive mode, replying to attacks with disaster and emergency response teams, law enforcement, and ambulances. The government agencies at all levels are not involved in defending a business directly against attacks on its facilities, personnel, or other business assets.

In terms of economics, this is no trivial matter. Examining the short-term impact of the attacks on September 11, 2001 (9/11) alone, show the cost to be tremendous. The loss of life and property cost insurance companies an estimated $40 billion.[2] However, the indirect economic costs were greater. Following are just a few examples of conditions contributing to significant economic losses:

- The lost revenue from business closures immediately following the September 11 attacks
- The reduction in the number of airline flights and passengers, globally and within the United States (fear factor)

Table 5-1 Terrorism Surge Since 2003

Event	2003	2004	2005
Total attacks	208	3,168	11,111
Deaths	625	1,907	14,602
Injuries	3,646	6,704	24,705

Source: U.S. House of Representatives, Committee on Government Reform, *Flash Report: The Bush Administration's Data on Global Terrorism in 2005* (April 28, 2006).

- The reduction in the number of vacationers to and from the United States
- The cost of increased security measures to business and government
- Delays in shipments of goods due to greater border crossing and shipping security controls for both imports and exports

In stark contrast to the economic impact and cost of terrorism is the expense incurred by terrorist groups in committing acts of terror. For example, the March 2004 attacks in Madrid, Spain, where multiple simultaneous bombs exploded on four commuter trains, killing 191 people, cost the terrorists approximately $10,000 to accomplish.[3] Using cell phones, detonators, and mining explosives, terrorists were able to kill a large number of people, paralyze the capital of a Western nation, and engender fear throughout the world, all for less than the cost of an average new small automobile. With only few resources, a determined terrorist group or even a single terrorist can inflict tremendous damage, both physical and psychological.

In April 2006, the U.S. State Department annual report on global terrorism showed a dramatic increase in the number of terrorist attacks (see Table 5-1). Although many organizations are tracking, analyzing, and reporting on global terrorism, all with their own methodology and in many cases producing varying results, in virtually all cases the assessment shows that global terrorism is on the rise. It has been argued that the war in Iraq is responsible for much of the increase in global terrorism. Supporting this position is the many daily acts of terror occurring within the borders of Iraq.

In contrast to this, the *Wall Street Journal* reports that between 1998 and the end of 2001 there were 2,991 fatalities from terrorism in North America, almost all on 9/11; since then there have been only three.[4] Although terrorism is an ever-present reality, it is occurring mostly outside of the United States. In any event, and regardless of root causes and perhaps even in spite of the coalition war on terror, terrorism, particularly in this highly mobile and advanced technological world, could be afflicting the globe for many years to come.

In Chapter 1 we presented many different definitions of terrorism, from the perspectives of different nation-states, world organizations, and academic researchers. Although most of these differ from one another to some degree, three features are common to all of the definitions we provided: (1) the use of violence, (2) political objectives, and (3) the intention of sowing fear in a target population.

Perhaps the most succinct definition offered is a legal definition used in Britain: Terrorism involves "the use of violence for political ends, and includes any use of violence for the purpose of putting the public or any section of the public in fear."

It is important to keep in mind the differences among terrorist groups. All too often, since the global war on terror began, the tendency has been to think of terrorism predominantly in the context of Islamic extremism. However, other terrorist groups have political goals and objectives vastly different from those of extremist Islam. For example, the Revolutionary Armed Forces of Colombia (FARC) continue to operate in Colombia, Venezuela, Panama, Ecuador, and Mexico. They also maintain active contact with Hezbollah in the Tri-Border area of South America.[5] The goals of FARC differ significantly from those of Islamic extremists. Their commonality lies in the methods they employ to achieve their differing objectives: terror. For a detailed listing of terrorist groups defined by the U.S. Department of State as foreign terrorist organizations, visit their website.[6]

What Does an Increase in the Number of Acts of Terror and the Spread of Terrorism Mean to Corporations and Businesses Operating in a Global Economy?

Should every business be concerned about protecting its interests and assets from potential acts of terror? Should only those companies operating in high-risk countries and regions (those areas with a high incidence of terror) be concerned, or should every business, particularly a global corporation, be concerned about the potential impact of terrorism? As significant as the data in Table 5-1 is, in reality most businesses will never become a direct target of terrorists. A larger number will become to some extent indirect targets of terrorist acts (perhaps *victim* is a better term than *target*).

For security executives not responsible for protecting global corporations but charged with providing protection for other global entities, such as nongovernmental organizations (NGOs),[7] that conduct activities in any high-risk country or region, the threat, vulnerability, and risk conditions encountered by global corporations are as potentially harmful to NGOs as they are to businesses.

☐ ☐ ☐ ▬▬▬▬▬▬▬▬▬▬▬▬▬▬▬▬▬▬▬▬▬▬▬▬▬▬▬

The recommended protective measures discussed within this book as applicable and useful to security executives protecting corporations will also be of value to security executives protecting NGOs.

▬▬▬▬▬▬▬▬▬▬▬▬▬▬▬▬▬▬▬▬▬▬▬▬▬▬▬ ☐ ☐ ☐

When we talk about global companies, we mean a multinational corporation operating as though the entire world were a single market. These companies serve a range of international markets through export and direct investment.

The World Is a Dangerous Place, so What Is a Security Executive to Do?

First and foremost, the primary responsibility for protecting a corporation against the threat of terrorism lies with executive management, who are responsible to company owners for the protection of the business assets from all threats, including, of course, threats from terrorist attacks. Ultimately, the chief executive officer (CEO) and the executive management team are responsible for protecting the company—its personnel assets, physical assets (such as facilities and equipment), and information.

As with all other critical functions, the CEO will have an executive on staff dedicated to manage each critical business function. For company security (leading the day-to-day protection of assets), the CEO will have a chief security officer (CSO). The CSO may be called something different at different companies. Whether called CSO, vice president of security, security professional, security manager, or security executive, the day-to-day responsibility for protecting the company's assets lies with the senior company security executive.

☐ ☐ ☐ ▬▬▬▬▬▬▬▬▬▬▬▬▬▬▬▬▬▬▬▬▬▬▬▬▬▬▬▬▬▬

Providing protection from terrorism for any company is not a government responsibility.

▬▬▬▬▬▬▬▬▬▬▬▬▬▬▬▬▬▬▬▬▬▬▬▬▬▬▬▬▬▬ ☐ ☐ ☐

Governments at all levels are concerned with providing protection from terrorism for their government agencies' assets. Their emphasis is on the greater community, not on a specific company or even group of companies. Beyond the general protections offered by governments to their society and communities, the responsibility for protecting specific business interests lies with the owner of the assets.

Before developing and implementing effective protective measures, a security executive needs to understand the conditions within which the company operates.

- Could the company be harmed by an act of terror?
- Is a terrorist event likely to occur that will cause harm to the company?
- In the parlance of business, is the company at risk and, if so, to what degree?

Terrorist Risk Assessment

Determining the degree of risk faced by a company is part art and part science. Unlike solutions to mathematical equations, the answers to risk assessments are imprecise. Risk assessments help security executives better understand the dangers faced by their companies. But because of unknown factors (such as exactly when and where a terrorist group will strike and how it will strike), a precise level of risk assessment is impossible to achieve. Notwithstanding the aforementioned, a risk assessment is a useful tool and offers the security executive sufficient information to develop and define reasonable and effective countermeasures.

There are essentially four components to a terrorist risk assessment.

- *Assets*—What are the company's assets that, if damaged, altered, or eliminated, would cause harm to the company? What are the likely asset targets by terrorists?
- *Terrorist threats*—What are the threats to those assets by terrorist threat agents?
- *Vulnerability*—Are company assets vulnerable? If so, to what extent are they vulnerable to successful attacks by terrorist threat agents?
- *Risks*—What are the chances that terrorist threat agent attacks will find asset protection vulnerabilities and be able to take advantage of those vulnerabilities to mount successful attacks and meet the goals of the terrorist threat agents?

Asset Risk Management

The first step in assessing the threat must be approached within the context of understanding what needs to be protected.

- What assets require protection, and what level of protection is required for each asset? All company assets have value.
- All assets do not have the same value.
- All company assets do not require the same level of protection.
- It is the responsibility of the security executive to know what the company assets are and where they are located and to determine the level of protection required to reduce the risk to those assets to a level acceptable by company leadership. For example, a "Western" company with 10 employees operating in a sales office located in Stockholm, Sweden, has a different asset protection profile (in terms of value and exposure to risk) than a manufacturing operation with 500 employees from the same "Western" company but operating in Saudi Arabia.

Generally, all businesses have the following categories of assets:

- Physical property
- Information
- People

The specific types of assets, where they are located, how they are used, and the risks to those assets vary from business to business. When developing protective measures for company assets, the security executive must determine the risks to those assets and the impact to the company if the assets were lost. The following is a listing of major and common general categories of assets. It is not all-inclusive and is provided as a baseline for the security executive to use in developing a company-specific inventory of assets.

- Physical property
  - Buildings and real property
  - Equipment (office, research, and manufacturing)
  - Raw materials
  - Hardware/software (information systems)
  - Product (what the company produces and sells)
  - Services (that are sold to customers)
- Information
  - Intellectual property
  - Proprietary information
  - Information owned by partners, suppliers, or customers
  - Personal information of employees
- People
  - Employees
  - Customers
  - Suppliers
- Good will: Reputation of the company (particularly important in the context of product tampering)

Once the security executive knows what assets the company has, where they are, what their value is, and what the impact to the company would be if those assets were damaged or destroyed, the next step is to understand the threat, if any, to those assets.

Terrorist Threat Agents

Men never do evil so completely and cheerfully as when they do it from a religious conviction.
—Blaise Pascal, French mathematician and physicist (1623–1662)

Do terrorists target corporations? If so, are all corporations equally threatened? These are difficult questions to answer, yet they are questions every security executive must ask about the company he/she protects. There are many factors to consider when determining the threat, if there is any threat at all, to a corporation from terrorism. For a security executive to determine the threats effectively, there is much that executive must know about the company he/she supports.

- Is the company a global corporation operating in areas of high risk?
- What type of business does the corporation operate?
- Are its products and/or services controversial (e.g., abortion clinic or producer of petroleum products), and are there groups of people in strong opposition to the actions and objectives of the company?
- Has the corporation caused harm in the past (such as with the December 1994 deadly gas leak at the Union Carbide plant in Bhopal, India[8]), or is it aligned with governments engaged in controversial polices and practices?
- Is the company perceived as part of a nation-state that a terrorist threat agent considers an enemy and therefore a "state" target?

A large corporation operating globally and producing controversial goods or service is more likely to be a direct target of terrorist attacks than a small company operating locally and producing noncontroversial goods or services (e.g., a local baker of bread and pastries), assuming they are not operating in an area of high or extreme risk.

□ □ □ ▬▬▬▬▬▬▬▬▬▬▬▬▬▬▬▬▬▬▬▬▬▬▬▬▬▬▬▬▬▬▬▬

The *Encarta Dictionary* defines *threat* as: (1) a declaration of intent to cause harm, (2) an indication of something bad; a sign or danger that something undesirable is going to happen, (3) a person, animal, or thing likely to cause harm or pain.

▬▬▬▬▬▬▬▬▬▬▬▬▬▬▬▬▬▬▬▬▬▬▬▬▬▬▬▬▬▬▬▬ □ □ □

World Conditions

In its Country Reports on Terrorism 2004,[9] the U.S. Department of State described one of the elements of Al Qaeda's ideologies as follows:

U.S. power is based on its economy. Therefore, large-scale, mass-casualty attacks—especially focused on U.S. and other Western economic targets— are a primary goal.

This statement alone clearly indicates that at least one group intends to target Western economic interests. Targeting U.S. economic interests specifically is viewed as a means of inflicting serious harm to the United States. Targeting Western interests extends the threat of terror to the entire Western world; where Al Qaeda is concerned, this is essentially the non-Muslim world.

Committing a significant act of terror does not require many resources. According to a United Nations study, the cost of perpetrating an act of terror is very low.[10] For example, the Al Qaeda network spent less than $50,000 on each of their major attacks since September 11, 2001. Only the acts of 9/11 required funding of more than $100,000. Most arms and explosives used were unsophisticated and easily accessed. With desire, committed personnel, and a few dollars, major damage can easily be accomplished by a small group.

☐ ☐ ☐ ▬▬▬▬▬▬▬▬▬▬▬▬▬▬▬▬▬▬▬▬▬▬▬▬▬▬▬▬▬

As a security executive responsible for defending the corporation's assets against terrorist threat agents, you will probably need to spend much more money on defending the company assets than it would take for a terrorist threat agent to destroy them.

▬▬▬▬▬▬▬▬▬▬▬▬▬▬▬▬▬▬▬▬▬▬▬▬▬▬▬▬▬ ☐ ☐ ☐

The impact of terrorism is not the same everywhere. Robert Shapiro, former undersecretary of commerce in the Clinton Administration, states in his article "Al Qaeda and the GDP" suggests that "where terrorism is pervasive and protracted it depresses growth (Colombia, Basque area of Spain, and Israel), but where it occurs occasionally the economic impact is modest, resembling ordinary crime."[11]

A major difference between terrorism and crime is that with terrorism there is an expectation of future acts of terror, instilling a lingering sense of fear and thereby dampening future investment and causing greater resources to be spent on security and other protective measures. Furthermore, Shapiro argues, terrorism scares investment away from industries and areas thought to be particularly vulnerable and toward those less vulnerable, "safer" sectors and locations. In less vulnerable areas, like the United States had once viewed itself, acts of terror are less likely to have as significant an impact on the economy as, let's say, a tax bill imposed by the U.S. Congress.

Remember, the majority of today's terrorist threat agents, extreme-Islamic-oriented based, do not want businesses to succeed, hire people, and help make them, the company, and the nation-state prosperous. They want poor economies in these nation-states and high unemployment among the young, who are most vulnerable to the propaganda spewed by these Islamic extremists. That way, they offer these disaffected youths a way to vent their frustrations and targets to attack, who can be blamed for the youths' impoverished conditions.

The economic model of terrorism is similar to the economic model of crime. Common theory of crime indicates that people commit crime in expectation of a greater payoff. This is also often the case for the commission of acts of terror. Radical Islam has as its higher goal ("payoff") the institution of a world Islamic state.

Terror vs. Crime

Regardless of the similarities in terms of economic impact between terrorism and crime, don't make the mistake of thinking of crime as terror. All countries have crime, and, although violent criminal acts can be terrifying, violent crime is not generally considered an act of terror. An act of terror by itself may be indistinguishable from a violent crime.

An act of terror is a crime in most every corner of the world. However, unlike violent crime, terror is intended to create expectations of more violence to come. It is the anticipation of future violence that creates a condition of fear. Fear is paralyzing. It causes people to change their behavior.

In a capitalist society powered by a free economy, the changes driven by fear can be economically devastating. Crime, unlike terrorism, is generally committed in the present *without* the expressed intent of future violence. What follows is a list of common types of terrorist acts as defined in the United States and the United Kingdom.

- Armed attack (use of firearms and/or small explosives)
- Bombing (often vehicle-borne)
- Suicide bombing
- Firebombing
- Arson
- Kidnapping
- Assault

The following are the common types of crime defined in the United States—Part I Crimes Index.[12]

- Murder, homicide
- Forcible rape
- Robbery
- Assault
- Burglary
- Larceny
- Vehicle burglary
- Motor vehicle theft

Next we list the common types of crime categorized in the United Kingdom.[13]

- Violence against the person
- Sexual offenses
- Robbery
- Burglary
- Theft and handling stolen goods
- Fraud and forgery
- Criminal damage
- Drug offenses
- Other offenses

Most of the crimes just listed have at least one common characteristic: the objective of profit for the perpetrator. Crimes such as theft, burglary, larceny, robbery, motor vehicle theft, fraud, and some drug offenses (manufacturing, distribution, and sales) provide a financial gain for the perpetrator. These crimes are committed to make money. Terrorists often engage in criminal acts using ill-gained profits to finance their ability to commit acts of terror.

◻ ◻ ◻ ▬▬▬▬▬▬▬▬▬▬▬▬▬▬▬▬▬▬▬▬▬▬▬▬▬▬▬

Today's terrorists appear to be mostly those espousing extreme Islamic idealism as a justification for their actions and their goal of building Islamic regimes (Taliban style) and countries throughout the world.

▬▬▬▬▬▬▬▬▬▬▬▬▬▬▬▬▬▬▬▬▬▬▬▬▬▬▬ ◻ ◻ ◻

When considering the threat of terror to a corporation, it is important to think of that threat by terrorist threat agents as a distinct threat in itself and not one of criminals per se.

Direct and Indirect Threats of Terror

Preparing against a direct threat of terror may require a different level of protection than preparing for an indirect threat. A direct threat of terror against a corporation is one where a terrorist group specifically targets a corporation because of what that corporation is, does, or represents. For example: An eco-terrorist group attacks an oil company drilling operation in a generally pristine environmental system. The attack is intended to disrupt operations and inflict adverse economic impact on the corporation. In this case the intended target (the corporation) was selected and attacked because of what it does.

Generally, situations such as this are rare and are intended to cause damage only to the target corporation, with the ultimate goal of putting that corporation out of business. Security executives really need to know and understand that such organizations exist. Security executives must also seek to learn if any of those terrorist organizations have the company in their sights. For example, if you are the senior security executive of a company producing nuclear power, it is important to know if any terrorist or potential terrorist groups are targeting you to further their cause.

An indirect threat of terror to a corporation is where a general threat of terrorism exists either in the country or region where the company operates or to the business sector (energy, defense, etc.) the company is part of. It is possible and even probable that a corporation may fall victim to this threat, but the corporation itself is generally not the intended target. There are many more situations where a corporation was an indirect target of terrorism than situations where a corporation was a direct target of terrorism. For example, the attack on the Bali Indonesia Marriott Hotel in October 2002 was not an attack against the Marriott Corporation. It was an attack on a location where a large number of Western travelers, businesspersons, and foreign tourists congregated. There is no evidence to indicate the terrorists intended to attack a Marriott Hotel because they wanted to cause direct damage to the Marriott Corporation. Instead, the terrorists intended to inflict harm to Westerners while they were in a predominantly Muslim country. Thus, the Marriott Corporation was an indirect target of terror, not a direct target.

It does not appear that United Airlines was the intended target of the terrorists who attacked the United States on September 11, 2001. However, United Airlines assets (airplanes) were used as tools (implements of terror) to commit a large-scale and horrific act of terror. To a victim of terror this may be an inconsequential distinction, but to the security executive trying to protect company assets it is very relevant because it aids in developing and understanding the probability that a terrorist event may be committed against the company. Knowing whether the threat is direct or indirect influences how the security executive develops and implements preventative measures; for example, the amount of risk may differ between indirect and direct threats.

Why is this even important? Unfortunately, direct and specific threats are seldom stated by those intending to cause harm. Part of causing terror in a large population is to create uncertainty. General and vague threats of terror cause greater fear than specific threats. It's much easier (in terms of expenditure of company resources) for a security executive to protect a single specific target from terrorism than it is to protect many targets based on a general threat. Terrorist groups seldom make specific threats or threats specific enough to allow a security executive to focus on a single asset or target. At best, broad and general statements may be made by terrorist groups, assuming any statement at all is made prior to the execution of the act of terror. Statements too specific take the advantage away from the terrorist, and they are not inclined to let this happen.

Assessing the Threat

Once the security executive has determined what assets the company has, where those assets are located, and what the impact to the company is should those assets be damaged or destroyed, then he/she must begin looking outside of the company for terrorist threat agents to those assets, followed by analyses of attack methodologies.

Are there external threat agents intending to exploit company vulnerabilities to achieve a purpose detrimental to company assets (there could also be internal threat agents intending to damage the company)? This is the essential question the security executive must answer with some degree of certainty to develop effective protective measures.

Effective assessment of threats to company assets requires the security executive to know the environment within which the company operates. Does the company operate in areas of high risk? If so, what assets are exposed in these areas? What must a security professional know before he/she can make a reasonable evaluation of the threat to the company? Table 5-2 presents a checklist of areas to consider when determining if there is a terrorist threat to the company. Developing answers for these checklist questions will help any security executive better understand his or her own company. An in-depth understanding of the company is crucial for the security executive when assessing potential or actual threats to the company from organizations or entities that may have issues with your company.

Developing a realistic threat assessment takes time and resources. Determining meaningful answers to the checklist questions in Table 5-2 also takes time. In the interest of saving time, one may ask, "Can't the security executive assume what the terrorist threats are or just develop measures and plans to protect against the highest possible threat?" This may seem like a reasonable question. After all, who does not want their interests protected to the maximum extent possible and with the least amount of time and effort?

The problem with this approach is that developing protective measures for the highest possible threat requires a large amount of resources, which most security executives do not have at their disposal. Furthermore, it's usually unnecessary and impractical to protect against a maximum possible threat. It is much more efficient to develop an understanding

Table 5-2 Relevant Questions for a Security Executive to Answer When Attempting to Assess the Terrorist Threat to His/Her Company

Question	Comments
1. What is the size of your company?	Larger companies generally have greater levels of exposure.
2. How many employees do you have?	Greater numbers of employees can mean more exposure to risk.
3. Are company operations geographically dispersed?	This can be good because disbursement prevents putting all one's eggs in one basket. However, it does depend on where the operations are dispersed to.
4. Where are the major operations or manufacturing centers? (All locations must be considered.)	Large operations are generally more visible than small operations, attracting the attention of more people.
5. How well known is the company? (Is your company brand recognized internationally?)	High-profile companies attract the attention of many.
6. What is the company known for?	How the company is perceived by outsiders may influence the threat to the company.
7. What types of goods and services are produced?	Not all products are perceived of as good for people, animals, or the environment.
8. Are any of the goods and services produced controversial? (Offensive or objectionable to other groups or countries.)	Controversial products and services may call attention to the company. For example, the maker of products used for human abortion may be seen as controversial by some and in different parts of the world.
9. Are any of the products and services harmful (e.g., manufacture of toxins)?	These products or services could cause harm to people, animals, or the environment.
10. What is the reputation of the company? (What do outsiders, national and international, think of the company?)	It is important to know how the host country perceives your company.
11. Are there any organizations with stated positions against company products, services, or personnel?	This could be a direct threat.
12. Does the company operate in countries or regions of high risk? High-risk areas include those security with the following listed conditions: • Political instability • Open conflict or war • High rates of terrorism • Lawlessness or conditions of anomie	Obviously, operating in a high-risk country or region increases the general threat to the company, causing an executive to expend more resources on protective measures than if the company were operating in a lower-risk country or region.
13. If the company does not operate in high-risk areas, do employees visit or solicit business in high-risk countries or regions?	Employees who travel in and out of high-risk areas operate at a greater risk to themselves.
14. Does the company conduct business with unstable governments?	Political instability can and often does lead to increased risk and potential conflict. Sometimes, companies within that environment fall victim to political turmoil.

(Continued)

Table 5-2 Relevant Questions for a Security Executive to Answer When Attempting to Assess the Terrorist Threat to His/Her Company—Cont'd

Question	Comments
15. Does the company represent Western interests, culture, prosperity, or values and operate home country?	This is particularly important to know when operating in countries or regions hostile to outside its Western interests.
16. Does the company do business with other controversial corporations or companies?	Risk by association.
17. Are any of the company senior executives, directors, or officers controversial and drawing negative attention?	Senior executives are generally the most visible people within a company and often viewed as being the company (e.g., Microsoft and Bill Gates).
18. Are there explicit or implicit connections with a specific religion or religious group?	Politics, sex, and religion bring controversy.
19. Are there terrorist groups operating in the country or region?	Countries or regions with known terrorist groups possess known threats.
20. Have the terrorist groups stated their intentions?	Direct or indirect threats.
21. Have there been prior acts of terror?	A track record, known past threats.

of the threat to your company and to build an appropriate protection profile against a realistic threat. Obviously, if a direct threat is made against your company, as a security executive you must take action. Understanding the nature of the threat and its source (credibility) will help the security executive make better risk assessments.

Vulnerability

Once a security executive has determined what company assets require protection, the value of those assets, and the threat to those assets, the next step is to determine the vulnerability of those assets.

- Just how vulnerable are company assets?
- Are they currently protected at all?
- Are they protected to a level that will effectively mitigate existing threats?
- If there is a direct threat, do existing protective measures counter that threat?

The security executive must conduct a vulnerability assessment to determine the effectiveness of existing protective measures. Vulnerability cannot be assumed. Assuming is much like playing the lottery: It's highly dependent on luck. Just because the threat of terror exists does not necessarily mean any company will become a victim of an act of terror. Protective measures may already be in place that could effectively mitigate any threat of terror. However, the opposite may also be true. Existing protective measures may fall short of providing a sufficient level of protection to mitigate a threat of terror.

The *Encarta Dictionary* defines *vulnerable* as (1) without adequate protection; (2) open to attack.

When assessing vulnerability, we can ask such questions as the following:

- How vulnerable is any company to terrorism?
- What is the likelihood that a terrorist attack against a corporation will be carried out successfully?
- Are corporations particularly vulnerable to acts of terror?

There is no simple answer to the question of vulnerability; nevertheless, it is a question that every security executive must answer. Keep in mind, vulnerability may be a weakness in physical security measures, a flawed system or process, and/or a human error.

Until a vulnerability assessment is made, the answer will be unclear. Assessing asset vulnerability against acts of terror begins from within the organization and must be the result of a comprehensive effort to consider weaknesses in protective measures applied to those assets. Protective measures, if inadequately applied, could result in asset damage or loss. Simply stated, when security executives think about protecting the company they work for, it is good to begin by answering a few simple questions to help keep the mission in perspective.

1. *What must be protected?* In terms of assets this question is addressed earlier in this chapter but is worth restating here. All businesses have assets in the form of physical property, information, and people. The specific types of assets, where they are, and how they are used will vary from business to business. The security executive is charged with developing protective measures for company assets and must determine the terrorist risks to those assets and the impact to the company if the asset was lost because of a successful terrorist attack.

2. *For whom is the company being protected?* Shareholders and stakeholders have an interest in the company's being protected. Corporations exist for the benefit of their shareholders and stakeholders. Shareholders are owners of the company (private or public owners of company stock) and expect company management to perform well, make profits, and enrich them (as owners). Stakeholders (employees, suppliers, customers, local community, etc.) benefit in different ways from the success of the company. Employees benefit because through the company they work for they have a means of earning a living. Customers benefit from the products and services produced by the company. The community may benefit from taxes paid by the company and any good works accomplished by the company for the community.

3. *What is the company being protected from?* Companies must be protected from any person or organization that would harm them or impact the ability of a company to serve the best interests of its shareholders (owners) and stakeholders.

The charge to protect company assets cannot be taken lightly. Shareholders and stakeholders depend on executive management to run the company effectively and efficiently and to turn a profit. The security executive is a major contributor to this effort. Without adequate and appropriate protection, the company operates at a higher risk than necessary. With too much protection, potential profits are unnecessarily eroded through inefficiency in the application of protective measures, essentially through poor risk management.

▪ ▪ ▪ ━━━━━━━━━━━━━━━━━━━━━━━━━━━━━━━━━━━━━━━

Assets: What assets require protection?
Threat: Determine the type and likelihood of an attack that could cause damage to or loss of assets.
Vulnerability: How well are you protected against an attack of this nature?

━━━━━━━━━━━━━━━━━━━━━━━━━━━━━━━━━━━━━━━ ▪ ▪ ▪

So, just how does a security executive determine the overall vulnerability of his/her company to an act of terror and the vulnerability of any specific assets to terrorism? Assuming a threat assessment has been made, the security executive's next step is to assess company vulnerability against that threat. If the threat is a direct and specific threat (a rare occurrence), the security executive's response must be to assess the vulnerability of the company or assets to the specific threat. For example, should a threat of a vehicle-borne explosive be made against a company operating in a high-risk country, then the first course of action for the security executive is to assess the vulnerability against that specific threat. Here, the security executive must determine if the company operations are vulnerable to an attack of this type.

Since the threat of an attack by a vehicle laden with explosives is generally a problem of physical security controls, the security executive's first course of action is to conduct a thorough assessment of physical security controls. Physical security controls extend beyond physical barriers and include processes and procedures used to control access into and near an asset. (Physical security measures are addressed in greater depth in the next chapter.)

If a general threat of terror is made, that is to say, a threat to which no specific target can be associated, the security executive must assess the overall security profile of the company, looking for areas with substandard security measures or weaknesses in the general security profile. This is best accomplished by conducting a security survey. An example of a general threat of terror is one made against a country or a group of people. Threats of this nature are all too common in high-risk areas of the Middle East, where threats are commonly made against "Westerners" residing or traveling in the area. In this case, "Westerners" is intended to mean any person who appears to be from a "Western" country or region (Europe, North America, Australia, etc.).

▪ ▪ ▪ ━━━━━━━━━━━━━━━━━━━━━━━━━━━━━━━━━━━━━━━

A recent study by university researchers, using available data for the period of 1995–2002 and examining where a publicly traded firm was specifically mentioned as the target of a terrorist act, concluded that companies experience a significant drop in stock prices after they have been the target of a terrorist attack or incident. Furthermore, this study included in the analysis incidents of the kidnapping of a corporate executive and concluded that such an act is more devastating to company stock prices than the bombing of an office building.[14] The study results go on to state that the average drop in value of a company stock is $401 million for each terrorist incident. Clearly, from the perspective of shareholders an act of terror is not good for business.

━━━━━━━━━━━━━━━━━━━━━━━━━━━━━━━━━━━━━━━ ▪ ▪ ▪

Risks

How prepared does a company need to be to protect against the threat of terrorism? This is a question every security executive must answer and a question the authors continue to ask, since it is the question every security executive must confront.

Essentially, a security executive must first understand the level of risk for his company. Is the company at risk, and what is the degree of risk? For a risk to exist there must be a threat (agent), a vulnerability to that threat, and an adverse impact to company asset(s) if the threat exploits any vulnerability.

In its simplest form, risk can be described as

$$\text{Threat} \times \text{Vulnerability} \times \text{Impact on asset value}^{15} = \text{Risk}$$

or

$$T \times V \times I = R$$

To elaborate: The threat against an asset when considered in the context of the value of the asset and the vulnerability of the asset leads to an assessment of risks. Figure 5-1 is a graphic depiction of this formula. In the matrix, the risk profile for three different companies is plotted. Company A is in a medium-threat environment, but its vulnerability is high. This could be due to inadequate asset protection measures being in place. Company B is in a high-threat condition and a highly vulnerable position. This could be due to operating in a high-risk region of the world or to operating within a country under an actual threat of terror. Company B is also operating with inadequate asset protection measures in place. Company C is operating under low threat with a low level of vulnerability. This condition could be due to an absence of a threat of terror in the region where Company C operates and because Company C has strong or at least adequate asset protection measures in place.

This simple matrix is an effective way to depict the risk condition of an asset, regardless of what the asset is or where it is located. This matrix is particularly effective

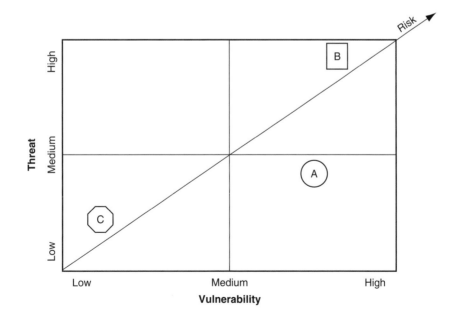

FIGURE 5-1 A risk assessment matrix.

in demonstrating to others the risk level of company assets when many high-value company assets are located in different geographical environments.

To make effective use of the risk assessment matrix, the security executive should categorize company assets into groups, selecting categories that best represent company assets (physical sites, high-value equipment, product storage/distribution centers, specialized capabilities, etc.) and then plot them on the risk assessment matrix in those groupings. This should produce a simple yet effective picture of company asset risk levels.

The risk assessment process is an iterative one. That is to say, threats, vulnerability, and the assets owned by a company continually change. To understand effectively the risk to company assets, the threat and vulnerability must be evaluated periodically. These evaluations are not one-time actions that can be executed, filed away, and referred to as needed. They must be revised and updated. Ideally, revisions and updates should be event driven (a known change in condition) or schedule driven using a schedule best meeting company leadership expectations.

Risk Mitigation

To be successful, a security executive must understand the company's tolerance for risk. Some companies (driven by ownership or management) have a higher tolerance for risk than others. Sometimes this is driven by the nature of the company business. For example, a pharmaceutical company may have a lower tolerance for risk than an entertainment company since a failure in the pharmaceutical business may pose a threat to human life, whereas a failure in the entertainment business may result in a canceled production. Both create a financial loss, but one may threaten human life.

A security executive taking big risks in a company with a low tolerance for risk creates a "risky business" situation for him-/herself. Once risk levels have been established, the security executive must begin to manage that risk. The options for managing risk are quite basic.

- *Transfer the risks*—This is usually accomplished through the purchase of insurance.
- *Avoid the risk*—Leave or stay out of high-risk countries or regions.
- *Accept the risk*—Operate as is and hope for the best.
- *Manage the risk*—Lower the risk to an acceptable (within company tolerance) level by taking or enhancing protective measures. Remember, the security executive can't protect everyone and everything.

Gathering Information and Producing Intelligence Related to Terrorist Threats

> *Knowledge is power.*[16]
> —Sir Francis Bacon

Earlier we discussed the risk equation:

$$\text{Threat} \times \text{Vulnerability} \times \text{Impact on asset value} = \text{Risk}$$

or

$$T \times V \times I = R$$

Perhaps the most difficult part of this equation is determining the threat. Without knowing the threat, it is difficult to assess vulnerability with any degree of specificity. Identifying company assets may take time, but the task is achievable. Determining a threat requires access to threat-related information that the security executive generally does not possess. In some ways, getting threat information can be easy. For example: a terrorist group may make a threat, usually via the press or a website posting. That information becomes public and is there for anyone to use as deemed appropriate. Unfortunately, information of this nature is more often than not broadly stated, lacking specificity, and highly unreliable.

In other ways, getting threat-related information is very difficult. For example, most governments obtain and develop threat information through their intelligence-producing apparatus. Most often this information is classified (access to it restricted through formal governmental controls) and is not shared with commercial businesses (with few exceptions).

Where does this leave the security executive? Terrorists don't share their intentions other than in general statements. Governments don't share developed threat information. This means that the security executive must either produce or purchase threat-related information through open-source providers. Useful threat information is not easy to obtain and is necessary for an effective threat assessment.

Collecting Information to Produce Meaningful Threat-Related Intelligence for the Company

The type of information collected is information that has potential value in the processes of making business decisions about risks, more specifically, risk to the company from terrorism, be that an act of terror or the threat of terror. The information collected is to be analyzed, with the intent of producing a usable product. That usable product contributes to the threat, vulnerability, and risk assessments developed by the security executive in an effort to understand the potential (or real) threat of terrorism to the company, its assets, personnel, and information in any environment it chooses to operate. That usable product will be referred to throughout this section as *threat intelligence* or *intelligence*.

Intelligence has value. The extent of that value will depend on its timely and relevant application and use. Having intelligence is of little value if it is not used properly or not used in a timely manner. Intelligence can assist the security executive in preparing to make good strategic and tactical decisions involving the protection of property, assets, people, and information from harm.

Intelligence has value in many areas of the business. However, it is vital to the successful decision-making processes of the security executive. Intelligence can be produced through the gathering of information from a variety of sources. This section discusses these sources along with the process for developing useful intelligence.

□ □ □ ▬▬▬▬▬▬▬▬▬▬▬▬▬▬▬▬▬▬▬▬▬▬▬▬▬▬▬▬▬

Intelligence, n. **5.** information received or imparted; news. **6. a.** secret information esp. about an enemy or potential enemy. **b.** the gathering or distribution of such information. **c.** the evaluated conclusions drawn from such information. **d.** an organization engaged in gathering such information: military intelligence.[17]

▬▬▬▬▬▬▬▬▬▬▬▬▬▬▬▬▬▬▬▬▬▬▬▬▬▬▬▬▬ □ □ □

Intelligence does not just happen; it has to be produced. However, there is nothing mystifying about intelligence. Like anything of value, it takes skill and hard work to create. Producing intelligence is not unlike producing many other products. It involves a defined process, disciplined and skilled workers, careful analysis, and proper application or implementation. It is as much an art as it is a science. The value of intelligence depends on where, when, how, and under what conditions it is used.

Intelligence may also be purchased from commercial providers. There are many commercial providers of intelligence, producing security-relevant information about political, economic, safety/security, and crime conditions in countries and regions around the world. Most provide general assessments of conditions in a country or region of the world, which are developed from public, open-source information and from in-country or in-region experts. This is done for a fee and made available to customers. Further, for additional fees, most commercial providers of intelligence will tailor information and reports focusing on the specific interest of a customer (political, geographical, economic, criminal, a specific company or business, etc.).

Many of the companies providing this type of service are good at what they do and have people all over the world capable of gathering information and producing useful threat-related intelligence. That is not to say that any of these providers of intelligence can and do produce specific threat-related intelligence. Most provide information related to a general threat or condition within a specific geographic region, developed from open, official, and unofficial sources.

Intelligence is more than just information or data. Collecting information, even massive amounts of information, does not create intelligence. Volume is not the key. Relevant information analyzed within the context of specific needs can lead to the creation of intelligence. Some information and data may have value as intelligence without further analysis. Data may be useful as intelligence just as it was obtained. Generally, however, that is not the case.

For most information or data to be useful as intelligence, it must be analyzed and applied within the context of what is known to help better understand what is not known. For effective analysis, the task needs to be performed by a skilled analyst or someone, at the very least, with subject matter expertise. Any data or information collected is most valuable when it is transformed through skillful analysis into results that are useful.

What Is Information?

In this age of electronic and digital information, people and businesses are inundated with data. More than any other time in human history, information is abundantly available to more people, businesses, governments, and institutions. So much information exists and the task of managing it is so complex that new disciplines such as knowledge management have evolved. Knowledge management seeks to better manage the body of knowledge contained within a company or organization and its people. Knowledge management can help a company manage what it knows and who knows what.

With so much information available, it is difficult to determine what information has value and what information does not have value. Moreover, with so much information available, valuable information gets lost within the sheer volume of it all. For practical purposes, if information is needed but not available when it is needed, then it may as well be lost.

In the April 2000, second edition of its *College Dictionary*, Random House Webster defines *information* as knowledge communicated or received concerning a particular fact or circumstance. Continuing on, *information* is further defined as knowledge gained through study, communication, research, etc.: data.

Information in and of itself has value. However, it may or may not be intelligence. Facts and figures by themselves may only be interesting. But when combined with other data, placed within a specific context, and analyzed with a purpose, the value of that information may increase. That information may become useful intelligence.

How Does Someone Get Information?

Information does not just fall into one's lap. Well, actually it may very well fall into one's lap, considering how ubiquitous it is, but generally information, particularly useful information, does not. Information needs to be acquired and developed. Collecting information is both simple and complex. Gathering information from public sources such as newspapers and journals requires only the purchase or borrowing of a copy and then searching through the publication for useful information. This is a time-consuming but simple process. Moreover, much of the information available may be vague or general and not specific enough to meet one's needs. Obtaining more specific or more narrowly focused information usually requires the use of less prevalent sources, such as commercial intelligence providers.

When seeking information, one should have an idea of the type of information needed. Since so much information is available, determining the type of information needed and then matching that to sources that may be able to provide that type of information is the simple and efficient approach. For example, if looking to gather information about the level of crime in a certain city, a good place to start is with organizations that study crime or organizations that monitor criminal activity and develop statistical data. In some countries, this data is open-source information; in others it is not. Where it is not, it may be necessary to seek commercial sources, NGOs, or organizations that have an interest in this.

When seeking information relative to the threat of terrorism there are two places to begin. The first is internal—right inside your own company. The second is external—any source outside of your company, and there are many. Each is further described below.

Internal Sources (Sources Within Your Company)

Within any company there are potential sources for acquiring information related to terrorism and the threat of terrorism. Here are some of the more obvious.

- *Company library:* Many large or medium-size companies maintain a small internal library where business-relevant publications are acquired and kept. This is usually a good place to start when looking for basic information since it is the most convenient. Company libraries usually contain current business, news, and political publications and journals. A librarian may even be available to assist in searches for specific sources or information.

- *Other employees:* Employees on assignment outside of the home country, or employees who frequently travel internationally, generally are exposed to or have access to relevant information. Talk to them. Engage the wider organization. If asked, they are usually willing to share what they know. The security professional should develop internal information sources and to the extent possible integrate them into an information network to help create a robust learning environment.

External Sources

These can be categorized into the following areas.

- *Commercial:* There are many commercial providers of intelligence. One only need consult the Internet to find multiple sources. Such companies sell their product for a fee. They generally produce a standard threat-based product useful to most businesses operating in different regions of the world. Moreover, they tend to focus on areas of high risk, since that is what most consumers of threat information are concerned with. They also produce specialized products to order that can vary from terrorist threat assessments to crime statistics.
- *News organizations:* There are many news organizations reporting on current events both locally and globally. They are particularly helpful in establishing trends and patterns.
- *Business colleagues working in the same business sector:* These can be useful for sharing what they know about the regions of the world they travel to and work in.
- *Government:* To some extent governments do make information available to their citizens through various means, including websites. The only disadvantage with government information is the "spin" put on that information. Often government information is biased, based on political objectives and not the blunt truth.

☐ ☐ ☐ ▬▬▬▬▬▬▬▬▬▬▬▬▬▬▬▬▬▬▬▬▬

Public information essentially refers to all information you can legally and ethically identify, locate, and then access.

▬▬▬▬▬▬▬▬▬▬▬▬▬▬▬▬▬▬▬▬▬ ☐ ☐ ☐

How Do You Transform Information into Useful Intelligence?

Developing or producing intelligence should be accomplished via a systematic process. It should not be a massive effort to collect huge amounts of information, hoping for the best as the information is sorted and evaluated. The process for developing useful intelligence should, at a minimum, traverse the following seven steps. (See Table 5-3 for a sample intelligence process checklist.)

- *Establish needs:* What must be known? What questions need to be answered? How will the results be used? Who needs the intelligence? These questions must be asked at the beginning of the information-gathering process. Answers to these questions will help focus time and energy on specific types and categories of information. Proceeding without posing these questions first will lead to wasted time and effort.

Table 5-3 Sample of an Intelligence Process Checklist

Process Step	Process Actions
Establish needs	• Who needs intelligence?
	• What information is needed?
	• Prioritize needs.
Collect information	• Develop research strategy.
	• Identify sources.
	• Collect information.
	• Review information to ensure you have what is needed.
Analyze information	• Ensure data is relevant to needs.
	• Analyze data.
	• Draw conclusions.
	• Conduct supplemental data collection if necessary.
	• Review analysis in the context of other known information.
Produce intelligence	• Package intelligence to meet user expectations and needs.
	• Protect intelligence—release only to those with a need-to-know.
Distribute to users	• Deliver intelligence in a timely fashion.
Apply intelligence	• Integrate intelligence into decision-making process.
	• Use in context with other relevant intelligence.
	• Protect the intelligence.
Receive feedback	• Was the intelligence supplied useful?
	• Was it delivered in a timely and relevant fashion?
	• Have users' needs changed?

- *Collect information or data:* Once intelligence needs have been identified and separated into specific categories or types of information, the process of gathering information can begin. The next step is to identify the specific sources for information. For example, if the question that needs to be answered pertains to the risk of doing business in the Congo with the threat of terrorism there, then sources where that information is expected to be found obviously should be tapped.
- *Analyze information or data:* The information collected must be analyzed within the context of the questions that need to be answered and in concert with other available relevant information. In other words, the new information must be analyzed along with what is already known within the context of the questions asked.
- *Produce intelligence:* The product of the analysis should be refined, or more useful new information should be produced. At the very least the product of analysis should contribute to increasing the body of knowledge in the areas where further understanding was sought. As additional information is acquired and analyzed, it too should contribute to enhancing the total body of knowledge.
- *Distribute intelligence to users:* Intelligence must be shared in a timely manner with the people who need it. For example, if a facilities and security team is making physical security enhancements to a site in Kuwait, relevant threat information is most useful to them prior to designing changes and enhancements. Regardless of how valuable new competitive intelligence is, unless it is placed in the right hands in a timely fashion its value may be diminished or totally degraded.

- *Apply intelligence:* Team members who receive intelligence must act on what they learn. Unapplied knowledge is not very useful.
- *Feedback:* Get regular feedback from all internal consumers of intelligence. Are they being supplied with the intelligence they need? What is the quality of the product they are provided? Has there been a change in their interest and needs? What additional intelligence do they need? These and other questions should be asked of the team members and regular feedback encouraged.

Summary

The world is a dangerous place, and all indicators suggest it will continue to be a dangerous place for many years to come. For the security executive responsible for protecting a company, particularly a global corporation, understanding and mitigating risks are primary responsibilities.

Essentially there are four components to a developing a risk assessment:

- *Assets*—What are the company's assets that if damaged, altered, or eliminated would cause harm to the company?
- *Threat*—What is the threat to those assets?
- *Vulnerability*—Are the assets vulnerable? And if so, to what extent are they vulnerable?
- *Risks*—A probability assessment of

$$\text{Threat} \times \text{Vulnerability} \times \text{Impact to assets} = \text{Risks}$$

Once a risk assessment is complete, the security executive must focus on mitigating risks. This can be accomplished through the following actions:

- *Transfer of risks*—This is usually accomplished through the purchase of insurance.
- *Avoid the risk*—Leave or stay out of high-risk countries or regions.
- *Accept the risk*—Operate as is and hope for the best.
- *Manage the risk*—Lower the risk to an acceptable level (within company tolerance) by taking or enhancing protective measures. Remember, the security executive can't protect everyone and everything.

Endnotes

[1] United States National Counterterrorism Center Report, "A Chronology of Significant International Terrorism for 2004," dated April 27, 2005.
[2] http://safespaces.com/SS.Security_htm/Security_Terrorism_Cost.htm; U.S. Department of State; *The Economic Cost of Terrorism,* by Brian S. Westbury (September 2002).
[3] http://www.theage.com.au/articles/2004/08/27/1093518081060.html?from=storylhs; *UN Calculates the Cost of Terrorism,* by Edith M. Lederer (August 2004).
[4] "Terrorism, Here and There," *Wall Street Journal* (September 15, 2006), p. A12.
[5] U.S. Department of Homeland Security, U.S. Customs and Border Protection, Office of Border Patrol: "Terrorist Organization Reference Guide" (January 2004).
[6] See: http://en.wikipedia.org/wiki/U.S._State_Department_list_of_Foreign_Terrorist_Organizations.

[7] NGOs are democratic entities generally formed around a focused set of goals and having no affiliation with governments or the business establishment. See: http://www.google.com/search?hl=en&lr=&defl=en&q=define:NGO&sa=X&oi=glossary_definition&ct=title

[8] See: http://www.bhopal.org/whathappened.html

[9] U.S. Department of State Publication 11248 from the Office of the Coordinator for Counterterrorism, released April 2005.

[10] See: http://www.theage.com.au/articles/2004/08/27/1093518081060.html?from=storylhs

[11] See http://www.slate.com/toolbar.aspx?action=print&id=2079298

[12] See: http://www.sanantonio.gov/saPD/pdf/UCRcategories.pdf

[13] See: http://www.homeoffice.gov.uk/rds/countrules.html

[14] See: http://newswire.ascribe.org/cgi-bin/behold.pl?ascribeid=20060523.083733&time=09%200; "Terror Attacks Against Companies Drop Stock Values Significantly, Study Shows."

[15] Andy Jones and Debi Ashenden, *Risk Management for Computer Security* (Elsevier Butterworth-Heinemann, 2005).

[16] Sir Francis Bacon (1561–1626), *Religious Meditations, Of Heresies*, 1597.

[17] *Random House Webster's College Dictionary* (New York: Random House, 2000).

Physically Securing Corporate Premises in Order to Mitigate Attacks

The superior man, when resting in safety, does not forget that danger may come. When in a state of security, he does not forget the possibility of ruin. When all is orderly, he does not forget that disorder may come. Thus his person is not endangered, and his States and all their clans are preserved.
—Confucius (551–479 BC)

To what extent should every corporation prepare to mitigate an act of terror? Must a fortress be built? Or is it only necessary to be better protected than your neighbor. How can the corporate target be hardened? What steps are necessary to harden the corporate target? These questions are addressed in this chapter.

Identifying physical measures and controls that can be used to harden the corporate target against acts of terror are two of the main defenses against successful terror threat agents' attacks. For the most part, the physical measures and controls discussed, when properly implemented, provide protection against many different security threats, not just potential acts of terror. However, considering the power of such terrorist tools as suicide bombings, improvised explosive devices (IEDs), and car bombs, it may be necessary that physical security defenses be extended as far out as possible.

It is important to keep in mind that there are no "silver bullets" available to the security executive for protecting company assets, people, and information against acts of terror—other than closing shop and going out of business, which is unrealistic. However, certain fundamental physical security controls when properly implemented will provide the foundation of a protection profile the security executive needs to build in order to protect effectively whatever requires protection. Physical security measures are the foundation for the protection program on which other security measures and practices (personnel protective measures and information protection measures) are built.

The concept of having different physical security measures and controls applied in layers is considered the most effective way to defend physically against terrorist attacks. A broad scope of different physical controls are discussed in this chapter, beginning with the most common measures employed at the outer perimeter of a facility and working through the various controls as they would be layered throughout an ordinary facility, from the exterior to the interior.

The use of external physical barriers such as fences, walls, gates, and other types of barricades are addressed. Moreover, the design of buildings and the use of internal barriers, including access control systems involving current security technology, are considered.

□ □ □ ▬▬▬▬▬▬▬▬▬▬▬▬▬▬▬▬▬▬▬▬▬▬▬▬▬▬▬▬▬

The focus should be on physical controls that can be effectively used to harden a facility or site, making it a less vulnerable and less desirable target of terrorists.

▬▬▬▬▬▬▬▬▬▬▬▬▬▬▬▬▬▬▬▬▬▬▬▬▬▬▬▬▬ □ □ □

It is important to make a distinction between the physical threat and the cyber-threat. All threats against a company must be taken seriously. The security executive must protect the company against all threats. That includes physical threats and cyberthreats. Extensive damage to a company's physical assets, information, or personnel can devastate and even destroy a company. Yet there is nothing more devastating to a company than loss of life. Protecting against the physical attack, the event with the greatest potential to cause harm to people, must be paramount in the security executive's efforts.

As damaging as an attack on information systems may be (thus the potential to damage information itself, its integrity, reliability, and availability), it is generally not as potentially life threatening as a physical attack. However, there are exceptions. For example, if cyberterrorists were able to compromise a medical facility's information system and change information contained within patients' medical records, causing the improper delivery of medical support to patients, a threat to human health and welfare could occur. In a worst-case scenario, even the death of patients could occur. Using a larger example, if terrorists were able, through a cyberattack, to disrupt a communications system such as an air traffic control system of a nation-state or region of the world, loss of information, property, or life could be the result. The security executive must prepare for all potential terrorist threats.

The threats that get the most attention (press and public) tend to be those that instill the most fear. It is much easier for the general public and for that matter many employees of businesses to understand the threat and consequences of a physical attack than those of a cyberattack.[1]

Physical Security Controls

No business is without security risks. These risks take many forms. From common crime and workplace violence to acts of economic espionage and terrorism, businesses can be, and often are, subjected to different threats. Effectively mitigating risks is not a happenstance occurrence. Problem elimination and risk mitigation require planning. They also require an understanding of needs, conditions, threats, and vulnerabilities. Assessing security risks and planning for an appropriate level of protection must begin with the basics: physical security.

Physical security is the most fundamental aspect of protection, that is, the use of physical controls to protect the premises, site, facility, building, or other physical assets belonging to a company. The application of physical security is fundamental to the protection profile of a company, and the process of using layers of physical protective measures to prevent unauthorized access and harm or damage or destruction of property is essential. In essence, physical security measures protect a property, plant, facility, building, or office and any of its contents from loss or harm.

Physical security measures also contribute to the protection of people and information. Generally, sophisticated protection measures other than physical controls are employed to protect information and information systems. Nevertheless, physical security measures are part of the overall protective package. They are the baseline security measures on which all other security measures are built.

Physical security measures help ensure that only authorized persons have access to company facilities and property. The measures employed must be appropriate for each separate operating environment. Manufacturing facilities, located in industrial areas, will require the use of physical security measures and controls that may differ from those at a downtown, large city sales office.

Company operations and assets located in high-risk areas will require greater controls than similar operations located in low-risk areas. All other security measures should be integrated into, or developed and implemented in coordination with, the various layers of physical security protective measures, thereby developing a protection profile of security suitable to the needs of the operation.

Security in Layers

What physical security measures get used will depend greatly on what assets require protection and the level of risk company assets are exposed to. Keep in mind the fundamental risk equation (see Chapter 5):

$$\text{Threat} \times \text{Vulnerability} \times \text{Impact on assets} = \text{Risk}$$

This is the basis for developing a protection profile intended to mitigate risks. The value of assets and the risk to those assets should be the basis for determining the type and mix of protective measures necessary for effective protection of all assets.

Ideally, the application of physical protective measures is accomplished in the beginning. That is to say, physical security measures should be incorporated into a facility during the design phase and built into the facility during the construction phase. Ideally, architects and security professionals would work together, taking into consideration all aspects of security applicable to the proposed operating environment. This type of planning would help create optimum security at the lowest possible cost.

If done properly, the security problems created by so many buildings being designed without any consideration given to security controls would no longer be an issue. However, the security executive must recognize that, over time, conditions change. Threats to a company may come and go. As conditions change, the security executive must reassess the risk to company assets by conducting threat and vulnerability studies and developing new risk assessments. As the threat increases, new physical controls may be necessary. As the threat decreases, it may even be practical and efficient to lessen some controls. All controls appropriate for high-threat or high-risk environments are not always appropriate for low-threat and low-risk environments.

If in the course of implementing new physical controls and measures the security executive is working not with new construction but with an existing facility or building with inadequate physical security controls, designing essential physical security measures and controls may not be possible. If retrofitting or renovation of the site or facility is necessary to accommodate a new business operating environment, then security may still be considered as part of the design. If not, physical security issues should be addressed prior to occupancy and before routine business operations begin. More than likely, security problems resulting from a failure to make security part of the design and construction phases will be of a structural nature and too expensive to undo or fix.

The only solution in this case will be the application of layers of protective measures in such a way as to minimize the negative aspects of physical controls on routine operations yet to enhance the security profile sufficiently to mitigate risks. This condition becomes problematic if there is a rapid change in threat conditions. Should a low-threat environment suddenly become a high-risk environment, the security executive may have to employ creative measures to enhance the overall security profile, thereby reducing the risk. For example, if the threat from vehicle-borne bombings suddenly increased, demanding of the security executive the implementation of security controls but with no built-in flexibility to move the perimeter, the security executive would be forced to seek less-than-ideal measures (e.g., temporary barriers and controls). Thus, because flexible security measures were not made part of the original design, a temporary and perhaps limited or less-than-ideal set of measures must be employed.

The application of physical security controls should be approached in layers. There is no single physical control that, when properly applied, will fulfill all security needs and, in particular, provide effective protection against terrorism. Layering controls from the outer boundaries of a facility (and beyond if possible) to the innermost boundaries will allow the security professional to build a security profile that meets the specific facility security needs. Figure 6-1 depicts the primary layers of a site requiring protection.

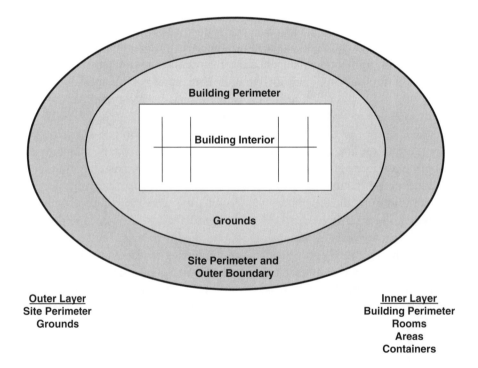

FIGURE 6-1 Layers of protection at a site, facility, or building.

Applying layers of protection to a facility or operation is influenced not only by the level of risk but by the environment and other conditions, such as the construction of the outer perimeter. For example, an office building located within a city may have only as its outer layer of protection, or perimeter, the walls of the building. In this condition the application of additional physical protective measures will be limited. After all, it's usually not possible to take over public areas and roads, rerouting or controlling traffic in order to keep people and vehicles away from a facility. Nor is it practical (or even possible) to take over areas occupied by adjacent businesses, thus expanding the zone of control. Therefore, the only options lie with reinforcing the structure itself and rigidly controlling personnel and, if possible, vehicle access. Structural, changes such as the installation of shatter-proof glass designed to minimize the effect of explosives or the installation of blast-resistant walls, essentially harden the building, thus reinforcing the perimeter, but may reduce the functional interior workspace. If the risk is still much higher than the security executives' ability to reinforce the structure and workspace, the only option left may be to vacate the premises and find a safer operating location.

In contrast, a manufacturing facility located in an industrial district may be situated on a large parcel of land and include open areas for parking and storage and general grounds surrounding the building or buildings. On a facility of this type the perimeter is usually the first barrier, often protected or constructed in the form of a wall or fence, located at or near the edge of the property line. An operating environment like this is much more conducive to the implementation of additional security measures and controls designed to keep intruders at a distance, thus reducing risk.

The perimeter of a facility may take many forms. For an office building it may be the building walls. For a factory it may be a fence line or a wall at the property edge. The outermost layer of protection could also be a natural physical barrier, such as a river, lake, or other body of water, or a man-made barrier. Whatever the barrier, it is the first layer of physical security. It may be at the perimeter's edge or inside the perimeter. Regardless of where it is situated, it is the layer of first control. Inside that outer layer, the use of other physical security layers may be necessary.

There may be times when the natural perimeter or barrier is as much a vulnerability as it is a barrier. Think of a lake or other body of water serving as a portion of a facility perimeter. That lake may prevent foot, car, and truck traffic, but it is susceptible to watercraft access. Other layers of protective measures may be required to reduce the vulnerability to watercraft traffic gaining access to the property.

Grounds

Not all facilities have grounds. Grounds may serve many purposes. They may be purely decorative, to create a pleasant environment for customers and employees. They may be functional and serve as a place to locate storage areas and warehousing facilities. They may also serve as a buffer or barrier between the perimeter of the facility and the buildings where work is done and where people, physical assets, and information are housed. If kept clear, grounds may serve as a buffer zone, allowing for unobstructed observation of the area. If used for storage or other purposes, they should be kept organized and maintained. In this way, disruptions are easier to identify and the risk of hazards is reduced.

When protecting against the physical threat of terror, grounds may serve as an ideal place for the installation of additional physical barriers designed and erected to reinforce the perimeter. For example, if ample grounds are available, a second fence line may be installed, serving as an additional barrier to prevent physical or personnel access. This layer may be particularly useful in helping to keep vehicles away from buildings that house people. Consider a situation where the desired condition is to have a decorative or soft look at the outer perimeter, with adequate grounds a more robust and fortified barrier or set of barriers may be placed behind the outer perimeter, thus maintaining the desired decorative look but reinforcing the perimeter and reducing the possibility of an intrusion.

In a high-risk environment, it may be necessary to do away with the decorative or soft-look perimeter and establish a hardened and fortified control at the outer perimeter. The operating environment and level of risk will influence the decision of the security executive here. It is also important to recognize the value of a fortified look in a high-risk environment. Unless your company is a specific target, terrorists and others with bad intentions will look for softer targets. A hardened look, in and of itself, may serve as one layer of security.

Roads and Highways

Roads are both necessary and problematic. They give employees, service and support personnel, and customers easy access to the facility. However, roads may also allow unauthorized personnel easy access to your facility. Roads are a particular concern where there is a threat of a terrorist attack using explosive-laden vehicles. Furthermore, should terrorists choose to target a facility from the ground, they will use roadways to get themselves as close to the facility as possible.

The degree of control necessary on all roads leading to your facility will vary. Any controls used will depend on the type of road and its use. More specifically, is it a public road or a private road? Public highways and roads do not allow for additional controls. They belong to the municipality, city, or state and exist to facilitate movement of vehicles and people. If a facility is adjacent to a public highway or road, controls can begin only where the highway or road ends and your property begins. However, in high-risk areas it may be possible to work with government authorities to make changes on public highways and roads, generally those roads less traveled and considered more vulnerable or close to sensitive sites. Don't always count on it.

Private roads allow for much greater control. Owners of private roads may install many different controls that facilitate restricting passage. Owners of private roads can make their own determination as to who has access and under what conditions. Ideally, controls on any road should begin as close to the perimeter as possible and extend as far away as practical and necessary.

In an office building environment, public highways and roads generally lead to parking lots, which are often adjacent to your building. This means perimeter controls begin at the parking area or at the walls of the building. Parking structures, particularly public parking structures, are inherently vulnerable to explosive-laden-vehicle attacks. One need only look at the first attempt by terrorists to attack the World Trade Center in New York City on February 26, 1993.[2] An explosive-laden vehicle was driven into the parking structure and detonated, causing extensive damage.

Fences, Walls, Gates, and Other Barriers

Two types of barriers are used for perimeter protection: natural barriers and structural barriers. Examples of natural barriers include rivers, lakes, and other bodies of water, cliffs, and other types of terrain that is difficult to traverse. Each has advantages and disadvantages.

Examples of structural barriers include highways, fences, walls, gates, concrete (reinforced) vehicle barriers, and other types of construction that prohibit or inhibit physical access. None of these barriers completely prevent access. They do, however, make it much more difficult for unauthorized persons to gain access. Remember, there is no single protective measure that can be implemented to achieve total control. When structural barriers are used with other layers of physical control they can be very effective.

☐ ☐ ☐ ━━━━━━━━━━━━━━━━━━━━━━━━━

One very important consideration to keep in mind is that today's terrorists perpetrate their attacks with no regard for their own lives, expecting to die (suicide attacks) in many attacks. Therefore, a security professional cannot assume that most physical barriers will be sufficient to deter and successful in stopping all terrorist attacks. Terrorist vehicles will not stop for locked or otherwise-closed gates. They will not stop for security guards. They will stop only when their vehicle reaches its destination and is exploded. So to protect against this type of attack, fences and gates must be able to withstand the force of vehicles ramming into them. Exterior windows, doors, and walls must be as blast-/bomb-proof as possible.

━━━━━━━━━━━━━━━━━━━━━━━━━ ☐ ☐ ☐

Fences

The most common form of barrier, other than the walls of a building, is the fence. Fences vary in type, size, use, and effectiveness. They can be erected quickly for a reasonably low cost, as in the case of the basic chain-link fence. In the event of a sudden increase in threat level, erecting a fence as an additional layer of security can be a relatively swift action. Fences may also be made more complicated and effective by adding barbed wire or concertina wire or alarm systems or using double fencing with alarmed clear zones in between. The type of fence selected should be determined by the specific threat and needs.

For fencing to be most effective it should rest no more than two inches above the ground; in areas where the soil is loose, a concrete trough or border should lie at the base to prevent gaps from erosion or human intrusion. Buildings, structures, and trees must be kept far enough away from the fence line as to offer no assistance to those who would attempt unauthorized entry.

Walls

Walls serve the same purpose as fences. They are man-made barriers (structures) but generally are more expensive to install than fences. Common types of walls are made of cement block, masonry, brick, or stone. Walls tend to have a greater aesthetic value, appealing to those who prefer a gentler and softer look. Regardless of the type of wall, its purpose as a barrier is the same as a fence. To be most effective, walls ought to be 7 feet high with three to four strands of barbed wire on top. This will help prevent scaling. For aesthetic reasons, management may resist the use of barbed wire. Nevertheless, it should be seriously considered, particularly in areas of high risk.

Walls also present a disadvantage, in that they obstruct the view of an area. Chain-link and wire fences allow for visual access on both sides—walls do not. This obstacle can be overcome by keeping clear zones for several feet on each side of the wall and by using video surveillance cameras. Use of roving patrols also increases visibility. When the wall of a building serves as a perimeter barrier in lieu of fencing, the issues are different. Scaling the wall to get to the other side is not an issue, but access to the roof is. Furthermore, controlling access to other openings becomes more critical, since the wall to the building may be the only outer barrier separating the outside world from the assets inside requiring protection. In situations like this, where the wall is the only barrier between company assets and the outside world, if risk is high, it may be necessary to consider relocating to a more desirable and suitable location. It would be prudent to move to a site in a lower-risk area (assuming the current risk is a long-term one) or one with enough flexibility and room to allow for adequate physical security enhancements.

Natural Barriers

The effectiveness of a natural barrier will depend on the barrier itself and how it is used. A body of water may be very effective in keeping pedestrian traffic away from your property but not very effective at keeping away boat traffic. In this case, a natural barrier may need to be augmented with a man-made barrier. In any case, natural barriers, like man-made barriers, need to be monitored. Cliff sides can be scaled, water can be crossed, and difficult terrain can be overcome with the support of tools and technology. Perhaps the largest vulnerability with natural barriers is assuming they offer more protection than they really do.

Natural barriers must be included in any vulnerability assessment of a company facility or site. Ignored vulnerabilities become a weak link in the company protection profile. For example, if the threat of terror to an oil-producing facility is high and that facility is adjacent to the shoreline of a major body of water, the vulnerability to watercraft access is high. Additional physical measures must be taken in the water and away from the shoreline to prevent a water approach attack. Security patrol boats and/or underwater surveillance and intrusion detection systems will be useful in reducing the risk of a water approach.

Gates

Gates exist both to facilitate and to control access. The most secure perimeter allows no one through. However, that is not practical or desirable. People must come and go. Unauthorized persons must be kept out. Employees, customers, and other visitors need to have easy access to your facility. Gates allow for this. Gates need to be controlled to ensure that only authorized persons and vehicles pass through. A variety of controls can be used. Guards, electronic interactive access-control systems, such as card, key, or password access, or remote control access with video camera observation can all be useful. What you select will depend on your specific needs and conditions. The number of gates to a facility should be kept to the minimum necessary, not the minimum desired. To control gates requires resources. The more gates, the more resources it will take and the more potential problems created, since any opening is always a potential vulnerability.

Gates not used should be locked or eliminated. Having the flexibility to open an additional gate when pedestrian or vehicle traffic demands are high is useful. Eliminating a potential vulnerability may be more important. If a periodic need for an additional gate does exist, then when the gate is not in use, it must be closed, locked, and monitored. Monitoring can be by video camera, roving patrols, or the use of an alarm system. Periodically, even monitored gates require physical inspection to ensure they are operable and secure.

Other Openings

Openings not designed for personnel or vehicular traffic are a vulnerability. They must be secured. Sewage pipes, drains, utility tunnels, large conduits, heating, ventilation, and air conditioning ducting, along with other purposeful openings, must be controlled. Where it is appropriate to lock them, they should be locked. Those that cannot be locked should be monitored. Monitoring may be in the form of an alarm system or a physical inspection. Any opening larger than 96 square inches should have doors, bars, or grillwork in place to prevent human access.

These can be installed permanently or made removable with locking devices. For example, to prevent access through heating, ventilating, and air conditioning ducting, man bars can be installed inside the ducting. This is not practical for openings requiring access by maintenance personnel, so removable grills or doors may be more practical. In any configuration, all openings must be assessed for vulnerability and an appropriate protective measure implemented. Regular inspection or monitoring to ensure tampering has not occurred is essential.

Buildings and Doors

For many facilities, buildings and doors define where the outer layers of security end and the inner layers of security begin. Within a site, buildings are the separation point between the outer and inner layers of security controls. In the area between a building and the outer perimeter (usually a fence line) of the facility may lie a variety of security controls that make up the entire outer layers of security. In this configuration, it is best to keep the areas adjacent to building and door exteriors clear. In essence, create a clear zone of 10–15 feet where no storage, parking, or regular work activity is authorized. Maintaining a clear zone allows for unobstructed observation by surveillance cameras and security personnel. Visual access to the clear zone becomes the first line of defense for the inner perimeter. When developing protective barriers intended to reduce the vulnerability of a terrorist attack, surveillance and surveillance systems are a critical component. Buildings, walls, and doors help keep unauthorized persons out but restrict area visibility. Surveillance systems can restore visibility. Buildings and doors as part of the inner layers of security are discussed later in this chapter.

Parking

Providing parking space for employees, customers, and visitors is generally necessary. Unless the business is small and located on a street with public parking access, parking needs to be provided. Parking should not be allowed within the outer perimeter. Parking areas can be problematic in many ways. From being used to facilitate theft of company property to the potential use of a mobile bomb, vehicles on or adjacent to company property present a heightened risk. Furthermore, unless all vehicles are inspected, it will be unknown whether items of contraband or weapons are brought onto the facility or into buildings. If, for lack of space, parking must be permitted within the outer perimeter, additional fencing should be erected to separate the parking area from the remainder of the facility. To protect against attacks from vehicles laden with explosives, it is essential to create an adequate clear zone, that is, the space between where vehicle access ends and the building perimeter begins.

Parking can be a very sensitive subject. Where people park is often linked with their status within the company. Municipal, state, or federal laws often require sufficient parking to be set aside for physically challenged persons. Visitors like to park close to the areas they visit. Parking can be difficult to manage and police.

Company-owned vehicles are the only exception for parking within the perimeter. As an asset of the company, these vehicles require protection. Protection is particularly important if the vehicles are loaded with merchandise, supplies, or raw materials. They should be parked in a secure, well-lighted area and locked. However, they ought not to be parked in the same area as privately owned vehicles, and access to them should be controlled.

Lighting

Lighting serves several purposes. Adequate lighting reduces the possibility of accidents and injury. It also serves as a deterrent to would-be intruders. With adequate lighting, the company premises, grounds, fences, walls, and buildings can be properly illuminated and clearly observed. Guidance for specific levels of illumination may be obtained through many government regulatory sources or any company that sells and/or installs exterior facility and parking lot lighting. Perhaps the best determination for assessing adequate lighting is to conduct an actual test. Is the existing lighting sufficient as assessed under controlled and practical conditions? If not, more lighting is needed.

Adequate lighting serves as a deterrent. Intruders are less likely to enter well-illuminated areas, fearing they will be observed. Lighting should be sufficiently protected to prevent tampering and destruction. Lighting should be kept within the perimeter to reduce the possibility of damage. Lights should be placed high enough to ensure that tampering must be deliberate and difficult. When used as a deterrent, lighting should have a backup power source in the event of a power disruption. Lighting requires little attention, in that it can be programmed to turn on and off at specific times. The control system can be sensitive to light, movement, or heat. It can be linked to alarm systems and support surveillance systems. After installation, it does require frequent inspection to ensure that all systems are operational.

Specific lighting needs vary with each site or facility. As part of a site physical security survey, lighting should be examined. Areas that require direct protection should have lighting that not only illuminates the area but does not interfere with security's ability to effectively monitor. Too much lighting can create a problem, in that it may provide bright spots that blind people and cameras. Doors, gates, and other entrances should be well illuminated. This allows for safe passage and for better observation by security personnel and cameras. Areas with heavy personnel and vehicle traffic also require adequate lighting. Lighting will reduce hazards and increase visibility in support of routine activities. Large, open areas with little traffic need less lighting, but the lighting must be sufficient to allow for general observation and a safe environment. To ensure that lighting remains effective and available when needed, lighting systems should be inspected regularly. At the very least, lighting should be checked daily just to ensure the "lights are on."

Surveillance

Surveillance is a critical tool for security in its effort to protect and is an essential component of the layers of security. Generally, surveillance is accomplished by using security personnel (guards) or surveillance cameras. Most frequently, a combination of both is used to achieve maximum observation and effectiveness for any facility. The use of surveillance is particularly critical in the effort to protect against acts of terror. Acts of terror are not random attacks; they are planned. Terrorists plan. As part of the planning process, terrorists will do their own advance work. They will conduct their own reconnaissance activities on their targets.

Prior to committing an act of terror, terrorists will usually survey their target and develop a plan to ensure they are able to accomplish their mission successfully. Part of that reconnaissance effort is to observe the routine operations and the effectiveness of security measures in place at the target site. More often than not, terrorists will actually visit the target site and make a firsthand assessment of vulnerabilities. It is this action, the actual visit to the target, where the terrorists are vulnerable. If the terrorist is observed and their intentions identified, it is possible to divert them or even, with the support of law enforcement, capture them.

Situational awareness is an important condition in defense of terrorism. In addition to understanding threat, vulnerability, and risks, the security executive must create an operating condition allowing for as complete a situational awareness environment as possible. Intrusion detection systems and other layers of security must be augmented with surveillance systems. Surveillance systems should be monitored and all irregular and suspicious activity reviewed. Security personnel must be trained to detect suspicious activity, activity that is out of the ordinary (e.g., a vehicle parked nearby for an extended period, a curious pedestrian loitering in the area with a camera, unusual overflights by small aircraft), and report or act on that observation.

The environment for terrorists is target rich. Hardening your target will cause terrorists to take greater risks or, more importantly for the intended target, to seek another, "softer" target.

A plan for site or facility surveillance should be developed. The plan should consider the following:

- Observation and deterrence
- Identification of critical or high-risk areas
- Camera and security personnel mix (technology and human mix)
- Location of cameras
- Need for hidden cameras
- Type of cameras needed: wide or narrow angle of view, low or high level of light
- Recording capability needed
- Establishing procedures for review and retention

Intrusion Detection Systems (IDS)

IDS are one of the many layers of protection for a facility. IDS augment barriers, guards, and other physical controls. They call attention to problems not stopped or prevented by barriers and not observed by humans. In essence they enhance the detection process. IDS serve an alert function. They sound the alarm to unauthorized attempts to access systems or to enter grounds, properties, or facilities. They cause a reaction to an event. They also serve a deterrent function. Since most physical security controls include the use of IDS, intruders can assume they are part of the protection profile. If intruders know IDS are in place, then, if determined, they must plan their attack accordingly. If not determined, they move to another target.

IDS are used to call attention to an immediate problem. Unlike physical barriers such as walls, fences, and gates, they are not a physical obstacle in and of themselves and are used to slow down or stop an intruder. They are an alerting mechanism used to call attention to an intruder or problem. Audible alarm systems may serve as a physical obstacle much more than do silent alarm systems since they let everyone in the general area know when there is IDS activation.

There are many types of IDS. Within the physical security profile, intrusion detection and fire detection are used the most. As part of the outer barrier, intrusion detection serves to indicate penetrations in or between the various layers of protection. Different types of IDS are available for fences, gates, and walls, and all provide an alert if any are compromised.

IDS can be used as part of the protection profile for both inner and outer layers of physical security. As part of the outer layer of protection they serve as either an advance warning indicator that an outer layer has been compromised, thereby making the inner layers more vulnerable, or they serve to protect property and assets stored within the outer layer by providing an indicator that an intruder is tampering with or in the area of the property being protected. In any case, IDS are only effective if there is a response, most often an immediate response. Someone must react to IDS activation. An IDS without a timely response capability is not effective. Responding to an IDS alert is essential; otherwise the alert becomes nothing more than an expensive annoyance. Perpetrators often test IDS by causing their activation and watching for a response. No response lets perpetrators know they have plenty of time in which to accomplish their objectives. In terms of a terrorist attack, there is little time to react before major damage can occur.

IDS provide balance for the overall physical security profile in both protection capabilities and costs. IDS can reduce the need for a large, stationary security force. They allow for a configuration of sensors, monitors, respondents, and some form of patrol. In some cases, IDS reduce and even eliminate the need for a stationary force. If IDS are not used, the function they serve must be fulfilled by means of a larger security force or through greater surveillance capability. Or the security executive can just assume a greater level of risk. When operating in a high-risk area for terrorist activity, not using IDS is unwise in most instances.

IDS normally cost more to install than to maintain. The cost of IDS is greatest in the acquisition and installation phase. Once installed, maintenance and monitoring costs are generally much less than personnel cost. A return on investment can be calculated and used as a selling point on the value of IDS. The savings in recurring costs of security personnel can be compared to the cost for acquisition and installation of IDS. Over several years, it is usually more cost effective to use IDS to augment security than to rely on a larger security personnel force.

Inner Layers

In the previous section, we discussed elements of security controls generally considered to be part of the outer perimeter. For the most part these are layers of physical protection that begin at the site or facility perimeter and lead up to the building walls. We also indicated that, depending on the environment, the outer perimeter may actually begin at the building walls. In this situation, the first layer or outermost layer of security is made up of the walls, door, and windows of a building. Office buildings in urban environments represent a common example of this situation. Outside these buildings is an environment with conditions that are not controlled by the building occupants. A single layer of outer physical security controls protects the inner layers. There is not much room for error. When the building wall is the outer layer of security, penetration of that layer allows access to the inner layers of security. This condition should lead the security executive to place a greater emphasis on the types of inner controls applied. When protecting against terrorist attacks in an environment where the outer layers of security are the walls of the building, it is critical for threat, vulnerabilities, and risk to be clearly understood. Effectively mitigating the vulnerability of a single outer layer of security is crucial. A failure here leads immediately to the interior of the facility or building, where physical assets, information, and personnel are housed.

Buildings, Doors, Windows, and Glass

Buildings serve as perimeters. In urban areas, the walls, doors, and windows of office buildings may be the outermost perimeter and possibly the only outer layer of security control for the entire facility. In other settings, buildings may serve as part of the outer perimeter or as the first layer of the inner perimeter. This will depend on the individual facility configuration. Whatever layer of protection they provide, full consideration must be given to all aspects of building protection, particularly for protection against acts of terrorism.

Since the method of operation of most terrorist groups when attacking a target has been with use of firearms and/or explosives, facilities where the building walls serve as the outer perimeter of protection are most vulnerable to such attacks. (*Note*: Remember to consider both vulnerability and threat. In this condition the vulnerability is high but the threat may not be.) Not having a *clear zone* separating the building from the perimeter allows greater ease of access for intruders using vehicle- or suicide-bombing techniques. (See Figure 6-1, which depicts the security-in-layers concept.) The closer the blast is to the structure, the greater the damage to it.[3] Where the threat of terrorism is high for a site, facility, or building, with only walls of the building serving as the outermost perimeters, these walls must be hardened or the higher risk accepted.

Generally, the greatest weakness in a wall is its windows. The threat from bomb blasts and explosions is one of the most difficult issues facing security professionals. A major cause of casualties during a bomb blast is flying glass. In a high-terrorist-threat environment, it is prudent to install blast-resistant glass. Blast-resistant glass is essentially glass that has a transparent polyester antishatter film applied to the glass either during manufacture or during a retrofit.[4] To harden the building walls completely, it may also be necessary to install blast-resistant doors and to augment the structure with blast structure protections.

As a general security practice, all building openings need to be assessed. Doors, windows, and passageways for ducting and conduit all need to be controlled. Power, communications, heating, ventilating, and air conditioning systems require entry points from the exterior of the building into the interior of the building. To ensure that they are not used for unauthorized purposes, controls need to be in place. Any other opening that serves no useful function should be permanently closed. Functional openings larger than 96 square inches should be modified to prevent human access. Windows should be locked and alarmed. Alarms should detect entry or tampering. In some cases, man bars or screening may be necessary. Screen and man bars allow for the passage of air and visual inspection but do not allow for human access.

Doors should be locked when not used and controlled when in use. Controls range from guards at the door monitoring entry and exit to mechanical or electronic access control systems requiring cards and card readers and/or access codes. Exterior or perimeter doors must be hardened and are generally built stronger than interior doors. It may be necessary to have interior doors of a similar strength and quality as exterior doors if those interior doors are part of an area used to provide specific protection to high-value assets. All associated materials for doors must be consistent with the strength of the door itself. For example, a high-security door is of little use if weak latching devices or cheap locks are holding it in place. High-security doors should have high-security locks.

Locks and Keys

Locks are an essential part of physical security protection. They are a cost-effective and simple means of denying access to unauthorized persons. The largest expense for locks is the initial purchase and installation. Depending on usage, little maintenance is required. Although any lock can be overcome, the higher the quality, the longer it will take. Simple locks can be picked or damaged easily. More sophisticated locks will buy time against any attempt to bypass them. Locks vary in quality and type. A wide variety of locking devices are available. Selecting and determining what is an appropriate locking device for any door, window, or other opening is based on planned usage, specific needs, and whether the asset itself requires protection. The level of protection offered by the locking device must be consistent with the level of protection provided by the door or window to which it is affixed. For example, it could be foolish to augment a window or door with blast-resistant material, only to secure that window or door with an inferior lock.

Perhaps the most vulnerable aspect of locks is improper protection of keys. Effective key control is critical. Poor key control can render any locking devices useless. Issuance of master keys must be severely limited. All keys should be accounted for. Keys should be issued in accordance with someone's need to perform his or her job. If there is no specific need, keys should not be issued. A permanent record of personnel issued or assigned keys must be kept. When keys are lost or stolen, the locks should be rekeyed. When a master key is lost, all affected locks should be rekeyed. There may be reasons when this is not necessary, such as if a key was inadvertently destroyed and its recovery or use poses no risk. Keys should never be issued on a permanent basis. An annual assessment of key needs and requirements should be made. This assessment will also assist in identifying lost or stolen keys that were not reported to security.

Roofs

It is important to remember that the roof of a building may be part of the outer or inner perimeter. Roofs generally have openings for maintenance, power, heating, ventilation, air conditioning, and for other conduits. The same principals applicable to barriers and walls are applicable to roofs. This includes, where necessary, reinforcing the structure to render it blast resistant. Openings must be controlled. Since routine access to roofs is generally not an issue, locking devices and barriers such as screens and bars are used. Moreover, ladders or stairs leading to roofs should be controlled. Access to the roof should be made difficult for unauthorized personnel. In some cases, rooftops serve as parking areas. Where this is the case, consideration must be given to the threat of vehicle-laden explosives.

From the vehicle bombing of the Oklahoma City, Oklahoma, federal building to the all-too-frequent vehicle-borne bombings occurring in Iraq, the use of vehicles as a means to transport and house explosives continues to grow. Where there is a threat of terrorism, there is a threat of bombings through the use of vehicle-borne explosives. The security executive must consider this common terrorist tool when developing a protection profile in a high-risk area. Failure to do so could produce dire consequences.

Access Control

Controlling access is a critical component of security in layers. Ensuring that only authorized personnel and vehicles enter and exit a facility reduces the risk of loss or damage to all exposed assets. Effective access control requires the integration of different security functions that serve as individual layers of protection. As part of an integrated system, the following are useful access control tools:

- Security personnel
- Locks—combination, code, or key
- Electronic access control systems using any of the following reader systems: magnetic stripe, optical bar code, proximity cards, signature, and biometric systems that include recognition of unique human characteristics such as fingerprints, face or hand geometry, voice, and retina geometry.

Part of the site vulnerability assessment should focus on identifying access control vulnerabilities and existing access control practices. When vulnerabilities and existing practices are compared with what is actually needed, an access control profile that best fits your site can be developed and implemented. The access control profile must address who should be authorized access to the facility and under what conditions. It should also identify the individual security process and tools needed to design and implement proper access controls effectively.

What Needs to Be Controlled?

The following areas should be considered when designing access controls.

Vehicles

All vehicles entering and exiting the facility must be controlled. Only authorized vehicles should be allowed onsite. Procedures establishing traffic flow and parking need to be written down and communicated. Violations of these procedures must be enforced. Not enforcing traffic and parking rules and regulations will quickly lead to a breakdown and abuse of controls. At the very least, vehicles should be subject to random inbound and outbound searches to ensure that anything entering or leaving the facility has proper authorization. In a high-threat environment, inbound- and outbound-vehicle searches should be mandatory. This point can't be emphasized enough. Vehicles have a capacity to carry large amounts of explosives. Keeping them away from buildings, people, and other assets in a high-threat environment is essential.

Employees

Employees need easy access to their work areas, and access control procedures should be designed to facilitate their swift and efficient movement in and out of work areas. Access control procedures should be the same for all employees, thereby creating a culture of respect and adherence to the process and practice. Requiring employees to use some form of identification to be authorized access to a site should be a standard practice. Employee identification badges, access identification cards, and other forms of physical controls can be used to validate that a person is actually an employee and quickly allow them entry to or exit from a facility. Furthermore, all employees should be subject to random entry and exit searches as determined by security. There should be no exceptions to this practice. In a high-threat environment, random searches should be changed to mandatory searches of all packages, briefcases, purses, and similar items that may contain weapons or explosives.

Vendors, Suppliers, Customers, and Visitors

Very few people who are not employees should be allowed free and complete access to your facility. In the event vendors or suppliers are assigned to your site on a full-time basis who require unrestricted site access to perform their work, they should be vetted through an established screening process (designed to prove they are who they claim to be with valid reason to be on site and meeting company suitability standards for unrestricted access) and provided with identification that indicates they are not employees. Moreover, this status should be subjected to scheduled periodic review to revalidate the need. Any identification provided to allow access should have an established expiration date.

Packages/Mail

Controlling packages entering a facility is a critical process. Packages can enter a facility or building in many different ways. Some are carried in by people. Others are carried into a facility via motor vehicles. Many are mailed through the postal system. The security professional must install a means of screening packages. In large facilities this can be accomplished by requiring all packages to be processed through a single screening center. That screening center can be equipped with sensing and x-ray devices to assist in the screening for explosives and other threats, such as chemical components (e.g., poison matter) or biological components (e.g., anthrax).

The threat of explosives-laden packages is all too common, as exemplified by events in the United Kingdom, where, in February 2007, a suspected letter bomb exploded, injuring two people at a business center southwest of London. One day prior to this event, a padded envelope exploded in another office building. Both buildings were associated with the processing of traffic fines.[5] Acts of terror are not necessarily associated with international terrorist groups. They may be perpetrated by angry locals with willingness to cause deadly harm. See Figure 6-2 for information concerning bomb threats associated with stand-off distances.

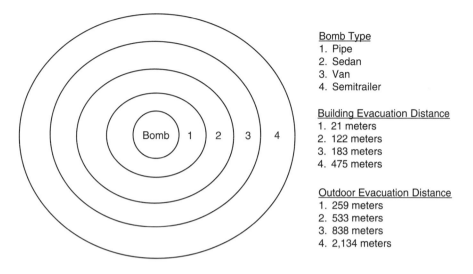

Bomb Type
1. Pipe
2. Sedan
3. Van
4. Semitrailer

Building Evacuation Distance
1. 21 meters
2. 122 meters
3. 183 meters
4. 475 meters

Outdoor Evacuation Distance
1. 259 meters
2. 533 meters
3. 838 meters
4. 2,134 meters

FIGURE 6-2 Bomb-threat stand-off distances. (*Note:* Numbers in the circles correspond to the numbers associated with bomb type and evacuation distances. Building evacuation distances are estimated based on typical U.S. construction standards. Outdoor evacuation distances are estimated based on fragment throw distances. For additional information, see the National Counterterrorism Center website at http://www.nctc.gov/)

Personal Identification and Identity Management

Badges are a useful tool for employee identification. They can be coupled with security technology, producing effective identity management tools. Smart-card technology and more traditional security technologies used for access control, such as magnetic codes, bar codes, and proximity cards, can be integrated into the badge, making it a highly functional tool supporting the identity management process. This tool can store and even process information pertaining to the specific characteristics of an employee. Identifying each individual by name and other specific personal information, such as photographs, encoded access authorization (something they possess), or biometric data (something they are) and linking that with a PIN (something they know) can be a useful and reliable tool.

To ensure reliability and effectiveness, the process of using a badge for employee identification must be controlled. Specific parameters for use must be established and followed for the badging process to maintain its integrity. Rules governing the following aspects of a personnel identification badging process will help ensure a very reliable system.

- Determine who is authorized to have an identification badge.
- Identify what data is needed on each identification badge.
- Security must control production, issuance, and accountability of all identification badges, which includes establishing/validating actual identity (they are who they claim to be) and establishing access authorization parameters (where they are authorized to go within the facility).
- Identification badges must be recovered from employees who leave the company.
- Lost or stolen identification badges are reported and removed from the system.
- Worn or damaged identification badges are exchanged for new ones.

- A tracking system is devised to ensure internal accountability of unused identification badge stock.
- A periodic audit of the identification badging process occurs.
- Identification badges made but not in use must be controlled or destroyed.
- Tamper-resistant features, such as holography, should be included to prevent counterfeiting.
- Employees must understand the need for the identification badge process and adhere to proper usage.

It may also be necessary to control the access and movement of visitors, suppliers, and customers. For this, an identification process for nonemployees is needed. It should be similar to that of the employee identification process but more restrictive; that is, it should clearly identify the visitor as someone who is not an employee and offer obvious indicators on the identification badge itself declaring appropriate restrictions. Some useful data necessary for the visitor identification badge includes escort required, expiration date, and specific areas authorized to visit.

Employees must be familiar with the company identity management process. They must be able to recognize the company identification badge. They should receive guidance and training as to how the process works, for employees and nonemployees. Employees should be trained to react to the site of an unauthorized badge and to alert security. Persons not wearing an appropriate identification badge or who violate the parameters of the process should be challenged. Without the active participation of all employees, any identity management process will be rendered ineffective or even useless.

Begin Planning with a Physical Security Checklist

In order to assist the security professional charged with assessing vulnerability for his/her site or developing mitigation measures to reduce that vulnerability, a checklist to serve as a quick reference is provided here.

Perimeter Control:

- Fencing (gate control)
- Alarms
- Guards (fixed post/mounted/mobile)
- Barriers (e.g., bollards, traffic diversions)
- CCTV
- Property access
  - Employees
  - Visitors
  - Maintenance, delivery, supplier
  - Rooftop
  - Windows
  - Sewers, storm drains, manholes

Protective Lighting:

- Perimeter lights
- Buildings (exterior)

- Buildings (interior and emergency)
- Parking lots and garages

People Control:

- Mechanical access control devices (turnstiles, roto-gates, gate arms, etc.)
- Badges and badge readers
- Automated access control systems
- Guards (posted and mobile patrols)

Intrusion Detection Systems (IDS):

- Doors
- Windows
- Loading docks
- Roof hatches and skylights
- Volumetric sensors
- Passive infrared sensors
- Microwave sensors
- Embedded (buried) sensors
- CCTV
- Duress alarms

Lock and Key Control:

- Accountability
- Locks
  - Key operated
  - Combination operated
- Keys
  - Doors
  - Desks
  - Vehicles
- Storage containers

Telecommunication Security:

- Telephone and network distribution room requirements
  - Construction
  - Access control
  - Operation
- Cabling requirements
- User access requirements

Utilities (gas, electric, water):

- Perimeter entry point controls
- Internal site distribution points
- Emergency backup systems
- Utility company access (repair, administration)

Vehicle Control and Parking Security:

- Delivery vehicles
- Employee vehicles
- Visitor vehicles
- Catering vehicles
- Fuel trucks
- HAZMAT vehicles
- Registration

Physical Defenses Against Terrorists

The foregoing examples of what to do from a physical standpoint is general in nature, to help get you started. However, it is important to remember that today's terrorists won't care about their own lives or any other lives. The physical defenses you now have in place or put in place must be hardened to the point of stopping terrorists with a truck of explosives and bombs attached to their bodies and not burglars.

Summary

In the current world environment, where terrorism continues to be a significant threat in many areas of the world and with no end in sight, companies operating in areas considered to have a high threat of terrorism must assess their risk and employ appropriate physical security measures to enhance the overall security of their assets.

☐ ☐ ☐ ▬▬▬▬▬▬▬▬▬▬▬▬▬▬▬▬▬▬▬▬▬▬

Physical security is the first line of defense to protect company assets. However, a security professional cannot rely on "normal" physical controls to prevent acts of terror. The most common acts of terror using firearms and explosives require reinforced and multiple layers of physical security to harden a potential target sufficiently.

▬▬▬▬▬▬▬▬▬▬▬▬▬▬▬▬▬▬▬▬▬▬ ☐ ☐ ☐

Additional controls for protection of information and personnel are added, creating a complete protection profile. No single physical security control can satisfy all of your protection needs. Physical security controls are applied in layers. Each layer of security serves a specific purpose by providing specific protections. Many controls used in conjunction with each other help to create a secure environment.

Before applying physical security control, one must obtain and understand the answers to the following questions.

- Apply the risk equation:

$$\text{Threat} \times \text{Vulnerability} \times \text{Impact on assets} = \text{Risk}$$

- What controls are already in place?
- What additional controls are needed?

Then you will need to:

- Design them.
- Implement them.

Endnotes

[1] For readings on information system security and cybersecurity, see Appendix B, Recommended Readings and References.

[2] See: http://news.bbc.co.uk/onthisday/hi/dates/stories/february/26/newsid_2516000/2516469.stm

[3] For more specific information on bomb threat stand-off distances, see: http://www.nctc.gov/

[4] For additional information on blast-resistant window systems, visit this website, where links to other, related sites can be found: http://www.dupont.com/safetyglass/lgn/stories/2205.html

[5] See: http://www.cnn.com/2007/WORLD/europe/02/06/london.letterbomb.ap/index.html

Protecting Employees from Terrorist Attacks

I arise in the morning torn between a desire to save the world and a desire to savor the world. That makes it hard to plan the day.
—Elwyn Brooks White

This chapter addresses ways a corporate security professional can develop and implement an effective antiterrorist protective program for employees.

When considering the threat of terrorist's attacks against employees and others associated with a corporation, these employees, associates, suppliers, contractors, customers, and visitors, may be vulnerable in many ways. Whether they are inside corporate facilities, commuting to or from those facilities, traveling on corporate business to some other location, representing the company, or conducting company business, their risk must be assessed and protective threat mitigating measures be implemented.

A corporate security executive, e.g., chief security officer (CSO), must decide, in concert with the legal staff and executive management, the scope and degree of the "protective umbrella" that is the responsibility of the corporation. Obviously, when employees and others are within the corporate facilities, the corporation is responsible for their protection from acts of terror. In addition, the corporation has some responsibility to protect the employees when they are traveling on corporate business. However, it is not practical or possible to protect employees from all threats when they are outside of the home facility. Nonetheless, an employer (corporation) can help reduce the vulnerability of traveling employees by providing them with information that increases their awareness of such vulnerabilities and threats, thus enabling them to better protect themselves.

Employee Protection Outside the Corporate Facilities

Since employees are valuable assets of the company, it is a good business practice to protect them. The company must provide assistance and support to them as part of any company antiterrorism protection program dealing with events outside the corporate facilities. When developing a protective program focused on protecting employees from threats, particularly, the threat of terrorism, it is a good idea to include experts other than security professionals in the process. Human resources, legal, risk management, finance, and safety professionals can help the security professional develop an effective program meeting the needs of the company and considering all aspects to protect the employee and the company.

Employees are more vulnerable when they leave the safe confines of a company facility. How to help ensure their safety when they venture into the often-dangerous world is a major challenge to security executives while at the same time balancing potential liability issues.

The corporation can best balance this protective effort by giving some guidelines and recommendations that provide employees with basic measures that can, and in some cases must, be taken to help mitigate the risk to them while they are outside the confines of the corporate facilities:

- At home
- While traveling—protecting the moving target
- On assignment (short-term)—operating in a foreign and often unfamiliar environment
- Expatriates (long-term)—living and working on a long-term basis in the foreign environment, to include the risk of "going native"

The amount of risks an employee is subject to will of course depend on several factors.

- Is the corporation a primary terrorist target?
- Is the corporation a secondary target, e.g., associated with a nation-state that terrorists consider the enemy?
- Where is the employee traveling to while on corporate business?
  - Is the employee traveling to a Western nation-state?
  - Is the employee traveling to a non-Western state?
  - Is the employee traveling to a hostile area, e.g., Middle East?
  - Which one?
  - Is that nation known for terrorist activities?
- How will the employee travel to the work destination, e.g., airplane, rail?
- Where will the employee stay?
- How will the employees be traveling between the business location and the place they are staying?
- Where will the employee go, e.g., tourist sites, restaurants?

Better Safe than Sorry!

One should not have to choose between being safe and secure and going about the business of working and living. It is a matter of awareness and practice that allows a person to incorporate safe and secure habits into his or her daily routine. Awareness is particularly important when the threat of terrorism is high and the vulnerability of the employee is real. Perhaps the best form of security a company can provide its employees, aside from that protection provided within the boundaries of the corporate facilities, is to empower them with a heightened level of security consciousness through security education and awareness training, thus enhancing their capacity for individual situational awareness and personal safety, especially outside the corporate facilities.

☐ ☐ ☐ ▬▬▬▬▬▬▬▬▬▬▬▬▬▬▬▬▬▬▬▬▬▬▬▬▬▬▬

Being able to recognize unsafe and unsecured situations is a valuable capability. Being able to avoid them is even better.

▬▬▬▬▬▬▬▬▬▬▬▬▬▬▬▬▬▬▬▬▬▬▬▬▬▬▬ ☐ ☐ ☐

Reasons Why a Corporation Should Protect Its Employees

Why it's important to protect employees should be obvious to every security executive and security professional. Employees are assets to the company. Remember how, in earlier chapters, we identified company assets as physical (i.e., buildings and equipment, also referred to as capital assets), information and information systems, and personnel (often referred to as human capital). It's imperative for the company to protect its assets. From insurance policies to physical barriers, companies go to great lengths to protect assets and reduce risks associated with those assets.

Providing protection for employees, in addition to protecting them as a company asset, addresses other potential costly risks for a business. If an employee is harmed, not only is that employee unavailable to work but he or she may, in some situations, have cause to seek recompense from the company for damages that may have occurred on company property or while on company business. This harm may or may not be due to company negligence or perceived negligence. Nevertheless, it is likely the employee will seek some type of compensation and in all probability be successful. Providing protection for employees reduces the likelihood that they will be harmed, thus reducing the potential liability to the company.

Another reason to protect employees is to maintain continuity of business. If employees, particularly large numbers of employees, are not available to work, the ability of the company to produce its goods and services is impaired and the continuity of business is disrupted. When planning for a contingency it is not uncommon to identify alternative work locations for employees, thereby, through planned alternative means, ensuring that employees are available to work, albeit under different circumstances, during a disruption to the business. However, if the employees themselves are harmed and unavailable to work, it's often more difficult to find skilled and experienced workforce replacements than it is to obtain buildings and business-related infrastructure.

It is much easier to have resources such as power generators available and ready to use in an emergency to restore power to a site or building, albeit somewhat limited, than it is to have a stable of employees waiting and ready to begin work on a moment's notice, replacing any employees who may have been rendered unavailable due to some sort of crisis. Protecting employees essentially contributes to the continuity of business. Protecting employees helps keep them available to work and to do what they do for the company, maintaining continuity of business.

It's easier for companies to protect their assets when those assets are under their control. For example, it's much easier to protect information when it's stored and used within company confines. If that same information were placed outside of the company, say, in the possession of a business partner or another third party, it's more difficult for the company security executive to ensure that the appropriate level of protection is being provided.

It's not any different for employees. It's much easier for a company security executive to provide protection to employees while they are on company property than it is to provide that same level of protection for them when they are at home, in transit, or working at company or customer locations throughout the world in support of company business. Since the security professional cannot be with all employees whenever they are traveling or working away from company property, the best that can be offered is to prepare them to protect themselves.

The Fundamentals

Providing protection for employees begins with establishing company policies and procedures that address basic protective measures. In many cases, having basic protective measures in place is required by government regulations (external drivers) or laws. The basic measures should be general security measures designed to harden a facility and afford a level of protection to all assets within that facility. Where external drivers (laws, regulations, contractual requirements) calling for protection of employees do not exist or are lacking, assessing the need for protective measures ought to be part of the security risk assessment.

In any event, even if government regulations and laws do require protective measures to be in place, it is prudent for the security professional to conduct a facility or site risk assessment since the required protective measures may not be sufficient for every type of business operating environment. Implementation of security measures should be based on an assessment of risk. Part of the risk may be failure to comply with government regulations and laws. It is the responsibility of the security executive to consider this when conducting a risk assessment.

Recognizing that work environments differ enormously, the following sections present a series of areas that should be considered when developing company policies that address basic protective measures, to include those measures necessary for protecting company employees. Some policies will be written with the purpose of establishing measures designed to enable employees to protect themselves. Each of these areas should be considered for development of individual company policies and should form the basic requirements, standards, and practices for company management, security, and employees to follow.

The policies should be constructed in such a way as to address the responsibilities of company management, the security organization, and the rank-and-file employee. All policies should be prepared in accordance with the results of risk assessments, which should be designed to consider all aspect of risks, including the threat of terrorism, and with the intent of complying with government regulations, laws, and contractual obligations.

The policies should also have subsections that deal with the various needs for protection based on the type of threat agents. Using this approach, there should be specific policies dealing with terrorist threats.

Physical Security of Company Facilities

This policy should define the basic guidelines for protection of company facilities, ranging from erection of physical barriers to implementation of access control systems. Essentially, the policy declares and documents the basic physical measures necessary to protect company assets at a minimum level. However, the minimum level should be that needed to defend the corporate facilities from the various known actual as well as potential future threats from terrorist attacks.

Providing protective measures beyond this minimum requirement ought to be based on a specific risk assessment. For example, if the threat of terrorism in the area or region where assets are located is based on the risk assessment, additional physical measures should be implemented to harden the protection of those assets. Essentially, the security executive is hardening the target against the threat of terrorism.

It is important for this policy to define the basic requirements and methods and to allow for additional controls to be implemented in accordance with specific risks that are most often identified through risk assessments. In some cases new or heightened risks will develop and become apparent to the security executive, without conducting a formal risk assessment. For example, changes in the political environment in high-risk countries may lead to strife. Conducting business in these areas becomes "risky business."

Prohibited and Restricted Items

This policy should provide specific guidance to all employees regarding the type of items that are prohibited on company property. Such items include, but are not limited to, weapons (not used as part of company business), explosives, and illegal drugs. There may be situations where security personnel are required to carry weapons as part of their protective duty obligations. Security officers working in a bank or security officers protecting energy-generating nuclear power plants are a prime example. However, other employees should not be allowed to carry weapons onto company property when doing so is not part of their responsibility.

A prohibited- and restricted-items policy is essential, and it should be used to clearly declare what the company determines are inappropriate items to bring onto company property. Preventing those devices from entering the facility reduces the probability of a successful terrorist attack from an internal terrorist threat agent. To ensure that employees know and understand the restrictions and the reasons for these restrictions, a written policy declaring specific guidelines is essential.

□ □ □ ▬▬▬▬▬▬▬▬▬▬▬▬▬▬▬▬▬▬▬▬▬▬▬▬▬▬▬▬

The policy on prohibited and restricted items must take into consideration the potential for such items to be used in support of terrorist attacks, for example, the terrorist hijackings on 9/11, where the hijackers carried with them onto the targeted airplanes weapons that were inconspicuous enough not to draw attention but effective enough to enable them to accomplish their mission. In this regard, the most recent items of concern for air travel have been liquid chemicals that when mixed create a highly explosive substance. As a preventative measure, airlines now restrict the amount and type of liquids that may be carried onto an aircraft.

▬▬▬▬▬▬▬▬▬▬▬▬▬▬▬▬▬▬▬▬▬▬▬▬▬▬▬▬ □ □ □

Just as terrorists continue to find more sophisticated ways to conduct their attacks successfully, CSOs and others responsible for defending corporate assets must continue to update their prohibited- and restricted-items policy and listing. Furthermore, such information, and the rationale behind it, must be brought to the attention of all employees.

The main difficulty that a CSO runs into is that there are usually so many items within a corporate facility that are used for normal business operations, e.g., chemical compounds and flammable materials. So what should the policy incorporate to mitigate this type of risk? If the corporation is a primary terrorist target, the least that should be done is to identify and control the materials that can be used to make explosive devices. Their quantities should be monitored, and no one person should have access to the most dangerous of these items.

You may be thinking that borders on paranoia. However, it goes back to risk and how much risk a corporation is willing to take. For example, in today's environment, where Islamic extremist terrorists are truly a global threat, a corporation doing business in the Middle East and employing many local people faces a higher risk of a terrorist attack from an insider than, say, a corporate facility operating in Alaska, where the threat of terrorism is quite low and there are no known extremist terrorist groups. For those with a concern for the "profiling" of people, keep in mind that it is the behavior of individuals that is of concern, not the persons themselves, and forecasting the potential risks.

For those corporations in high-risk areas and associated with what the terrorists consider an enemy nation-state or otherwise a primary terrorist target, the policy and actions taken will differ from those of corporations who consider themselves a secondary or tertiary target. Again, it is a matter of risk and threat from different terrorist organizations/agents, the vulnerability of the corporation as a target, and the level of risk company executive management is willing to assume in the effort to protect assets.

Employee and Visitor Identification Process

This policy provides guidelines for employees on how to properly identify persons authorized to be within a company facility or on company property. Most businesses have areas of the office, factory, facility, or site where they control access. To eliminate ambiguity as to who is allowed where, provide guidelines within company policy that will help ensure that all employees know the rules. Furthermore, employees should receive some form of awareness training to ensure they understand the rules and are sensitized to challenging persons who are in areas where they should not be.

Recognizing people who are "out of place" and challenging or reporting them contributes to reducing the threat of terrorism. In an earlier chapter we discussed terrorists' method of operations and the practice of advance work, that is, scouting a potential target prior to hitting that target. Recognizing and reporting unauthorized access and behavior could prevent an act of terror.

It should also be policy that all those entering the facilities pass by screening devices, for example, those that may alarm when explosives are "scented" or other types of screening devices that will alert security personnel to a potential threat agent, whether an employee, suppliers, or a visitor.

It should also be policy that all vehicles entering the facility to deliver goods or services be ideally x-rayed. However, this is probably not practical for a corporation today until the technology becomes cheaper and more convenient to use. However, all such vehicles entering corporate property should be isolated and searched to ensure that they are carrying authorized products or are there to provide authorized services.

Pre-employment Background Investigations

This policy establishes the basic criterion for vetting a potential employee prior to being hired, to ensure that the potential employee is who he or she claims to be and that there is nothing in that person's background or history indicating risk to the company (e.g., a history of violent behavior) or appearing on a government terrorist watch list. Many governments maintain terrorist watch lists. Within the United States, a Denied-Parties List is available for businesses to check to determine if persons they are doing business with or hiring have any affiliation with terrorist groups or are considered themselves to be terrorists.

Most commercial providers of pre-employment background investigations include as part of their basic background investigation a check against the Denied-Parties List.

Doing so, helps reduce the probability of hiring a known terrorist. The check does nothing to reduce the possibility of hiring an unknown terrorist.

Vetting employees helps company management determine the suitability of each potential employee before that person actually becomes a permanent employee. Within the policy, a common set of criteria should be declared so that all potential employees are subjected to the same type of review. This will help prevent the possibility of discrimination against any particular group of employees. It also applies a standard for all of management to use as they make hiring decisions.

The areas investigated must be areas where it is likely one would find potential derogatory information—information that can be linked to terrorist threat agent profiles.

The investigative process must be conducted in accordance with the laws of the host country. Different countries have different limitations on the type of information an employer can have access to and can use to make an employment decision. Within the United States it is generally acceptable to seek and obtain information in the following areas in order to assess the potential employment candidate's suitability for employment.

- Education
  - What schools?
  - Where are they located?
  - Verify period of attendance.
  - Type of degree, professional licenses, or trade school certifications.
- Employment
  - Verify claims of employment for most recent period (7–10 years is usually sufficient).
  - Verify self-employment through court and tax records.
  - Verify significant gaps in employment.
- References: Obtain responses from at least two character references.
- Criminal checks
  - Only verify conviction information.
  - Conduct review of court records where applicant resided and worked during most recent period of employment or 18th birthday.
- Department of Motor Vehicles (DMV)
- Credit check
  - Conduct for financial-related positions.
  - Conduct through national credit bureaus.
- In some cases it may be necessary to conduct a civil records check, particularly with financial concerns. Civil records can provide information related to the following areas, which indicate potential financial issues:
  - Divorce
  - Child support
  - Alimony
  - Bankruptcy
  - Assumed names

- Other personal data
  - Date of birth
  - Place of birth
  - Employment-related identification data, e.g., Social Security number
  - Proof of citizenship or legal residency
  - Other data and records checked based on corporate antiterrorist program needs, e.g., immigration

When establishing any employee vetting process, the security executive must ensure that the policy and processes are coordinated with representatives from the human resources department and the legal department. Laws governing the hiring of persons and the types of personal information that may be obtained by a company and used to evaluate suitability for employment differ widely.

Although the foregoing is not specific for screening for potential terrorists, it is at least a starting point. Of course, when discrepancies are noted, further inquiries must be made and resolved, in the interest of asset protection.

Of course, it is a double-edged sword to use profile techniques and also probably illegal in many nation-states. For example, one may want to use the profile of today's Islamic terrorists and exclude all those who practice that religion, e.g., Muslim, male, between 20 and 40 years old. Not only is that basically illegal, a violation of individual rights, but it may be a poor business decision, in that it will exclude some very fine employment applicants. Such an action could exclude people who would make a significant contribution to the business. In addition, such profiling means that some others could be hired who do not fall into that profile but nevertheless may pose a threat of terror.

Employee Safety and Security Guidelines

Many countries require companies to have in place basic safety measures and practices in accordance with the nature of their business. Essentially, the company must take proactive measures to ensure the workplace meets basic safety requirements. As such, many of these actions contribute to securing the work environment, thus reducing the overall vulnerability to terrorist acts.

Those measures may also affect security as the security organization works to implement antiterrorism-supporting measures, such as controlling access to dangerous work areas or ensuring controlled substances used in research and development or manufacturing processes are properly managed and protected.

Since a good part of employee safety is based on personnel actions and behavior, it may be prudent to develop, in addition to a company policy, a practical handbook or guide for all employees to use—something brief, easy to use, and capturing the essential concerns for all employees while they are in the workplace, in transit, at home, or in unfamiliar and new locations. This should be a quick reference and not a lengthy or detailed risk assessment, just a reminder of basic precautions an employee can readily access and perhaps even memorize.

Personal Safety and Security Practices

The following is an outline of areas that may be useful for employees of a global business operating in the service sector that supports an antiterrorist program for the corporation.

- Office safety:
  - Include general office safety guidelines.
  - Include office safety guidelines unique to the type of business.
  - Include safety guidelines incorporating antiterrorist-related defenses.
- Home safety: This section should address simple measures that employees can take in their home to help make them and their families as safe and secure as they deem appropriate. Particular emphasis should be placed on disaster preparations and those incidents related to terrorist attacks, e.g., chemical or biological attacks.
- Planning should include preparations for the following:
  - 10- to 14-day supply of emergency food and water
  - Emergency medical/first aid provisions (to include prescription medications)
  - Portable AM/FM radio, flashlight, waterproof matches, multipurpose tool such as a Swiss-Army knife
  - Emergency cash (small bills, since during a crisis financial institutions may not be accessible)
  - Portable shelter and emergency and protective clothing
  - A predetermined safe location for family members to meet when away from home
  - Photocopies of important documents, stored in a safe, alternate location:
    —Identification documents: driver's license, passport, and birth certificate
    —Ownership documents: title to home and title to automobiles
    —Financial documents: copy of will or trust documents; list of bank and financial institution account numbers; list of credit card numbers; copy of all insurance policies
- Street safety: Include guidelines such as the following and, if possible, area-specific guidelines.
  - Remain alert, with at least one hand free.
  - Avoid being alone at night while walking or while on public transit.
  - Stay in lighted and open areas to the extent possible.
  - Keep a low profile (blend into crowd if possible).
- Driving safety: Include basic tips on staying safe in one's vehicle.
- Parking safety: Include the following:
  - Use of valet parking and limiting access to vehicle key only
  - Parking in well-lighted areas
  - Checking inside the vehicle and surrounding area before locking and unlocking
  - Keeping valuables in the trunk
  - Being alert for suspicious individuals
- Identity theft protection should include the following categories:
  - Protecting information unique to each individual (e.g., date of birth, driver's license number)
  - Protecting financial information (i.e., account and password information for banking and credit)
  - Destroying (preferably shredding) information no longer needed (e.g., preapproved credit offers, old checks, bill and invoice copies, bank statements)
  - Periodic checks of credit reports through major credit reporting agencies

- Scams and fraud perpetrated in person, over the telephone, or via the computer and Internet with intent to lure potential victims into bank fraud, pyramid scams, Internet fraud, international lottery scams, phone scams, chain letters, fraudulent business opportunities, and telemarketing fraud

Employee Travel Guidelines

Many employees travel in support of company business or on vacations. Sometimes such travel takes employees out of their home country and into areas of the world with varying degrees of risk. Traveling out of familiar confines and into parts of the world with greater risk may make employees more vulnerable to terrorist attacks. Before traveling, employees should be made aware of the potential risks they face.

A company policy for travel should define who is responsible for what. For example, the policy should declare to employees what they must do prior to, during, and after each trip. It should also define what security must do to ensure that employees are as prepared and aware as possible, to reduce their vulnerability to the terrorist risks they will face.

☐ ☐ ☐ ▬▬▬▬▬▬▬▬▬▬▬▬▬▬▬▬▬▬▬▬▬▬▬▬▬▬▬▬▬▬

It is essential to establish rules for travel to ensure that employees are familiar with what they can and should do in addition to what they can't and should not do, to minimize the risk of terrorist attacks, e.g., kidnappings, bombings.

▬▬▬▬▬▬▬▬▬▬▬▬▬▬▬▬▬▬▬▬▬▬▬▬▬▬▬▬▬▬ ☐ ☐ ☐

Moreover, employees ought to understand what support is available to them should they experience a problem. Guidelines for these areas should be clearly addressed within a company policy.

Similar to the guidelines for employee safety, a simple and informative handbook or pamphlet reminding employees what they must know and do to remain safe while traveling may be very useful. Employees can take it with them when they travel. What follows is an outline of areas that may be useful for employee travelers of a global business operating in the service sector.

Employee Travel Guide

- Planning: Consult company travel and security policies.
  - Consult with your company security professional for specific antiterrorist guidance.
  - Ensure family member and/or business associates know your plans and how to contact you.
  - Obtain necessary passports and visas.
  - Medical assistance: Learn what the company provides and what the employee can expect and who to contact while out of the home country.
- Traveling:
  - Luggage:
    —What to take and what not to take
    —Avoid use of company name on luggage

- ○ Airline security and seat selection: Avoid airlines with poor records of safety and security.
- ○ While at the airport:
  —Check in early, and go directly to one's gate or a secure zone.
  —Keep a low profile.
  —Know what areas to avoid.
  —While en route, limit personal contacts and avoid discussing business.
- ○ On arrival:
  —Have prearranged transportation if possible.
  —Claim your baggage, and ensure it has not been tampered with.
- ○ Reception: Know your host and how to make contact with them.
- During your stay:
  - ○ Hotel room safety, including:
    —Familiarize yourself with emergency exit routes and procedures.
    —Secure important items and documents when not in your room.
    —Have important items and documents readily available when in your room— making a quick exit.
    —Know emergency phone numbers.
    —Carry a small flashlight in the event of an emergency.
  - ○ Conducting business:
    —Know who you are doing business with.
    —Keep conversations focused on business and not politics.
    —Share business schedule with your home office.
  - ○ Vacationing:
    —Avoid excessive behavior (e.g., alcohol indulgence) and illegal behavior (e.g., illicit drug usage).
    —Become familiar with the common crimes of the country.
    —Avoid calling attention to yourself.
  - ○ The terrorist threat:
    —Know risks associated with the specific country or region.
    —Have an emergency evacuation plan.
    —Know how to contact company security support.
    —Know where your home country embassy or consulate is located and how to contact them.
    —Know where or how emergency medical support can be obtained.
    —Do not attract attention to yourself—to the extent practical, blend in with the local surroundings.
- On your return:
  - ○ Report unusual or suspicious incidents or contacts to security.
  - ○ Report any involvement with law enforcement or government personnel.
- Emergency contact information: Carry it with you.
  - ○ Travel assistance: company point of contact and travel agency numbers
  - ○ Security: company security office, ideally, and 24/7 number
  - ○ Home country embassy or consulate
  - ○ Immediate family member or emergency family point of contact
  - ○ Medical assistance numbers, local and home country

Employee International Assignment

It has been the authors' experience that having a policy in place establishing guidelines for international assignments is not always a common practice. All too often, employees are given a new assignment and provided with information on pay, transportation, relocation costs, and housing and helpful tips on the culture of the country where they will be assigned yet not provided with relevant safety and security information useful to them while in the new location, e.g., the terrorism threats.

Where formal policies exist, they often address operational and human resource issues and not security issues. Establishing comprehensive guidelines for international assignments, including written security guidance for employees, that include antiterrorist defensive actions provides the employees with necessary and even essential information for staying safe.

Relocating to another country is difficult in itself. Doing so without knowledge of terrorist threats and dangers makes the process increasingly difficult and risky. All employees should have a standard protocol they must follow to ensure that they are prepared for all aspects of their new assignment. Within the policy the unique responsibilities for all involved parties should be clearly established. This includes security and a definition of its role in supporting the reassigned employee. All reassigned employees should be required to pass through security and receive a briefing on all security issues associated with the reassignment and provided with security and threat-related information specific to the country or region to which they are transferring.

Any policy addressing employee international assignments should be developed in coordination with the company departments of human resources, security, risk management (insurance), legal, and the senior executive from the business unit managing international business. The policy should address the following areas.

International Assignments

- Approval authority and the approval process
- Applicability:
  - To whom this policy applies
  - The roles and responsibilities for all supporting functions
- General information about international work assignments
- Compensation: general information applicable to all employees on assignment
- Employee benefits, including medical benefits
- Medical treatment/exams: prior to assignment and while on assignment
- Travel: business and personal
- Temporary living expenses
- Permanent living arrangements
- Absences
- Changes in conditions of employment
- Security:
  - General security guidelines
  - Country-specific security guidelines
  - Kidnap and ransom guidelines
  - Guidelines in the event of a terrorist attack
- Risks: general and specific to the country or region

All employees designated for international assignments should be briefed on the specifics of this policy. Furthermore, a "handbook" version of the policy, with additional practical guidelines, should be made available for the affected employees to take with them on assignment.

Business Continuity Program Guidelines

A policy establishing guidelines for company contingency planning should include the following components:

- *Emergency response*: the act of trained personnel responding to any type of emergency, that includes from a terrorist attack
- *Crisis management*: the process of managing a terrorist and other crisis from its escalation as an emergency into a crisis and until the crisis has ended
- *Disaster recovery*: the short-term restoration of business after a terrorist attack or other type of disaster. Often heavily focused on restoration of information systems
- *Business resumption*: the long-term restoration of business (generally, back in business operating as the business did prior to the crisis)

Within this construct, planning should consider all of the types of crises a company is likely to encounter based on geographical conditions, environmental conditions, social and political conditions, and events unique to the nature of company business. For example, an energy company drilling for oil offshore must be prepared to manage and contain an oil spill. When managing an active oil field in a high-risk country (such as Iraq, Yemen, or Nigeria), that same company must plan for and be prepared to respond to terrorist attacks.

The goal is to ensure that security executives establish a company policy defining the basic components of a business continuity plan and as part of that plan address the need to be prepared to manage a crisis caused by an act of terror. Furthermore, for employees operating in areas outside of their home country, they should have in place emergency evacuation and repatriation plans in the event the risk of terror increases or an act of terror occurs. Emergency evacuation plans must consider evacuation for medical, political, and elevation in risk levels. Each condition calls for a different approach for safely relocating employees.

Security Awareness, Training, and Education (SATE) Program

In support of company practices that incorporate and address terrorist threats, attack methodologies and defensive measures used to protect employees should be part of a formal security awareness and training program that incorporates the information just provided. Through such a program, the security executive can ensure company rules and guidelines established through company policy are communicated and reinforced with all employees.

Let's face it, how many employees actually read company policies and procedures? Most refer to them as needed but do not take the time to seek them out and learn all they need to know. Perhaps the exception to this is a few overly cautious employees or those few who, after a bad experience, become much more proactive and diligent in the quest to protect themselves. Thus, in an effort to ensure that employees know and understand how best to protect themselves in today's high-risk environment, they must understand and comply with security rules and regulations. Compliance is necessary so that employees are reasonably prepared to contribute to their own protection.

A good security awareness and training program should do more than reinforce company rules, guidelines, and policies with employees. It should be designed to help raise employee general security consciousness and awareness as well as explain the dangers they may face under various circumstances, that is, get them thinking about security and developing good safety and security practices and habits.

It should also be designed to enable employees to help themselves. Methods and mechanisms should be made available to employees that encourage and facilitate their efforts to enlighten themselves. For example, there exist many web-based and reliable sources of useful protection methods and other security- and safety-related information easily accessible to company employees. Any interested employee with access to a computer and the Internet can seek them out. As part of a good security and awareness training program, the security executive can make the best of those resources available to employees.

More specifically, many governments provide useful information related to safety and security for their citizens who travel abroad. In the United States, the Department of State provides travel advisories for Americans planning to travel abroad (and anyone who chooses to access their website and read the information posted). General travel security and safety precautions are provided along with other useful information. This includes information on safety and security from terrorism. Other government agencies, such as the United Kingdom's[1] Foreign and Commonwealth Office and the Australian Government's Department of Foreign Affairs and Trade, Travel Advisory, and Consular Assistance[2] provide similar information useful for citizens as they plan and prepare for protecting themselves and their family as they travel and venture into areas with a risk of terrorism. Most of this information is posted on websites and is organized by category (e.g., security, travel, safety) and by country. This allows the user to access current and country-specific information pertaining to conditions within the area, region, or country of interest.

The security executive should design the SATE program in such a way as to reach employees via many different mediums. In today's technologically advanced world, with so much information available to people, almost to the point of saturation, the security executive has a difficult task of getting relevant and useful information out to employees and making that information stick. The message must be clear, concise, and timely and sometimes, when appropriate, delivered with humor, which will help catch the attention of employees and increase the likelihood that they will capture and retain the essence of the message. Ideally, the security executive will use multiple approaches for reaching employees to ensure that the message does reach them. The following are offered for consideration.

- *Face-to-face briefings and exchanges*: These are labor-intensive, which
  means costly, but offer the employee an opportunity to ask questions of the

security professional directly. Face-to-face exchanges also allow the security professional to assess if the employee really understands the essence of what is being communicated. In some situations, usually when the information being communicated is sensitive and related to a specific situation, face-to-face exchanges are necessary to ensure that the message is communicated effectively.

- *Publications*: These are useful for employees as take-away resources. Publications offer the employee something they can hold on to and refer to at a later date. Once created, they require periodic review and updates.
- *Electronic messages and announcements*: This is perhaps the fastest way to reach a large number of employees. Electronic messages are perhaps the best to get the word out quickly in the event of a rapid situational change, e.g., increased risk caused by a potential or actual terrorist attack. The downside of electronic communication is overload. So many messages are sent to employees electronically that many of them go unread or, at best, not read in a timely manner.
- *Web-based tools*: Access to web-based tools allows the employee to seek out the terrorist information most relevant to them. Web-based tools also allow the security professional to establish a single source, a company security website, for example, from which the employee can be directed to many other web-based and potentially useful resources offered by the company, local, state, or federal governments, and recognized advocate sponsors, such as professional associations.
- *When delivering critically important messages*: Multiple methods of communication should be used. Furthermore, through the various communications methods, employees must be told of the importance to their own safety that such information provides. In today's environment and especially in many nation-states after attacks in their countries, e.g., 9/11, subway attacks in the UK, train attack in Spain, bombings in Indonesia, it is easier to get an employee's attention because it may truly be a matter of life or death.

Most commercial providers of intelligence information, selling their services to security executives in companies around the world, also provide information on the risks of travel to many regions of the world. Many of these intelligence providers will arrange (for an established fee) for the security executive to establish a link to the company website that will take employees to the intelligence provider's website, thus allowing the employee to access up-to-date safety, security, and terrorist- and antiterrorist-related information directly. Since the process is web-based, employees can access the information they need, when convenient for them, and from wherever in the world they are, as long as they have Internet access.

Through the SATE program, the security executive opens a dialogue with employees and, essentially, offers them awareness resources (tools or toolbox may be a more useful characterization) that can be delivered to the employee or obtained by the employee via a convenient self-serve process. Part of increasing the security awareness of all company employees involves empowering them to help themselves. It is important to provide them with tools to do this in a simple, convenient, and quick way.

Protecting Employees in the Workplace and on Company Property While in the Home Country: A Summary

☐ ☐ ☐ ▬▬▬▬▬▬▬▬▬▬▬▬▬▬▬▬▬▬▬▬▬▬▬▬▬▬▬▬▬▬

Protecting employees in the workplace begins with having an effective company-sponsored security program in place. Where there is a risk of terrorism, the program should incorporate antiterrorist measures consistent with the established risks of attack and vulnerability of the enterprise.

▬▬▬▬▬▬▬▬▬▬▬▬▬▬▬▬▬▬▬▬▬▬▬▬▬▬▬▬ ☐ ☐ ☐

Essentially, the company and the security executive must work to create a safe and secure work environment, one that employees can enter knowing they are generally safe and secure from the hazards of the world and can focus on doing the work the company is paying them to do. But just how safe must the work environment be? An essential challenge to the security executive is to ensure that the right amount of asset protection is provided to protect the workforce and all company assets effectively and efficiently. Thus, a risk assessment must be conducted for the company and its different facilities or sites.

Given the results of the risk assessment, the security executive puts in place the general security measures designed to create a safe work environment and a workforce suitable for the company. Moreover, the security executive must incorporate into the security profile those measures needed to mitigate any threat of terrorism. Recall that suitability refers not only to the employees' ability to perform their job assignments but also to any risk they may create for the company. For example, a company may not want to hire an individual on the government terrorist watch list—this may be a legal issue, so it is best to consult with the listing agency and the company legal staff prior to rejecting such an applicant.

In order to protect employees effectively from the threat of terrorism and potential terrorist attacks, the security executive uses the security program in place and builds on it in a way that specifically addresses the vulnerability to terrorism and the threat of terrorism. This is not the case when building a new facility while facing an existing threat of terror or when renovating or refurbishing a facility in a high-terrorist-risk environment. Here the threat of terrorism must be taken into account during the design and construction or reconstruction period.

With a safe and secure work environment, filled with suitable employees, the security executive's focus should be on maintaining the security program and working to make it more efficient (process improvements, or doing things "faster, better, cheaper"). The security executive should also be focused on change, that is, on changes in conditions that will require a mitigating action and, more specifically, on changes within the environment that will affect the effectiveness of the security program, thus diminishing the security executive's ability to protect company assets. For example, if the risk level for a terrorism event increases, the security executive must be able to assess the potential impact to company operations and take appropriate actions to enhance company security—essentially, work to harden the target. To do this, the security executive must learn as much as possible about the new threat or elevation of a current threat and assess the vulnerability of the company against that threat. Essentially, the security executive assesses the risk to the company from the changing threat conditions.

Part of the process of making the company facility more secure is reaching out to employees, advising them of the changes in risk conditions and the actions company security has taken to mitigate these conditions, and providing employees with guidance on what they may do to contribute to the protection of company assets and to the protection of themselves and other employees. Keep in mind the necessity of continuing to improve the situational awareness of all employees.

Leaving the Protective Confines of the Home Country

Employees are vulnerable to the unfamiliar and the unknown, so when they enter areas they don't know the risk to their personal safety and security is increased. Employees are dependent on the company they work for to provide them with information and tools needed to mitigate any increased vulnerability and risk to them so that they, the employees, may accomplish their mission in support of company business while remaining safe and secure. This is particularly so in the case of terrorism.

General information regarding the threat of terrorism is regularly made available in the media. Television, radio, and print media regularly provide information to viewers, listeners, and readers on changing threat conditions in different parts of the world. The information provided is seldom specific, unless it relates to a specific event following the occurrence of that event.

☐ ☐ ☐ ━━━━━━━━━━━━━━━━━━━━━━━━━━━━━━━━━━━━

When employees leave the protective confines of company property in their home country and venture off into other areas of the world they become more vulnerable.

━━━━━━━━━━━━━━━━━━━━━━━━━━━━━━━━━━━━ ☐ ☐ ☐

Specific information, particularly newly developed information related to specific increases in the threat of terrorism, developed by government intelligence providers, commercial intelligence providers, and security practitioners is not shared with the media but may be highly valuable to the traveling employee though not readily available. Security practitioners can, and often do, have access to some or much of this information and can shape or customize it, making it relevant and available to employees. Some or much of this specific intelligence is, or can be, made available to the security professional, recognizing that all will never be available from any one source.

There exist many producers of intelligence related to the risk of terrorism. Much of the work is done by governments who do not share that information freely. How governments share threat-related information varies and is usually done so on a need-to-know basis. Commercial intelligence providers, with capabilities far less robust than most governments, sell their information only to a list of vetted clients (not just anyone off the street). Security professionals use the information they receive, purchase, or develop to inform company management and employees. Essentially, specific and useful terrorist threat–related intelligence is not readily available to everyone. However, some useful terrorist threat–related information can be obtained or developed by security professionals, but they must make the effort to do so.

So, is it reasonable to expect employees to take on the responsibility of preparing themselves for the many risks they may face when they head out on company business? The answer to this question is both yes and no. All employees are responsible for their own safety and security. As employees they are obligated, when away from the company, to behave and prepare in a manner that contributes to protecting company assets, which usually means protecting themselves. However, to varying degrees, employees will have a basic understanding of how to protect themselves while in unfamiliar areas.

What they generally do not have is an in-depth and specific knowledge of risks in the areas where they venture. That is where the security professional comes in. Drawing on the various providers and producers of threat and risk information to include specific threat information related to the risk of terror, security practitioners make relevant and specific information available, thus reducing the risk to employees. After all, it is the responsibility of the security professional to mitigate risks to company assets.

In an earlier section of this chapter we presented multiple approaches the security executive can use to communicate to employees to ensure safety and security information gets to them. Furthermore, we addressed how to use the different approaches in some combination as the most effective means of ensuring that the message gets out and is received, for example, briefing employees prior to departure from their home country and providing them with written material to take with them as a quick reference.

All methods of communication fall into two categories: information that is *pushed* out to employees and information that employees *pull* from the company, the security department, and/or other designated resources.

Pushed information is information the security executive delivers in some way to the employee, be it face-to-face communications, electronic communications, printed material, or some other form of getting information into the hands of the employee. Pushed information targets the employee. Pulled information is information employees seek out on their own. They go to a source—a security professional, a website, a library, or some other source housing relevant information—and get that information.

While on Travel

Before employees embark on any company business–related travel, they should be made aware of, in accordance with company policy as recommended earlier in this chapter, all general travel precautions, company restrictions, requirements, and basic safety and security guidelines relevant to their journey. Essentially, these are the precautions, restrictions, and guidelines relevant to employees for all travel outside of the home country. When traveling to areas where concern for employee safety and security is greater, employees should receive from the security organization specific guidance related to the areas discussed in the following sections.

Concerns for Areas of High Risk

This information can be compiled using the various sources of commercial intelligence providers with whom the security executive has chosen to do business. Moreover, relevant information may be obtained from guidance provided by and posted on various government advisory websites. Ideally, the information should come from the host/home country websites. The focus should be on relevant information associated specifically with the level of risk and the areas of risk that may affect the traveler.

Specific Country or City Threat Assessments

These assessments should be more focused on the specific area the employee will travel to and within. For example; though much of the Middle East is a high-risk area for terrorism, an employee traveling to Riyadh, Saudi Arabia, needs to know and understand the specific risks associated with being in Riyadh. Moreover, the guidance provided should reach beyond safety and security measures. The assessments should include all information related to warnings, public announcements, and key local customs and laws. Ensuring that travelers are aware of the most common potential pitfalls and hazards will help them through their initial foray into the area. Once there, the travelers can easily learn more about the country they are in through their business contact or by consulting their home country embassy or consulate.

Registering with the Embassy

When traveling abroad, U.S. citizens are encouraged to register their "stay" in the country they are visiting with the U.S. Embassy, thereby ensuring that their presence is known in the event of an emergency situation. It's a voluntary way of letting the U.S. government know that an individual American citizen is in a foreign country. In the event of an emergency, the U.S. Department of State uses the information provided as a means of communication. The type of emergency could range from relatives trying to contact the traveler, through the embassy, about a family emergency to the embassy's alerting the traveler to a change in threat conditions. The registration process is web-based, for easy access.[3]

Other countries offer a similar service to their citizens. It is recommended that the security professional include information related to home country embassy support for travelers while they are out of the country.

Real-Time Tracking of Employees

Large global companies may have many employees engaged in international travel at any one time. In some cases, employees may be on travel for extensive periods. While they are traveling from country to country, global, regional, and country risk conditions may change. Some of the changes could be potentially detrimental to the employee. For example, if an employee is traveling in a politically unstable developing nation, the political conditions of that country could change in a very short period of time. Consider the situation in Thailand in September of 2006.[4] Here the country's military leaders staged a coup suspending the constitution and declaring martial law. Foreign travelers, particularly those doing business with the ousted government leaders, have a real need to know the current situation and how to react.

Tracking of the traveler can be accomplished by having the security executive work with the company travel manager and developing a process designed to track which employees are traveling where, including all stops between departure and return. Via this process, the company can know where each employee is at any point in time during travel and, when necessary, contact that employee or push (usually electronically via e-mail or messaging) information out to that employee, alerting him or her to changes in travel, safety, or security conditions.

Tracking traveling employees can be a very simple process. If the security executive chooses not to develop an internal process, there are many commercial providers of traveler tracking services. From companies engaged in the travel business to providers of commercial intelligence services, there are many standard products for traveler tracking and traveler notification. Furthermore, most providers offer customized traveler-tracking services, taking their standard capabilities and developing an enhanced or modified process specific to the needs of a particular business.

When using the traveler-tracking service of a commercial provider of intelligence services, the security executive can couple two different processes and capabilities into a single package. More specifically, if a single commercial provider of traveler-tracking services and risk and intelligence services is to be used, that company not only tracks the traveler but, when risk conditions change, is capable of pushing relevant information to the traveler on a real-time basis. This capability is particularly useful when dealing with the threat of terrorism. Most commercial providers of intelligence monitor global events around the clock. Some have personnel on the ground in many regions and countries of the world. These providers generally have the capability to learn of events as they are developing. Thus their capability to maintain constant global situational awareness, produce risk assessments, and push out relevant information to a traveler on a real-time basis can be a highly valued asset to any security executive. Being able to purchase multiple services from a single provider and to link together those services (traveler tracking, intelligence reports, risk assessments, and changes in global risk conditions), thus providing to the traveling company employee the support needed to remain safe and secure while on company business, is a tool so valuable it will be difficult for the security executive not to use.

Employees on International Assignments

It is very common for global companies to have employees (expatriate employees) assigned to different countries and regions of the world in support of the business. These employees represent the company outside of the home location for extended periods of time. Generally, these employees fall into two categories in terms of the time they will spend out of their home country supporting company business in global regions:

- Employees on short-term assignments—less than 60 days
- Employees on long-term assignment—more than 60 days

These employees, due to the length of time spent away from the home country and often in areas of higher risk, are more vulnerable to hazards and dangers than those company employees who remain within the protective confines of company home offices. Even when employees on assignment are operating in areas of low risk, just being away from the home country, detached from many of the company support structures, can create a greater vulnerability. Therefore, it's critical that company human resources and security executives know what employees are on international assignment and stay closely connected to them. The process of managing the welfare of employees on international assignments starts with knowing who they are, what they are doing, where they are doing it, and for whom they work.

Once an employee is designated for assignment, a formal approval process should be initiated whereby, according to company policy, all appropriate management and executive approvals are obtained and the employee signs a written agreement with the company acknowledging his or her understanding of the obligations associated with this international assignment and commits to fulfilling work assignment. The approval and written agreement process reinforces with the employee the obligations that must be fulfilled. Moreover, establishing the ground rules prior to the actual assignment reduces the possibilities for misunderstanding or error.

After the international assignment is approved, the next action for the security professional is to have the designated employees provide all relevant personal data, which will be used by the security professional in preparing special security briefings. This information should also be used by the security professional to develop an emergency evacuation plan for the country or region where the employees will be assigned. Prior to the employees' actually arriving at their international assignment, an emergency evacuation plan should be in place. For high-risk regions, this is particularly important, and it may be prudent for the security executive to have in place a primary plan and a secondary plan in the event of a major crisis, such as a terrorist attack. Emergency evacuation plans should consider exit from the area via air, land, and sea (for those countries not landlocked). The plan should also include consideration that movement within the country or area may not be safe and that it may be best to plan on having the employees' shelter in place.

Emergency evacuation plans can be developed and designed for implementation by company security and other company support personnel, or the services can be purchased through one of several companies offering worldwide emergency evacuation services. Generally, there are two types of providers of worldwide emergency evacuation services: companies that provide emergency medical evacuation services and companies that offer nonmedical emergency evacuation services (usually associated with area instability caused by natural disasters, political conditions, or armed conflict). For high-risk areas, these companies offer a unique expertise and skill set for getting into difficult areas and moving people safely from them. It is the wise security professional who takes advantage of this unique capability, thus letting those most prepared for the situation handle that situation.

One other area of consideration must be made when preparing to protect employees from acts of terror. Kidnap and ransom is a practice used all too often by terrorists. Kidnapping for ransom is a method used by terrorist to acquire funds for their other activities. In southern Iraq, a news service provider (Iran Focus) focused on events in Iran and reported on Iranian terrorists systematic kidnapping of Iraqis for ransom, demanding large ransoms for their return.[5] In Mexico, violent kidnappings for ransom and extortion have reached near-epidemic proportions. Nearly everyone, rich to middle class and those of lesser means, face the threat of kidnapping by organized gangs.[6] It is not uncommon for terrorist groups to engage in drug trafficking, kidnap and ransom, extortion, and other criminal activities to help fund their terrorist activities.

What does this mean to the business traveler or expatriate operating in an area of the world where terrorists are engaged in criminal activities to help fund their acts of terror? The threat of terror reaches beyond the high-profile bombings and attacks, such as the events of September 11, 2001, and threatens the individual, the ordinary employee, in the process of living and working in a high-risk area. The security executive can no longer be concerned only with the potential for a high-profile executive's being a victim of kidnapping and ransom. This concern must now extend to any company employee or representative. With this increased risk, the security executive must prepare to mitigate that risk. In the case of kidnap and ransom, mitigation preparations must begin with increased security education and training targeting those employees operating in areas with higher risks. All employees at risk should receive training focused on preventing them from becoming a target of kidnap and ransom.

Training employees in how to avoid becoming a victim of kidnap, ransom, and extortion requires some specialized knowledge. For the security executive unfamiliar with this growing phenomenon there are several global companies operating in Europe, the Americas, and Asia that specialize in crisis management for such situations. Moreover, most offer programs designed to train employees on how to avoid becoming a victim. They also offer training programs for security professionals on how to prepare for and manage such a crisis should a kidnapping-and-ransom event involve one or more of their company employees. In terms of risks to company assets, there are insurance providers who offer coverage for such events, thus providing another way to help mitigate the risk to the company.

In no way do the authors suggest that insurance is the best or only method for mitigating potential losses from a kidnap or ransom event. First and foremost, full consideration should be given to the safety of any employee or company representative who becomes a victim. However, in addition to having plans in place to manage a kidnap or ransom crisis, prudent executives will have insurance to help offset any financial damage to the company.

Case Scenario

During a risk assessment directed by a chief security officer (CSO) with the objective of determining the risks to corporate employees operating in a corporate facility in Jakarta, Indonesia, it was determined that the risks to the American and other Indonesian-foreign employees at that facility were extremely high. This assessment was based on the increased terrorist threats and actual terrorist attacks, e.g., bombings throughout Indonesia, from Jakarta to Bali, which included restaurants, hotels, and other businesses in areas frequented by corporate employees.

All areas of Indonesia were identified by the risk assessment team as being at high risk. This assessment was reviewed with and agreed to by local Indonesian security and law enforcement personnel, who had provided some of the information. Furthermore, this assessment was reviewed with the U.S. Embassy staff's security personnel, who concurred with the assessment.

As a CSO, what would you do to address this risk to corporate employees in Indonesia? The following is an example of an approach.

Based on the risk assessment team's recommendations, which were agreed to by the CSO, the CSO decided that a company should be placed on contract, with another company as a backup, that would immediately extract these Americans and other non-Indonesians from a hazardous environment in Indonesia.

The CSO discussed the results of the risk assessment with his boss, the vice president of human resources, who concurred with the recommendation and set up an executive management briefing to be conducted by the CSO.

The briefing by the CSO included the risk assessment methodology used, how the results were determined, all general recommendations, and a CSO-recommended plan of action that included the extraction of corporate employees with support of a third-party company.

One of the matters discussed was the level of employment at which the contract should be applied, e.g., managers only, Americans only, other than local nation-state employees. It was recommended by the CSO, and supported by HR and Legal, that all corporate employees other than local Indonesian national employees were to be included for extraction. All expatriate employees required safe relocation from the area. Obviously, local national employees would not be extracted because they are citizens and residents of Indonesia.

Executive management asked if this was the only location where such risks appeared. The CSO said that all employees, particularly those overseas, share an increased terrorist threat and thus were operating in a higher-than-normal risk environment. But the other plants were located in areas currently operating under a lower-terror-threat environment than the current condition in Indonesia. However, the CSO explained that risk assessments at all overseas facilities was ongoing to establish the risks from terrorist threats and that those results would be provided to executive management in a subsequent formal report. The estimated risk assessment completion time was about two months, with the report coming within three months.

The executive management members, of course, wanted to know why it would take so long, and the CSO explained that the resources with the applicable expertise were limited, as was the budget. The managers did not object to that explanation.

The contracts included the following specifications.

- Two companies, a primary and a backup, would be contracted to arrange air transport for all employees identified for evacuation.
- Each must be able to respond to an incident within 48 hours anywhere in the world.
- Each company would arrange to have its transport vehicles at a prearranged airport at a prearranged time ready to transport a prearranged number of employees to a safe location, a location outside the country at risk.
- Provisions must be made for a secondary location and a secondary mode of transportation (land or sea) should air evacuation be hindered from reaching the primary prearranged location in any way. In other words, a backup evacuation process must be proposed.
- Each company is responsible for making all necessary arrangements with local and national governments to ensure safe passage (in and out) of the country.
- All employees are to be taken to a "safe" zone (country) and rerouted from there to their home location (assuming all are not American citizens and some are third-country nationals, e.g., Canadians, Germans)
- In the event medical support is necessary, each company must be prepared to provide emergency medical support.

The CSO, in cooperation with the corporate contract officer, finalized the proposed contract specifications, and then the contract office staff sent out a Request for Proposal (RFP) to those companies identified[7] who appeared to meet the criteria established by the CSO's risk assessment team. The criteria were based on potential contractors being responsive and responsible. In other words, they had the capability to fulfill the contract's requirements and their proposal accurately addressed the RFP specifications.

The executive management also approved a budget for this contract as part of the CSO's security department's budget, but as a fenced line item so that the funds could not be used for any other purpose. This authorized the CSO or designated others to quickly notify the contracted company in an emergency without having to deal with budgetary needs. After all, lives would be at stake and the bureaucracy should not get in the way of saving lives.

The proposals were reviewed by the CSO, legal staff, and the contracting officer. Winning bidders were identified and notified. A contract was signed and put in place, with annual evaluations and renewals based on the current company needs and world conditions, specifically, the increased or decreased global threat of terror as it affects company global operations.

Summary

Throughout this chapter the authors have placed much emphasis on training and awareness for employees in order to raise their individual and collective security consciousness, general security awareness, and situational awareness capabilities.

Having in place an effective security education and training program cannot be overemphasized. Keeping employees safe and secure and protecting them from terrorism and other risks they may face while conducting business is best accomplished when those same employees understand the importance of protecting themselves.

The ultimate goal of protecting employees from terrorism may best be achieved by creating safe and secure conditions in the workplace and a culture of safety and security within the behavior and mindset of all company employees. That is, the security executive, through the use of the tools, methods, and processes described in this chapter and incorporated into the company security program, creates a heightened sense of security and safety within the consciousness of company employees.

In this environment, employees, management, and executives all understand the need to acknowledge that the world can be a dangerous place and that all company employees play a role in mitigating risk to company assets. This includes all employees, for they too are an asset to the company.

Endnotes

[1] See: http://www.fco.gov.uk/servlet/Front?pagename=OpenMarket/Xcelerate/ShowPage&c=Page&cid=1007029390572

[2] See: http://www.smartraveller.gov.au/index.html

[3] See: http://travelregistration.state.gov

[4] See: http://news.bbc.co.uk/2/hi/asia-pacific/5361512.stm

[5] See: http://www.iranfocus.com/modules/news/article.php?storyid=1135

[6] See: http://www.mexidata.info/id217.html

[7] If your corporation is in need of such extraction services, you should, by means of an Internet search engine, be able to find applicable companies who are in this business.

Preparing for a Terrorist Attack: Emergency Planning and Implementation

Wisdom is a variable possession. Every man is wise when pursued by a mad dog, fewer when pursued by a mad woman; only the wisest survive when attacked by a mad notion.
—Robertson Davies

This chapter covers the measures that must be taken to prepare a corporation to respond to an act of terror. If an act of terror is perpetrated against a corporation, what can and must be done in response? How does a company recover from such a tragedy? What is the impact on employees? Is terrorism like lightning, seldom striking in the same place twice?

In today's world, following the tragic events of September 11, 2001,[1] and the subsequent global war on terrorism, the need for business contingency planning in the event of terrorist attacks should be ingrained in the mind of every security executive. That need is reinforced by the existence of a plethora of hazards facing contemporary security executives, from natural disasters such as earthquakes, tsunamis,[2] and hurricanes[3] to the threat of a new pandemic.[4] Other potential disasters, such as political strife[5] and financial collapse,[6] threaten business around the world.

Each hazard has the potential to disrupt the continuity of business operating in the affected geographic regions or market sector. Actually, in today's global environment, a disaster caused by a successful terrorist attack in Asia has the potential to affect businesses based in Europe, the Americas, and other locations, depending on global markets or suppliers. For example, imagine the impact to southern California if the shipping ports of Los Angeles[7] and Long Beach[8] were rendered inoperable for a period of 30 days due to a terrorist attack. Considering combined port operations support more than 250,000 full-time and part-time jobs in the state of California and more than 1.3 million jobs within the United States, an extended port shutdown would have a devastating effect on the national economy.

Whether in business, not-for-profit, or government service, all organizations must have contingency plans in place. Those plans need to be designed in such a way as to allow for prompt response to an emergency and effective management of a crisis. Furthermore, contingency planning must take into account the need for prompt restoration of critical processes and long-term restoration of the business or organization operations.

When developing contingency plans in preparation for an act of terror, planners must consider the possibility of terrorists striking following an unrelated crisis. For example, an effective time for terrorists to strike may very well be while efforts are focused on recovering from a natural disaster. Contingency planners must consider the importance of planning to recover from one crisis and recognize the potential that another one might occur during the recovery effort.

Since security organizations by definition are designed to respond to an emergency and manage a crisis, it is becoming common practice to see security executives charged with the design and implementation of contingency plans.

Contingency Planning[9]

The traditional role of security in the contingency planning process has been to develop emergency evacuation plans for the organization or enterprise and to respond to emergency situations and manage any situation escalating from an emergency into a crisis. Acting as the eyes and ears of an organization or business and usually maintaining a 24-hours-a-day, 7-days-a-week presence, the security organization is generally the most prepared and capable entity to respond to any emergency such as a terrorist attack. Security is certainly the most available.

Because of this posture and the recent increased emphasis on emergency preparedness following the tragic events of September 11, 2001, in New York City, many security organizations have expanded their contingency planning capabilities to include the following components:

- Emergency response
- Crisis management
- Business recovery
- Business resumption

The combination of these four areas constitutes the major components of a business continuity program. The fundamental elements of each component and the need for an effective integrated business continuity program is essential if a corporation is to have antiterrorist defenses in place. Furthermore, the categories and types of crises, along with basic preparation and awareness, must be considered.

The discipline of contingency planning has its own jargon, which includes terms such as:

- Business continuity
- Disaster recovery
- Business resumption
- Crisis management
- Emergency response

Other terms may have different meanings to different professionals within different businesses or organizations, both public and private.

To help eliminate confusion, especially when government agencies and corporate security personnel are responding to a terrorist attack, the security executive and the security staff and the government agencies who would be responding to a terrorist attack should have decided on and agreed on the definitions of key terms well in advance.

In the event of a terrorist attack, there will be enough confusion and miscommunication. No need for various people to add to it by using different terms and definitions for the same thing.

Definition of Terms

Regardless of the scope of the effort, a business continuity program must consider many types of terrorist attack methodologies and related activities. Depending on the size and complexity of a business, the process of contingency planning can be quite extensive.

▢ ▢ ▢ ━━━━━━━━━━━━━━━━━━━━━━━━━━━━━━━━━━

Planning for a contingency generally means assessing and understanding all aspects of a business and all categories of potential types of terrorist attacks and their associated risks.

━━━━━━━━━━━━━━━━━━━━━━━━━━━━━━━━━━ ▢ ▢ ▢

To plan effectively requires the participation of many people from different disciplines within the business. This includes organizational leadership, executives, management, employees, suppliers, and sometimes even customers—yes, customers. It's important to remember that customers have a stake in the success and continuity of a business. Businesses with few or highly valued and significant customers (significant in the sense of how much they purchase from or depend on the business) may find these customers are actively concerned with the continuity of business from a primary supplier.

The planning process may also include representatives from other organizations external to the company, such as executives of an insurance underwriter, planning experts from the local fire and police departments, medical experts, and other experts familiar with the unique threats posed by terrorist organizations possessing chemical, biological, or nuclear weapon knowledge, technologies, and material. Having so many people involved from many different functional disciplines within an organization calls for establishing common parameters. To be effective, everyone involved must have a common understanding of the elements and objectives of the contingency planning process.

When discussing any aspect of contingency planning it is essential that all parties have a common understanding of what is being discussed. Just what is meant when someone refers to the contingency planning process, business recovery, or any other elements of this process? Next we present a useful and effective working set of definitions. These are examples of those that may be used by business enterprises or organizations, and they provide the basis for a common understanding of terms. As stated earlier, common terms and definitions should be used by all respondents.

In any event, all people involved in the contingency planning process will need a common baseline, common points of reference, and a common language. Establishing definitions at the onset of your planning process will help accomplish this.

- *Business continuity*: Minimizing business interruption or disruption caused by different contingencies. Essentially, business continuity means keeping the business operating. Business continuity plans encompass actions related to how a company prepares for, manages, recovers from, and ultimately resumes business after an interruption.

- *Business recovery*: This refers to the short-term (less than 60 days) restoration activities that return the business to a minimum acceptable level of operation following an interruption to the business. Often used interchangeably with the term *disaster recovery*.
- *Business resumption*: The long-term (more than 60 days) process of restoration of routine business activities after an emergency or disaster that returns the operation to a pre-event condition. (Keep in mind that restoration to the exact pre-event condition may not be necessary or even desirable. However, making this determination may not be possible without proper planning or going through the actual resumption process.)
- *Contingency*: An event that is of possible but uncertain occurrence or is likely to happen as an adjunct to other events, e.g., terrorist attacks.
- *Contingency planning*: The process of planning for response to an event or emergency, managing the escalation of an emergency into a crisis condition, recovery and resumption of activities from an emergency or crisis for the infrastructure, critical processes, and other elements of a business or organization. Contingency planning is the process of building all elements of a plan focused on mitigating any interruption to business operations.
- *Crisis management*: The process of managing the events of a crisis to a condition of stability. This task is best accomplished by an integrated process team (IPT) made up of members from different disciplines throughout the company. This IPT serves as the company or enterprise deliberative body of experts for development and implementation of emergency response and crisis management plans.
- *Critical processes*: Activities performed by organizations internal to the business or enterprise that, if significantly disrupted due to an emergency, crisis, or disaster, would have an adverse impact on the company's operations, revenue generation, customer schedules, contractual commitments, or legal obligations.
- *Emergency response*: The act of reporting and responding to any emergency or unplanned disruption of business.
- *Terrorism or act of terror*: Any adverse action committed by a terrorist or terrorist organization leading to or causing a disruption in business operations or harm to enterprise assets in any way.

Contingency Planning Program[10]

The purpose of contingency planning is to better enable any business or organization to maintain continuity of operations. Should a successful terrorist attack cause disruptions somewhere in the world—and this occurs much too often—a business must be able to resume normal activities as quickly as possible. The inability to restore normal operations will have an adverse economic impact on businesses and other organizations. The extent of the impact will correspond to the extent of the disruption or damage. If the damage is severe and the mitigation of such damage has not been properly planned for, the effect could be catastrophic. Essentially, the business could fail.

Having a company policy on contingency planning is the basis for a sound and functional program. In Chapter 7, we identified many types of company policies necessary to establish formal controls and procedures to help keep the work environment safe and secure. Contingency planning is one of those areas where a formal written company policy is essential. Contingency planning is generally not considered part of the normal daily operation of most employees, departments, or organizations. Therefore, it is not automatically or routinely addressed. Employees and management tend to focus on the priorities of their specific jobs and departments. Seldom do they consider the potential effects of a disruption of business and the need to have contingency plans in place. Contingency planning for most company employees is not perceived as part of their job responsibilities.

If a contingency planning program is required by company policy and specific responsibilities are identified and assigned, then the process stands a greater chance of becoming part of the normal business routine. Contingency planning should be viewed as a critical business process in and of itself. This may take time. Ultimately, to become completely effective, contingency planning needs to become part of the business and company culture.

A security executive can help the process of contingency planning become part of the company culture by including a segment on contingency planning in the company security awareness training and education program. Emphasis can be placed on the importance of the program, the critical elements of the program, and individual responsibilities as part of the program, along with the benefits to the company and its employees by having a quality contingency planning process in place.

Contingency planning is a continual process. It is not something done once and put away, to be retrieved only when needed. It is a continual process requiring periodic updates and revisions as appropriate to and consistent with changing business conditions and changing terrorist-related risk conditions. For example, contingency planning prior to the events of September 11, 2001, in New York City generally did not emphasize preparations for response and recovery to a terrorist attack in the United States. This has changed. The process of contingency planning should be designed to achieve the following.

- *Secure and protect people*: In the event of a terrorist attack, people must be protected.
- *Secure the continuity of the core processes and elements of the business*: The infrastructure must be protected and, when damaged, quickly restored. Disruption of critical processes must be minimized; when disruption does occur, restoration must be swift and prioritized according to company needs.
- *Secure all information systems that include or affect supplier connections and customer relationships*: To the extent necessary, this could include the availability of alternative "hot" systems (that is, redundant and ready for immediate use).

Throughout the remaining sections of this chapter, elements of the contingency planning process will be presented and explained (see Figure 8-1).

Contingency Plans

Contingency plans formally establish the processes and procedures for protecting employees, core business processes and elements, information systems, and the environment in the event of an emergency, business disruption, or disaster. These plans must

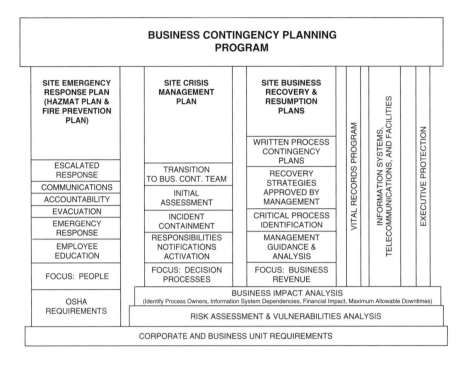

FIGURE 8-1 The building blocks of a business contingency planning program and their relationship to one another.

discuss specific types of emergencies, crises, and disasters, including those resulting from acts of terror or changes in operations due to a heightened terrorist threat and address the mitigation, preparedness, and response actions to be taken by emergency response and crisis management team members, executives, management, and employees, along with identifying the specific organizations charged with response and recovery tasks.

Plans must contain basic guidance, direction, responsibilities, and administrative information. Plans need to be developed, maintained, and shared in writing (hard copy or electronic) with management and employees. To develop contingency plans, the preparedness process must include the following considerations and elements.

Assumptions

Basic assumptions need to be developed in order to establish contingency planning ground rules. It is best to use as a baseline for planning several possible worst-case scenarios relative to time of event, type of event, available resources, building/facility/site occupancy, evacuation of personnel, personnel stranded on site, and environmental factors such as weather conditions and temperature. The scenarios differ depending on the nature of the event. Consideration should be given to establishing response parameters for terrorist-caused emergency events. Define what constitutes, for your business, a minor emergency, a major emergency, and a disaster.

Risk Assessment and Vulnerability Analysis

The crisis management team should have the responsibility of identifying known and apparent vulnerabilities, including the degree of risk from acts of terror associated with the type of business and geographic location of the enterprise. An assessment of risk and vulnerabilities should be made prior to developing any contingency plans. Chapter 5 provides a methodology for use in assessing risk. Simply stated, the threats against an asset, when considered in the context of the value of the asset and the vulnerability of the asset, lead to an assessment of risk:

$$\text{Threat} \times \text{Vulnerability} \times \text{Impact on assets} = \text{Risk}$$

All planning should be accomplished in accordance with a thorough understanding of actual and potential risks and vulnerabilities of assets. For example, if your company operates in an office building that is very old and constructed completely of wood and other combustible materials, then it may be vulnerable to fire. If that same building happens to be located in an arid geographical area where there is a high risk of fire, then planning needs to be done to address the hazard of fire. Here both the likelihood of fire and the vulnerability to fire are high. Therefore, the risk of potential damage is high. Furthermore, if that building is located in an area with a moderate or high risk of terrorism, the potential consequences of a terrorist attack must be considered.

If a company site is located in an area with a low threat of terrorism, then mitigation planning against terrorist attacks and threats should reflect the low-risk condition. Keep in mind that when the threat of terror is low, the security executive still has a responsibility to have adequate antiterrorist measures in place to ensure a safe and secure work environment. These measures must be consistent with company policy and the level of risk that company executives are willing to tolerate and accept.

A risk assessment and vulnerability analysis should also include an assessment of the policies and practices of the company's critical relationships. This means involving suppliers, customers, and critical stakeholders in the contingency planning process. Regardless of how prepared a company may be, if a critical supplier or many key suppliers are not also prepared for various potential contingencies, their inability to recover will adversely impact your company. Ideally, critical suppliers should be integrated into the contingency planning process.

Types of Hazards

Planning for each and every type of hazard is not practical or desirable. Grouping them into similar or like categories will allow for planning to address categories of hazards. Since many hazards have similar consequences and result in like damages, it is best to plan for them in categories. Following is a list of common related hazards any company may face. It is not all-inclusive and can be modified to fit the needs and conditions of any company.

- Medical emergency
- Fire
- Bomb threat
- Explosion
- Power interruption
- Hazardous material (HAZMAT)
- Aircraft crash

- Terrorist threat/activity—This includes the potential for the following types of attacks:
  - Military-type assault
  - Bombing
  - Biological, chemical, or nuclear (dirty bomb) attack
  - Disruption of critical infrastructure (power, water, fuel, etc.)
  - Kidnap, ransom, and extortion

Critical Process Identification

All critical processes must be identified. These processes must be ranked in accordance with their criticality and importance to the productivity and survivability of the enterprise. The process of recovery should be focused on those critical processes that, when resumed, will restore operations to a minimally acceptable level. In essence, these processes are identified as the first processes restored in the event of a major interruption to business operations. Failure to restore them presents the greatest possibility of damage or loss to the enterprise.

Business Impact Analysis

A business impact analysis must be accomplished to determine accurately the financial and operational impact that could result from an interruption to the business processes. Moreover, all critical interdependencies, those processes or activities on which critical processes depend, must be assessed to determine the extent to which they should be part of the contingency planning process. The business impact analysis, considered in conjunction with the company risk assessment, provides the security with sufficient information to develop effective and efficient contingency. The business impact analysis can also serve as a point of comparison with the risk analysis. Both should identify consistent assessments of the impact to the business in case any or all company assets are damaged or destroyed.

Emergency Response

It is essential to establish precisely who will respond to emergencies and what response capabilities are needed. This point is particularly critical because, since all emergencies are not the same, different responses may be necessary. For example, responding to a natural disaster such as a fire or an earthquake requires different skills than responding to a chemical attack perpetrated by a terrorist organization. Moreover, man-made disasters may introduce conditions, such as chemical, biological or radiological conditions, not normally encountered during a natural disaster. This is particularly significant when planning for emergency response in an area at high risk for acts of terror.

All participants in the emergency response process must understand what is expected of them. These expectations must be well defined and documented. Guidance for all employees on how to react in the event of an emergency and what their individual and collective responsibilities are must be documented and distributed. Organizational responsibilities must also be established to include the development of department-level emergency plans. Events such as building evacuation and roll-call assembly need to be well defined so that in the event of an actual emergency there is no confusion or uncertainty as to what must be accomplished.

Incident Management and Crisis Management

The company security organization or fire department is usually the first to respond to any incident. Security is usually responsible for incident management. As an incident escalates, the crisis management team should assume responsibility for managing the crisis. How this process works and who has what responsibilities must be clearly stated in the contingency plans. In the event of an actual emergency, some people will attempt to manage the incident or participate in crisis management who should have no role whatsoever in this process. Without established and well-defined incident management protocols and procedures, chaos or disorder is likely to occur. Such is even more likely during or in response to a terrorist attack. Remember, a primary objective of terrorists is to instill fear in the affected population. Unlike a natural disaster, which, when over, causes a concerted response and restoration effort to be initiated, a terrorist act instills fear and anticipation of the next attack. Trained personnel operate better under uncertain conditions than untrained persons.

Incident/Event Analysis

When an emergency incident or event occurs that interrupts or disrupts the business process, the organization charged with responding to and managing the scene should also conduct an incident/event analysis. This analysis is conducted to determine the immediate extent of damage and the potential for subsequent additional damage. The appropriate resources must be notified and activated to assist in damage mitigation.

Business Resumption Planning

The process of planning to facilitate the recovery of designated critical processes and the resumption of business in the event of an interruption to the business process must be performed in two parts. The first part focuses on business recovery in the short term; the other part focuses on business restoration in the long term. This process should establish priorities for restoration of critical processes, infrastructure, and information systems.

Postevent Evaluation

It is important to make an assessment of preceding events to determine which response and mitigation actions worked well and which worked less well and then to determine what improvements to existing plans and processes should be made. Learning from real events is an unfortunate opportunity. There is no better way to learn how to handle an emergency than actually to handle one.

Emergency Response

When an emergency occurs, and one may occur at even the most prepared businesses, being able to respond effectively is critical. As indicated earlier in the chapter, the types of emergencies that occur vary widely. From medical emergencies to terrorist-related events, being prepared to respond quickly and effectively will usually lessen the damage or impact of the event. At the very least, a prompt and effective response will help contain potential damage.

Preparedness takes many forms. Being prepared to respond to a medical emergency is different than being prepared to respond to a natural or man-made disaster. The medical emergency may require merely the application of first aid to a victim, or it may require the assistance and services of a paramedic. A natural or man-made disaster may require support from emergency medical services along with police, fire, and hazardous material crews and the local hospital; depending on the nature of the event, military support may be needed.

The purpose of preparing an emergency response plan is to document the planning accomplished in preparation for an emergency. This documentation provides the ground rules or parameters for emergency response. It also serves as a reference for all who need to know how the process works. The plan should identify general and specific responsibilities for emergency response personnel and for all employees, both management and nonmanagement. Having a plan will assist the return to normal business operations by minimizing the initial disruptive effects of an emergency or disaster. The emergency plan should address the following areas.

Reporting Emergencies

Employees must know how and to whom emergencies should be reported. If your company has a security organization capable of responding to emergencies, including medical emergencies, it may be best to have employees contact security first. If handling the emergency is beyond the capability of the security organization, additional assistance can be sought. For example, a victim of a terrorist attack may require immediate medical attention. If paramedic capabilities exist within the security department, then the in-house paramedic should be the first respondent. If the situation calls for more sophisticated expertise and capabilities, external emergency medical services can be called for.

In the event an employee discovers a suspicious package, it is best to contact security first. Security professionals should be able to make an initial assessment and inquiry to determine if assistance from the local police department bomb squad is necessary or if someone just left a package unattended. In any event, having an established reporting protocol with a single emergency number for employees to use will lead to prompt reporting of emergencies and facilitate rapid response.

This process can also be used for reporting of suspicious activities. As part of the company security awareness training and education process, employees should be trained and sensitized to reporting any suspicious activities they observe. Suspicious activities should be reported immediately, with a prompt response from security. Suspicious activities may be a precursor of events to come. Consider the method of operations for terrorist organizations. For example; prior to conducting an attack such as the 1993 attack on the World Trade Center in New York City,[11] the terrorists spent time at the World Trade Center site studying the layout and at many other locations purchasing materials and equipment to be used in the bombing. Had any of this suspicious activity been promptly reported and promptly investigated, this bombing might have been averted.

Emergency Communications and Warning Systems

Fire Alarm Systems

These systems are generally the most widely used. Linked to a variety of sensor detectors and manual-pull stations, fire alarms do just that: sound an alarm. These systems are sufficiently unique in sound and volume as to indicate clearly the need for building and facility evacuation. Employees must be conditioned to respond immediately.

Public Address Systems

These systems can augment the fire alarm system. Announcements can be made alerting employees to the danger of an emergency situation. Public address systems are particularly useful during emergencies where a building or facility evacuation is just the opposite of what is needed. For example, in the event of a chemical, biological, or radiological incident or other external environmental hazard, it may be necessary to keep people inside the facility and to shut down all air-movement systems, thereby preventing employees from exposure to hazardous airborne substances. Since employees are conditioned to evacuate a building or facility when a fire alarm is sounded, they can be conditioned to wait and listen for specific instructions provided over a public address system.

Floor Wardens

The use of employees to augment the emergency notification system has much value. Specially selected and trained employees can be given responsibility to act during an emergency to spread the word to evacuate a building or facility during an emergency. Assigning each a specific area of responsibility (or floor, hence the term *floor warden*) ensures complete coverage of the building or facility. Communications between floor wardens and emergency response personnel or a security emergency operations center can be easily established. Floor wardens can be alerted by pager, cell phone, instant messaging, or other means in the event of an emergency and be instructed to react to the specific situation. Floor wardens can and should be empowered and trained to react on their own in the event they recognize danger. Authority should be given to floor wardens (clearly stated in the company policy for contingency planning and emergency response) to evacuate a building or facility based on their judgment and assessment of an emergency situation. In the event of a complete communications failure, it may be necessary to empower them to dispatch people to a safe environment.

Response to Emergencies

The emergency plan should address response protocols for different types of emergencies. As stated earlier, emergency situations are not all the same. Some may require evacuation of a facility, while other emergencies may require sheltering in place. Since security officers are generally located throughout a facility, they are usually the first respondent to most incidents. Being first or quickly at the scene of an incident, the officer can assess the situation and make a determination as to whether additional assistance is necessary. In some cases, the officer may not be able to make an assessment and may require support from others. For example, in the event of a terrorist attack involving hazardous chemicals, it will be necessary to have on scene an expert in environmental and safety issues to make the assessment. It may even be necessary for a hazardous materials (HAZMAT) crew to respond to handle the event. Cleanup should be done only by skilled and certified personnel. In other cases, such as an explosion, the security officers' first reaction would be to assist in the evacuation of people to a safe area. In any emergency or category/type of emergencies, clearly defining who has what response capabilities and responsibilities will impact the effectiveness of any response.

Department-Specific Emergency Plans

It is best to have one corporate emergency response plan and subsets for each unique facility. This will serve as a master plan and provide a common framework for all sub-elements of the plan. Within the subelements, consideration must be given to response to likely threats. In an environment with a high threat of terrorism, plans specific to responding to terrorist events must be developed.

In general, all emergency plans should identify the following specific information:

- Common and unique responsibilities for all department personnel in the event of an emergency
- A roster of department employees
- Emergency contact/notification roster (not all emergencies occur during working hours, so it may be necessary to reach people at home)
- Floor warden(s) if a floor warden program is in use
- Evacuation routes, procedures, and assembly areas
- Roll-call instructions: *This is a critical process because it may help determine if someone is missing or did not evacuate a building.*
- Procedures for evacuation of people requiring assistance
- People identified as members of a search-and-rescue team
- Additional manager- or employee-specific or unique responsibilities

Incident Management

Emergency personnel manage the incident at the scene. If the incident escalates to a crisis, a crisis management team should be convened to manage the crisis. Generally, the senior emergency person at the scene manages the incident, with the assistance of specialists as appropriate. In the case of suspected terrorist attack, a senior law enforcement official or other member of a government agency will probably take command of managing the incident.

Evacuation and Assembly

A critical objective during any emergency is obviously employee safety. If it is necessary to evacuate a building or facility, having an established and orderly process is essential. Once a warning system sounds a notice to evacuate, employees must be aware of pre-established procedures for quick evacuation, including primary and alternate evacuation routes and where to assemble. Maps or diagrams with this information should be included in the plan and posted throughout the work area.

A floor warden or an employee with the assignment to facilitate evacuation should make a sweep of the area, assuming conditions permit and it is not unsafe to do so prior to his or her own evacuation, to ensure that all personnel have exited the building or facility. Once in the predetermined assembly area, a roll call must be taken. Primary, secondary, and tertiary responsibilities should be assigned to ensure that someone is available to take roll call and report the results to security. If someone did not evacuate the facility, a search-and-rescue team or other emergency personnel may be required to reenter the facility and provide assistance.

Emergency Evacuation Drills

The efficient and complete evacuation of personnel in the event of an emergency is such an important action that periodic drills should be conducted to reinforce the process and its importance. In some areas, local codes or laws require annual or periodic evacuation drills in certain types of buildings. For example, many American cities require evacuation drills to be conducted for all high-rise buildings and skyscrapers. At the very least, each building or facility should undergo an annual evacuation drill in which employees respond to a warning and completely evacuate the building or facility. A roll call should be conducted and the results reported to security. Security should conduct an assessment of the test and take corrective measures as determined to be appropriate.

Search and Rescue

In the event of serious damage, such as a fire, explosion, or collapse of a building, it may be necessary to search for unaccounted persons. Search and rescue is the responsibility of responding emergency personnel who have proper protective training and appropriate certifications and are properly equipped. Persons not trained or certified in search-and-rescue techniques and who lack proper equipment should not enter hazardous areas and conduct searches. Under some conditions, such as a suspected or actual terrorist attack, law enforcement or military personnel may determine who is responsible for search and rescue.

Return to Work

The process for returning to work after an emergency should be included in the emergency plan. After any incident where employees are required to leave their work area, evacuating from a building or facility, a process for having them return to the workplace and their normal routine is necessary. For example, if a building was severely damaged due to a terrorist attack, e.g., bombing, and cannot be occupied for an extended period, posting daily direction and guidance for employees on an 800 number information line will allow employees to call each day for specific instructions. For this process to be effective, employees must be aware of the process, know how it works, and know or have easy access to the emergency phone number. Finally, any information line designed to communicate messages and status from the company to all employees must be updated regularly. Failure to update and maintain the process properly will lead to a loss of credibility for that process. Any process lacking credibility is likely to be ignored or disregarded.

Action Following an Emergency

When any event occurs that necessitates evacuation of a building or facility, results in injuries or major damage, or presents the possibility of major business interruption, an after-action report should be prepared. The primary focus is twofold:

1. Promptly assist the applicable government agencies in documenting the events, circumstances, and chronology from your perspective. Documenting the process serves several purposes. It provides a written record, prepared close in time to the actual event, allowing for meaningful analysis postevent. Documenting the process may also support the criminal justice process in the event a crime was committed. Finally, documenting the process will be useful in the event of civil litigation.
2. Support the preparation of the government agencies' lessons-learned review and also conduct one from the company's perspective and for its use. Include key personnel involved in responding to and managing the emergency so as to assess what occurred and how could it have been handled better.

Crisis Management

Crisis management is the processes of managing the events of a crisis to a condition of stability. Crisis management is not incident management. Emergency response personnel at the scene of an incident manage the incident. If the incident escalates, becoming a crisis, it is then necessary to have a different group take charge. Ideally, a crisis management team, consisting of experienced personnel from multiple disciplines, would come together to manage any incident that develops beyond the capability and decision authority of emergency response personnel. Essentially, they manage the crisis to closure.

As discussed earlier, crises can take many forms. From managing the events surrounding the tampering of a product, such as the 1982 Tylenol crisis,[12] where seven people in Chicago died mysteriously from ingesting Tylenol capsules laced with cyanide, to responding to an act of terror involving the use of explosives, crisis management teams must be prepared to handle a wide variety of situations. To be effective, crisis management teams should be established integrated process teams whose members come together during a crisis but have planned, drilled, and worked together before any crisis has occurred.

After emergency response planning, crisis management planning is the next step in the continuum of the contingency planning process (see Figure 8-2), and a crisis management plan should address the following activities and concerns.

Crisis Management Teams

Crisis management teams are perhaps the most effective way to manage a crisis. The larger the organization, the more sense it makes to use them. Managing a crisis can't be left to emergency personnel only. When an incident escalates into a crisis, the situation becomes more complex, affecting different aspects of the business if not the entire business

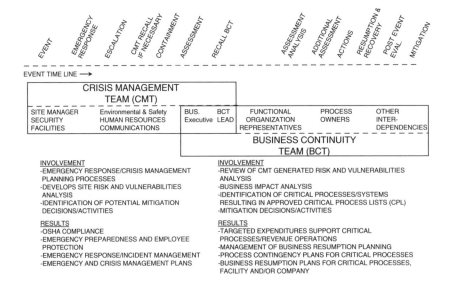

FIGURE 8-2 Event time line, from an emergency through recovery and resumption, along with responsibility assignments and necessary actions.

and requires different skills to manage. Employees with a broad understanding of the enterprise and its mission, goals, and objectives are much better suited to manage a crisis than those with a narrower perspective on the business. For a medium-to-large business or organization, bringing together different people representing different aspects of the enterprise and possessing different skills creates the strongest possible deliberative and decision-making body for handling a crisis. This is particularly important when we realize how many different events can occur and develop into a crisis. For example, in the event of a kidnap-and-ransom situation, the likelihood of having within the company any persons skilled in managing such a crisis is low. Outside expertise will most likely be required and needed fast.

Ideally, a crisis management team works like any effective integrated process team. Skilled professionals representing different disciplines come together on a short-term basis to work a specific issue or tasking. In the case of crisis management teams, the task is to serve as a deliberative decision-making body to plan and prepare (pre-event) for a crisis and, when a crisis occurs, to manage that crisis so as to mitigate any damage and the impact to company assets. Crisis management teams generally should be made up of representatives from the following departments or organizations: security, human resources, site management, safety and environmental services, facilities, business management, and communications. Larger companies will have professionals working in all of these disciplines; smaller companies may not. Deciding what the proper makeup of a crisis management team is will depend on many factors.

Disaster Operations

If a crisis turns into a disaster, it is to be expected that some personnel may not be able to leave the site immediately. Employees may have no choice but to seek shelter at the workplace for hours or days. Or in the event of a biological or chemical contamination, employees may be forced into a lockdown or confinement situation requiring them to remain in place until the area can be decontaminated.

Immediately following a disaster, emergency personnel may be needed onsite for an extended period to assist in recovery operations. For example, immediately following hurricane Katrina, recovery operations began on a massive scale, requiring the support of more recovery personnel than the geographic area had to offer. Outside support was necessary to begin recovery operations. Being prepared to deal with multiple disaster scenarios is essential. Preparation will include ensuring sufficient supplies to meet the needs of a reasonable number of stranded or support personnel on hand. Sufficient food, water, medical supplies, and emergency sanitation and shelter facilities are available. All of these items can be acquired and placed in a long-term storage condition providing they are regularly checked for serviceability and spoilage and maintained within the expected shelf life.

During a terrorist-related crisis, much uncertainty exists. Consequently, it will be necessary to communicate to employees, keeping them as up-to-date as possible with the situation and events and providing guidance concerning their safety and work expectations. During a crisis, employees are naturally anxious. This anxiety is made worse following a terrorist attack, for uncertainty looms while anxious and fearful employees await another attack. Prompt and clear communications can help reduce this anxiety and keep employees informed.

Communication may need to extend beyond the duration of a crisis into an undefined subsequent period. For example, if a natural disaster, such as a hurricane, causes damage to a building or facility during a weekend, employees will need to be advised if they should report to work the following Monday. Using the previously referred to emergency 800 number process, which all employees can call 24 hours a day, 7 days a week for information is very effective. Messages can be updated regularly as needed so that the information is fresh and relevant. Also, information broadcast on local news radio stations can reach a large population of employees.

At the point in time when an incident escalates into a crisis, the crisis management team becomes involved in managing the crisis to closure. At some point during a crisis, a de-escalation of events will occur, and eventually the crisis will terminate. If the impact or damage from the crisis is significant, the crisis management team will commence with restoration activities. These activities may be led by the crisis management team or passed on to a business continuity team. How this can work is discussed further in the upcoming section "Business Continuity."

Media Relations

During a crisis, there is no doubt that the local, state, national, and even international media will become interested in events. Regardless of scale, any suspected or actual terrorist attack will draw global media attention. Even isolated events such as workplace violence can draw significant media attention. It is therefore important to have a media relations plan.

If your company has a communications or public relations organization, their representative should be part of the crisis management team. If not, the crisis management team itself should establish protocols for handling the media. Since there is always a degree of unpredictability during a crisis, it is best that all crisis management team members understand how to deal with the media and be prepared to do so should they be thrust into such a situation. Under these circumstances, it is best to let the responding government agencies deal with the media and the corporate staff provide them with support.

Damage Assessment

During a crisis, emergency personnel will make ongoing damage assessments, reporting status back to the crisis management team or management. These assessments are useful in determining actions to be taken next. However, these assessments are situational and, due to the circumstances and nature of a crisis, do not have the luxury of thoroughness. The true extent of damage is not determined until after the crisis has terminated and a complete building assessment or facility or site assessment can be made. Immediately following a crisis, a damage assessment for infrastructure safety and functionality must be made. Without this, a return-to-work decision cannot be made. The damage assessment is also the starting point for all restoration and resumption activities.

Business Continuity Team

Earlier reference was made to the transition of responsibility from a crisis management team to a business continuity team. This is an important step in the effort to resume business. While the crisis management team's focus is on managing through the crisis, the business continuity team's focus it recovery and resumption.

After-Action/Postevent Assessments

After every crisis, an assessment of what occurred should be conducted. The chronology and circumstances of the event should be recorded. The crisis management team should review what went well and what did not. Performance to plan should be reviewed and a lessons-learned document should be created for all team members and supporting personnel to review and hopefully learn from. The need for after-action assessments will be the same for each phase of the emergency response, crisis management, and disaster recovery (business continuity) process.

Individuals and/or teams will need to assess what went wrong, what worked well, and what did not work well to ensure they learn from crises and disasters and are better prepared to handle future events. Failing to learn from real experiences is inexcusable. Failing to learn and take reasonable corrective actions to protect company assets could lead to future litigation. An argument could be made that company executives, from prior experiences, were aware of necessary actions to mitigate future damage from a crisis or disaster but failed to do so. This would not be good for the company.

Business Continuity

At the beginning of this chapter we defined business continuity as the effort to minimize business interruption or disruption caused by different contingencies. Should contingencies occur, business recovery and resumption need to happen swiftly. In essence, business must continue and the old adage of "time is money" becomes quite real. Business disruptions can be costly and even catastrophic. Customers, shareholders, and stakeholders demand that the business remain viable. Preparation to deal with contingencies is a critical component of keeping the business going and maintaining the viability of the enterprise.

Business continuity is a two-stage process. Business recovery is the first stage. Business resumption is the second. The recovery effort is the process of getting the business up and running again but only in a minimally acceptable condition. Essentially it's much like an injured old athlete managing to limp along. It is not a recovery to an exact pre-event condition. It is a recovery to keep things going. Produce product, make deliveries to customers, and accomplish the basic activities to keep the business viable.

The business resumption stage is the effort to recover from a contingency and to resume business in a pre-event condition. This is not to say that all critical processes and other processes will be exactly the same as they were pre-event. Resumption planning may call for new or modified processes. The intent is to resume business operations at a level similar to the pre-event operations level but not necessarily exactly the same.

Business Continuity Teams

A business continuity team should be established to provide oversight of the development of business resumption plans. Representation from each of the major business functions should be part of this team. Manufacturing, business management, engineering, information technology, human resources, legal, and other major areas and disciplines within the business need to participate. Business resumption teams lead the effort and planning process to ensure that the business is prepared to recover from contingencies and resume full business operations. In some cases it may be necessary to have a major supplier or customer participate as a member of this team. Furthermore, it may be necessary to bring in outside experts to help with the recovery process. For example; in the event of a biological contamination due to an incident where anthrax was delivered in a package to a company site (a terrorist event), it will be necessary to bring in skilled hazardous material specialists to assist in the cleanup.

Business recovery planning and resumption planning have common elements. The difference is the stage of recovery and the time necessary to get there. The following sections detail the common elements of the recovery and resumption process.

Business Impact Analysis of Critical Processes and Information Systems

The most fundamental aspect of recovery and resumption planning is conducting a business impact analysis of critical processes. Critical processes must first be identified. Knowing what they are and having the business continuity team agree to their criticality will allow for proper planning and prioritization. Failure to identify critical processes properly may lead to wasted time, effort, and money. Even worse, noncritical processes may be given priority over critical processes, leading to further delays in recovery and the unnecessary expenditure of resources.

It is not uncommon for organizations to identify their processes as critical when, on further examination, they are determined not to be critical. Process owners have a tendency to believe all of their processes are critical. After all, who does not think what they do is essential or critical to the company. This is precisely why it is necessary to have the business continuity team make this assessment. Teams tend to be more objective than individuals. When developing recovery and resumption plans, the areas detailed in the following sections must be considered and addressed.

Define Critical Processes

Each major business area, function, and discipline should provide to the business continuity team a listing of all critical processes. The business continuity team should then review these processes for criticality and prioritize them, creating an official Critical Process List. Planning for recovery of the critical processes is the primary concern. Noncritical processes should be recovered and resumed after the critical processes. Resource and time limitations do not allow for resumption of all processes at the same time. Processes critical to the business must have top priority. Any processes determined not to be critical should be planned for during the later stages of the resumption effort.

Critical Process Interdependencies

As part of the critical process assessment, particular emphasis must be placed on information systems and process interdependencies. For example, an information system, in and of itself, may not be determined by its process owner to be critical. However, if it supports a critical process and that critical process can't be completely restored without the information system, then that information system itself becomes critical. Examining processes as part of a system is essential in the assessment of criticality. Interdependencies need to be identified in order properly to assess criticality to the business. Other interdependencies may exist in the form of relationships with organizations outside of the company. These too must be considered. Different methodologies can be used to estimate the potential impact a contingency or disaster may have on a critical process. When considering the criticality of a process, the financial effect, operational effect, and any less tangible or quantifiable concerns, such as customer satisfaction, must be addressed.

Resources

Critical process recovery requires an assessment of resources. Planning for process restoration means considering what resources may no longer be available and will need to be acquired or obtained to get the critical process up and functional again. What type of facilities will be needed and where? Will additional hardware, software, or equipment be required? Will people capable of managing and working the processes be available? Will there be effective means of communications? If not, what must be done to provide a minimum capability of communications until full communications can be restored? These are some of the resource issues and questions with which the team must grapple.

Mitigation Strategies

For those processes identified as critical, pre-event actions can be taken to help mitigate the impact, both operational and financial, of interruptions to the business. When developing contingency plans for critical processes, strategies will become apparent that may be implemented prior to an event that will lessen the impact of an event if and when it occurs. A cost/benefit analysis may be required to assess the feasibility of implementing a pre-event action; if the analysis shows it to be an effective action, it should be taken. For example, an old building that is not up to current building codes may be vulnerable to damage from many different events. If that building supports a critical process, it may be more cost effective to retrofit the building with the necessary structural supports to bring it into compliance with current standards than to risk severe damage in the event of a natural or man-made (terrorist) act that might render a critical process inoperative.

During any retrofit, a risk analysis for the site, facility, or building should be made. This includes an assessment of the current terrorist threat. Recall our earlier discussion about how world conditions change frequently. An area considered at low risk today may tomorrow experience a new threat from terrorist activity, thus elevating the risk to the business. The risk assessment should produce a better understanding of the threat and be used to develop proper mitigating actions. It would be foolish to spend time, money, and effort on resolving a single vulnerability while ignoring others. Management may choose to mitigate only one or several of a number of vulnerabilities, addressing only the most likely, or management may take mitigation actions based on cost, choosing to mitigate as much risk as possible for as little cost as possible. That is fine as long as the decision to do so is informed and based on data from a risk analysis. Recall our earlier discussion about how different businesses have different levels of tolerance for risk. Some companies may choose or need to keep risk to a minimum, while others may have a greater tolerance for risk. For example, a hospital or pharmaceutical company may be willing and able to accept a level of risk that is much lower than what a producer of video games might.

Vital Records

The ability to recover vital records is critical to the recovery and restoration process. Having a vital records protection and management program will enable the recovery of essential information during any contingency.

Customers and Suppliers

The importance of considering input, participation, and impact to customers and suppliers cannot be overstated. Any business continuity planning must take into consideration customer and supplier relationships.

Communications

Communications during the recovery and resumption process can be just as important as communications during other phases of a contingency. Employees who may have been affected by the events of a crisis or disaster need to be kept abreast of developments affecting them and their employment. Customers and suppliers need to understand the progress made toward resumption of business because it may have a serious impact on their operations. Even external worlds stakeholders and shareholders have an interest in these events. A communications plan should be part of this process. However, all communications plans will not be the same. For example, in the event of a terrorist attack, the company will be faced with the added condition of managing employee expectations and fear.

Certain types of terrorist-related emergencies, crises, and disasters will generate greater levels of fear among the employee population than others. People tend to have a better understanding of more common events, such as fires and floods, than they do of terrorist attacks and pandemics. The latter will instill greater levels of fear in people, making it more difficult for a company to communicate effectively with them without playing to that fear. What a company does not want to do while trying to keep employees and stakeholders informed is to increase levels of fear. Keeping people informed without frightening them will be a difficult task.

Lessons Learned

An old adage says that lightning doesn't strike twice in the same place. If only that were certain and true and applicable to the critical processes of a business; however, it is not. Therefore, much can be learned for each phase of managing and recovering from a contingency. Document the process of recovery and restoration. Identify the things learned, both good and bad, and share this through learning sessions. It will go a long way toward dealing with other crises when they occur.

Business Recovery

Recovery plans focus on getting the business up and running. In essence, emphasis must be placed on what needs to be accomplished in the first 30–60 days to restore critical processes and resume limited business operations. During this period, the most critical processes supporting infrastructure and product delivery and keeping damage or loss to the enterprise to an absolute minimum should be the major focus. This includes identification of all critical personnel needed to support the most critical processes. As difficult as it may be, a prioritization of people/employees needs to be part of this equation.

Some may be preoccupied with their own issues of recovery and restoration and may not be able to support the company. Generally, you can expect this to be limited to a few, but it could be a critical few. Part of the critical process planning should take this into consideration and identify alternatives. In some situations, special provisions may be necessary or considered for certain critical personnel.

Vital Records

Recovery of vital records is very much part of the recovery process. Being able to access offsite records storage, hard copy and electronic, is critical to moving this process forward expeditiously. Many companies use outsourced providers to handle, store, and retrieve their vital records. This process allows for separate storage, away from company facilities, and reduces the possibility of damage to or destruction of these records. There are many capable and reliable companies throughout the world who perform the handling, storage, and recovery of vital records.

Business Resumption

Issues and areas of focus and concern that are common to recovery and resumption were addressed earlier. This section discusses areas specific to resumption and the long-term process of returning to normal business. Long-term priorities are addressed in business resumption plans, with the intention of restoring operations to a pre-event condition, which does not necessarily mean that all is the same as or equal to the conditions prior to contingency occurrence, crisis, or disaster.

During the process of recovery and restoration it may be learned or discovered that the implementation of a critical process or other processes can be accomplished differently—different in the sense that improvement can be made, making the restored processes more efficient and more cost effective. Consequently, changes can and should be made. Furthermore, it may be learned that some processes can be eliminated altogether. Recovery and resumption in many ways are similar to a reengineering process. Process owners are usually the best source for ideas, and because they participate in resumption they may develop new approaches to and methods of implementing and executing their process.

If the process is a simple one, changes can be implemented quickly with little or no additional review from management or the business continuity team. If the process is complex, affecting or dependent on other processes, a cost/benefit analysis is warranted to assess accurately the impact of any proposed changes.

Case Scenario

As the chief security officer for a major international corporation, you were asked by the CEO to ensure that the corporation had plans in place to deal with a terrorist attack. What steps would you take to ensure that such plans were not only in place but current?

You would need to determine the current level of security risk in all geographical areas where the company operates, which includes the following actions.

- Review existing plans.
- If recent risk assessments have not been conducted, do so.
- Assess the current political and economic climate. Has there been a change?
- Have any threats been made against the company recently?
- Seek the perspective of local government and security experts.
- Consult with local company management to determine if they have any concerns.
- Get an independent, up-to-date intelligence assessment of the local area (available commercially).

Once the risk assessment is conducted and analyzed, develop mitigating actions.

Summary

Contingency planning may not be a traditional security process, but in today's global business environment corporate security is assuming a much greater role and greater responsibility for its implementation. With a long history of responding to emergencies and managing escalating events, security was a logical early choice to lead contingency planning efforts. Moreover, many in the security profession possess experience in working with a wide variety of crises, ranging from natural disasters to acts of terror.

Prior to the terrorist attacks in New York City on September 11, 2001, many organizations were becoming more conscious of the need to have contingency plans. September 11th accelerated the process for many. A complete contingency planning program has three major elements:

1. Emergency response
2. Crisis management
3. Business continuity
   - Business recovery
   - Business resumption

Since September 11, 2001, emergency response plans have required that greater consideration be given to responding to terrorist-related incidents and crises and to managing these complex and dangerous conditions to restore stability. Initially, only company resources may be available for response and support. But as events escalate, crisis management teams must be able to work with government responders.

Once events are stabilized, disaster recovery and business resumption teams take over to restore business operations. The ability to restore normal operations will in large part be affected by earlier preparations. Good planning before an event will facilitate a faster recovery.

Responding to and managing a terrorist-driven emergency or crisis may be more complicated than responding to and managing other events. This is due primarily to terrorists' demonstrated willingness to use unconventional methods (aircraft crashing into buildings and other high explosives) and the potential use of chemical, biological, or nuclear agents for the purpose of wreaking maximum damage. Preparing for such events is complicated and expensive.

It is critical that the business recover and resume normal (pre-event) operations as soon as possible. Customers, shareholders, and stakeholders expect nothing less. Executive management has the obligation to ensure that contingency planning is properly considered and addressed within their company. The consequences of not planning for a wide range of contingencies a business may encounter can be catastrophic.

Endnotes

1 See: http://en.wikipedia.org/wiki/September_11,_2001_attacks
2 The 2004 Indian Ocean earthquake, which had a magnitude of 9.3, triggered a series of lethal tsunamis on December 26, 2004, that killed approximately 230,000 people, making it the deadliest tsunami as well as one of the worst natural disasters in recorded history. See: http://en.wikipedia.org/wiki/Tsunami#2004_-_Indian_Ocean_tsunami

[3] In reference to the Atlantic hurricane of 2005, see: http://en.wikipedia.org/wiki/Hurricane_Katrina

[4] For information on pandemics, including the potential of an avian flu (H5N1 virus) pandemic, see: http://en.wikipedia.org/wiki/Pandemic

[5] "Bethlehem Mideast Violence, Political Strife Affect Tourism: Lots of Room at the Inn." See: http://www.topix.net/content/kri/0633047826231197326726095628170745637411

[6] There was a stock market crash (or "correction") on October 19, 1987, known in financial circles as Black Monday, when the Dow Jones lost 22 percent of its value in one day, bringing to an end a five-year bull run. The FTSE 100 Index lost 10.8 percent on that Monday and a further 12.2 percent the following day. The pattern was repeated across the world. See: http://en.wikipedia.org/wiki/Stock_market_crash

[7] See: http://www.portoflosangeles.org/about_economicimpact.htm

[8] See: http://www.polb.com/about/overview/economics.asp

[9] See: http://www.ACP-international.com

[10] See: http://www.contingencyplanning.com

[11] In the World Trade Center bombing (February 26, 1993) a car bomb was detonated by Arab Islamist terrorists in the underground parking garage below Tower One of the World Trade Center in New York City. The 1,500-lb urea nitrate fuel oil device killed 6 people and injured 1,042. See: http://en.wikipedia.org/wiki/World_Trade_Center_bombing

[12] See: http://www.personal.psu.edu/users/w/x/wxk116/tylenol/crisis.html

Operational Security Methods for Mitigating Terrorist Attacks

Three may keep a secret, if two of them are dead.
—Benjamin Franklin

This chapter addresses the operational security methods security professionals can use to help mitigate a terrorist attack against a business's or corporation's facility, products, information, employees, or any of its other assets. How operational security is part of the security-in-layers approach of using systems, controls, and processes designed to protect people, assets, and information are discussed and examined.

Under certain conditions, particularly while operating in areas of high risk, operational security (OPSEC) methods can be critical to mitigate vulnerabilities to terrorism. OPSEC is a process, actually more of a tool, used as part of the layers-of-security concept to provide protection to company assets. OPSEC alone does not eliminate all risks. OPSEC as part of the total security program contributes to risk reduction. OPSEC when properly used will help mitigate the vulnerability to the threat of terrorism.

OPSEC is used to help mitigate vulnerability to many different types of threats, thus contributing to an overall reduction in risks. Essentially, OPSEC should be a tool already in the security professional's tool kit. OPSEC was specifically developed to help deny unauthorized persons from gathering information about an organization or business that may ultimately make that organization or business more vulnerable.

Increased vulnerability could occur in many areas. The unauthorized or inadvertent exposure of information could lead to an increased terrorist threat and vulnerabilities, e.g., greater security risks from exposure of weak or inadequate physical security controls in place to protect against the threats of terrorist agents.

In terms of protecting against terrorism, particularly in high-risk areas, OPSEC can help mitigate vulnerability to the threats of terrorism, thus reducing risks associated with terrorism. This includes the different types of threats from terrorists previously addressed in this book, e.g., not only the common acts of terror committed by terrorist groups, such as assaults with weapons and explosives, but also common types of criminal activity terrorists engage in to raise monies for funding their terrorist activities (separate from the common acts of terror committed for the sole purpose of instilling fear, as opposed to financial gain).

Historically, military organizations have been the most active practitioners of OPSEC. Concealing activities to deny others knowledge of their activities and plans gave them an advantage of surprise. In a formal or institutionalized sense, OPSEC came into being in modern times during and following the American conflict in Viet Nam. With Operation Purple Dragon[1] military analysts discovered operational security vulnerabilities leading to the unauthorized sharing of critical military aircraft flight plans. After losing aircraft and following unsuccessful bombing raids, analysts began examining the problem.

It did not take them long to learn that critical information revealing specific flight data about aircraft flight patterns and schedules was being shared, as required, with civilian air traffic controllers. The U.S. military itself was sharing this information in accordance with standard aviation guidelines and requirements. However, this sensitive information being freely shared with authorized persons was subsequently released without U.S. authorization by air traffic control personnel to the North Vietnamese, thus allowing them to prepare their defenses for the planned attacks. Out of this failure, the modern discipline of OPSEC was developed.

Armies throughout the world and over history have informally used OPSEC as part of their protective process. During World War II, Allied forces used the slogan "Loose lips sink ships" as a means of sensitizing citizens to be careful what they said about activities they were involved in or knowledgeable of in support of the war effort. In a practical way, this action was a form of OPSEC. It was intended to make people conscious of protecting important and critical information. In today's global war on terrorism, the coalition forces operating in the Middle East routinely employ OPSEC measures to keep the enemy as uninformed as possible.

The risk of being exploited through poor OPSEC is greatest for high-profile, high-value large targets, such as global corporations. For a business operating in a part of the world with a high risk of terrorism, having good OPSEC measures and processes in place may help the company keep a low profile and stay out of the view of terrorists. Consider the abduction and horrific murder of Lockheed Martin employee Paul Johnson. Johnson was working in Saudi Arabia on Lockheed Martin's Apache helicopter. A message attributed to his captors on an Islamic website alluded to the Apache helicopter's use in Iraq.[2] Was Johnson more vulnerable because terrorists were aware he worked on Apache helicopters? Or was he just an unfortunate victim?

Using OPSEC to protect effectively against terrorism is not confined to military operations in the Middle East. Consider the U.S. National Security Agency's (NSA's) effort in support of the Salt Lake City Olympics. Here, NSA OPSEC personnel trained officials on operational security and developed an OPSEC video for the public that was played at Olympic venues and on inbound commercial aircraft. Subsequent to supporting the Olympic Games, the NSA's Interagency Operations Security Support Staff (IOSSS) returned to Utah to host a National OPSEC Conference and Exhibition and provided OPSEC training and information to federal, state, and local first responders, helping prepare them to prevent and respond to acts of terror more effectively.[3]

What Is Operational Security?

Operational security can be considered many things. In some ways it is the design and implementation of security controls to be added to the existing layers of security used by an organization for the protection of that organization's assets. Another way to think of

OPSEC is as a counterterrorism activity. In this context, a security professional works to design and implement operational security measures that help protect corporate assets against the threats of terror by denying terrorists and their supporting organizations access to critical information.

☐ ☐ ☐ ▬▬▬▬▬▬▬▬▬▬▬▬▬▬▬▬▬▬▬▬▬▬▬▬▬▬

Even minutiae should have a place in our collection, for things of a seemingly trifling nature, when enjoined with others of a more serious cast, may lead to a valuable conclusion.[4]
—*George Washington, known OPSEC practitioner*

▬▬▬▬▬▬▬▬▬▬▬▬▬▬▬▬▬▬▬▬▬▬▬▬▬▬ ☐ ☐ ☐

Unauthorized persons can include anyone not part of the organization or business. In some circumstances, unauthorized persons may be part of the organization or business but be in a position where they need no access to specific assets. Generally, OPSEC measures are intended to prevent intelligence gatherers from learning anything about your corporation except what you want the public to know.

Intelligence gatherers and intelligence producers collect information and develop intelligence. That is, they gather seemingly common or unimportant information from many sources, mostly open sources, and compile it into a bigger picture in hopes of revealing critical information that is more useful than the information they had gathered, in order to learn more about their target's operations, plans, or vulnerabilities. (See Chapter 5 for more details on collecting information.)

Intelligence gatherers and producers may or may not be the user of intelligence information. It is possible that they are sharing or selling their information to interested parties. In a competitive context, this occurs all the time. In fact, the commercial world includes a recognized society of competitive professionals who develop competitive intelligence for the organizations they represent: the Society of Competitive Intelligence Professionals (SCIP). This global organization is involved in creating and managing business knowledge, with the intent of enhancing membership success through education, advocacy, and networking.[5]

In most business sectors, companies regularly gather information about their competitors through open sources and try to develop intelligence. They try to figure out their competitors' strengths and weaknesses. They also seek to learn more about any advantages a competitor may have in technology or strategy. If successful, the company gathering information will improve its competitive position. The company losing information may have its competitive edge dulled. Losing a competitive edge can be a significant cost to any business, but, compared to revealing information about operations or vulnerabilities to potential terrorists, where lives may be at stake, losing a competitive edge does not seem so bad.

Earlier we stated that most businesses, global or not, are unlikely to be direct targets of terrorism. However, some businesses may have a higher probability of being a target due to the nature of their business, their geopolitical relationships and associations, or their geographical situation (operating in high-risk areas and representing an unwelcome presence, e.g., being a Western business operating in an environment hostile to Western interests). It is these companies that will benefit most from the use of OPSEC methods. We are not suggesting some companies will not benefit from good OPSEC practices. All companies will, to some degree, benefit by employing good OPSEC practices. We are saying that some companies, particularly high-profile businesses operating in a high-risk environment, will benefit most.

What Is the Objective of Operational Security?

Employing OPSEC measures helps the security executive protect an organization by denying access to or making it more difficult for others to gain access to corporate assets, e.g., information that may have intelligence value, primarily critical information or bits of information that when put together become critical information and tell a larger story. In the case of protecting against potential acts of terror, revealing information about routine operations, security capabilities, or facilities' vulnerabilities may lead to increased terrorist threats and greater risks as observant terrorists perceive a weakness and choose to strike.

In today's global environment, where movement of personnel, information, and other assets across borders is commonplace, so too is the exposure to greater risk. A recent Canadian Security Intelligence Service study appearing in the Canadian Press[6] concluded that a dirty bomb is the most likely means of deliberately spreading deadly radiation. The article suggests that the spy agency is surprised that terrorists have not yet exploded a radioactive bomb in North America, considering the ease with which they can be made and transported.

Considering this revelation by Canadian Intelligence Services, law enforcement officials charged with protecting communities and security executives charged with protecting businesses must consider their vulnerability to radiological occurrence from the use of a dirty bomb. Furthermore, companies engaged in the production of radiological materials must factor the desire of terrorists to obtain such materials into their risk analysis and OPSEC process and ensure that securitys measures in place will effectively deter terrorists from seeking such material.

Ways in Which Information Is Revealed

OPSEC is about preventing unauthorized persons from learning more than they know about an organization or company. It is about denying those who want to know more the opportunity do so. To effectively prevent others from obtaining critical information about an enterprise, it helps to understand how they gather that information. Collection processes can vary widely. From simple observation of activities (such as watching vehicles enter and exit a facility) to the more complex gathering of information via technically sophisticated electronic methods (such as intrusion into information systems), collection of information is accomplished in as many ways as information can be revealed.

More often than not, information is revealed without an understanding of the potential impact. For example, while at a trade show, employees of company A may casually discuss specific technical details about a new product. But when overheard by employees of company B (a competitor), that information may help company B better understand the product development strategy or technological advancements made by company A. Obviously, this is not good for company A. Now, consider the same employees of company A, but operating in a region of the world with a high risk of terrorism. In this case, company A is an oil production company. Its employees are having lunch in a local restaurant, which happens to be a location known by many to be a favorite hangout of company A employees. While there, the employees are discussing changes in the process of moving oil from a production field to a port. Could this discussion be heard by others? Could the revealed information be useful for a terrorist group intending to disrupt oil supplies? Is it a good security practice for company A employees to discuss information of this type in a public location known as a popular hangout of theirs?

Let's consider another example: Employees of a Western construction company are working in a South American country where several drug cartels are known to maintain their production operations. Now, drug cartels often engage in acts of terror, particularly kidnap and ransom. The construction company employees are supporting a government contract with the host country, assisting them in the building of surveillance capabilities designed to monitor air and ground traffic in areas of the country with suspected drug production activity. Furthermore, much of the local population is on the payroll of one of the drug cartels that often uses terrorist tactics. Would it be wise for the construction company employees to share freely with others, particularly part of the local population, specific information about the type of work they do? Would doing so increase the construction company's vulnerability to attack?

Now consider a more common situation: As a matter of practice, a regional manager of a Western manufacturing company operating in a major city in a Third World country makes regular trips to a local bank. The banking transactions often involve receiving electronic money transfers from the home office, located in a Western country, in order to meet a local payroll. The regional manager makes a weekly visit to the same local bank on Monday mornings, traveling the same route. Is the regional manager vulnerable to a kidnap-and-ransom attack, never mind a simple robbery?

The preceding examples illustrate either a lack of OPSEC measures in place or situations where company employees are placed in a position of high vulnerability and risk.

The following is a list of sources from which information may be unintentionally released. These sources are also candidates for exploitation by those with bad intentions.

- *Company employees:* They have knowledge of sensitive information and, when not cautious, may unintentionally disclose some of that information to unauthorized persons, most often in casual conversations with known parties that may be heard by others or with persons unknown to them but exhibiting curiosity or interest in what they know.
- *Media releases:* Organizations seeking positive publicity and new customers often release information to multiple media sources. There is danger if the release of such information is not centrally managed or controlled by persons with an understanding of potential corporate asset vulnerabilities.
- *Websites:* Any information placed on a website is accessible to anyone using the Internet, unless that website is access controlled. If information is placed on a website, consider it released to the world, including to terrorists.
- *Information systems:* Information systems with connectivity to the Internet are vulnerable to intrusion. Even with robust controls in place, information systems are vulnerable to sophisticated intrusion attempts and careless employees who upload unauthorized files from unauthorized sources. Once an intruder penetrates a company information system successfully, that intruder may have unlimited access to data on that system.

- *Cyberfraud:* Cyberfraud is a popular and effective way that terrorists use the Internet to help fund their operations. In February 2005, *USA Today* reported that security experts uncovered many incidents where terrorist groups have stolen credit card numbers over the Internet, laundered money, and hijacked websites for their own use.[7] Furthermore, on April 27, 2006, the Associated Press reported that "five relatives of a U.S. citizen suspected of being a senior Al Qaeda operative were arrested in California and Utah on charges of defrauding banks of hundreds of thousands of dollars. The FBI said it was investigating whether any of the money was used to finance Middle East terrorism."[8]
- *Financial reports:* Much business financial reporting is required by law, particularly for publicly owned companies. Annual reports to shareholders and other such reports, if not carefully crafted, may reveal more information than necessary.
- *Customers*: With good intentions, customers may reveal information about suppliers' activities and capabilities, not fully understanding the potential negative consequences.
- *Suppliers:* Much like customers, suppliers with good intentions may nonetheless reveal information about customers' activities and capabilities, not fully understanding the potential negative consequences.
- *Waste and trash:* All company-sensitive information should be destroyed when discarded or no longer needed. Shredding and burning are generally effective methods for destroying sensitive information and ensuring that it does not fall into the possession of unauthorized persons. Here are two prominent examples. (1) Law enforcement has often been successful in finding criminal evidence by searching through trash. (2) The growing problem of identity theft is fueled by people not protecting their personal and sensitive information and often disposing of it in trash containers.
- *Routine daily operations:* Company activities occurring off company property are subject to observation by anyone in the area or with means to observe remotely (camera, listening device). For example, shipping and receiving activities are easily monitored. Shift changes for security officers protecting a facility perimeter can be easily observed, particularly in a metropolitan or industrial area. Moreover, movement of company personnel on and off company premises can easily be monitored. Terrorists often visit the target to improve their understanding of the layout and operations. Consider the April 19, 1995, bombing of the Oklahoma City federal building. In a series of reports prepared by Gary Hunt[9] the following assessment was offered: "As was evidenced by certain statements made, this site was selected because of the large number of windows in the front and the closeness to the road. It would appear, then, that it was intended that the blast would break windows and create havoc." Clearly, Mr. McVeigh or an accomplice visited the site prior to executing the bombing.

By developing and implementing OPSEC measures for each of the areas just addressed and in accordance with unique company operational practices, most vulnerabilities in these areas can be mitigated. Does this mean OPSEC is the perfect tool? No, just one effective tool out of many protective measures a security executive can employ to reduce vulnerability and risks, particularly risks due to terrorist activities.

Why Is Operational Security Needed?

If the world were a perfect place with no dangers, organizations and businesses would not need to be concerned with protecting their interests and assets. But the world is not a perfect place, and, some would argue, it is growing more dangerous and unpredictable as we move deeper into the 21st century. The dangers facing businesses are not just the local threats. In a fast-paced global business environment influenced by geopolitical, social, religious, economic, and other world conditions, companies, particularly companies operating internationally, face many threats.

Recognizing and understanding terrorist threats, particularly threats specific to your business, is the first step in protecting against them. Part of understanding the threat is to know the sources of threats. For example, a security executive may know his/her company is operating in a high-risk region of the globe; however, it's better to know what the specific terrorist threats in this region are in order to develop and implement the most effective mitigating measures.

Part of a complete risk assessment is discovering what adversaries the company is facing and how they exploit or may seek to exploit the business for their own gain. In some cases that exploitation may be economic damage (business interruption due to an act of terror). Fundamentally, a security executive needs to answer the following six questions to begin implementing adequate protective measures.

1. What do terrorists want (from you or to do to you)?
2. What are you trying to protect from terrorist attacks?
3. Who are you trying to protect from terrorist attacks?
4. How can terrorists be successful against your corporation?
5. How are you protecting your assets from successful terrorist attacks?
6. What are the gaps in antiterrorist protection?

How Does Operational Security Work?

Start with the premise that accumulation of small bits of information, particularly sensitive information, could be revealing and compromising. Many bits of information, when compiled, could "paint a bigger picture." Sorting out what information needs protection can be difficult. All information has value, but not all information by itself is sensitive or critical. Not all information, when compiled with other bits of information, tells a more important story.

Applying OPSEC measures should augment other layers of security. One of these other layers of security is the process for protecting sensitive information. In Chapter 7 we addressed the need to have in place a company policy for protection of information. OPSEC measures augment that policy. OPSEC measures are layered onto other controls, making the overall security profile stronger.

Developing and applying OPSEC measures can be a simple and intuitive process, a process so simple and intuitive that many people practice OPSEC in their daily life. For example, when people travel from home for extended periods they often take the following actions:

- Stop postal deliveries to their home or arrange for someone, a neighbor or family member, to pick up their mail.
- Stop delivery of all newspapers or have a neighbor pick up newspapers daily.

- Leave a light on in the house to make it look like someone is there.
- Place some lights on timers; having lights turn on and off at different times creates the illusion that someone is home.
- Ask a neighbor to check the house for any irregular activity.

Individually, the foregoing actions seem simple and don't appear to provide an extra layer of home security. However, together they create an intended illusion that someone is home and the house is not empty. The protective measures serve as a deterrent, and they protect the truth. These OPSEC measures cover the fact you are away from home by providing signals or bits of information to a would-be intruder suggesting someone is at home.

The following sections present the basic components of an effective OPSEC plan.

Identification of Critical Information

Identifying sensitive and critical information is the first step. All information is not sensitive or critical. All information can't be protected, nor does all information usually require protection. There may be situations when all information associated with a specific activity requires protection, but that is usually an exception and not the rule. Since security resources are limited, the security professional must focus on expending resources to protect the company's most important information. This includes information that, when compiled with other information, may reveal much in total. Essentially, the value of the whole is much greater then the sum of the individual parts.

Perhaps the most difficult part of protecting sensitive or critical information is identifying, within the entire company universe of information, what is most sensitive or critical. Can any one person know all of the information within a company and, of that information, what is most important? Not really. For the security executive to be successful, he/she must enlist the support of employees. Within the company there are functional, technical, and process experts. Together they are aware of the company's information, and within their area of expertise they know what is sensitive and critical. The role of the security executive is to enlist expert support to develop a methodology for the company to categorize and appropriately mark information and then to train all employees in the process.

Identifying sensitive information that may be of interest to terrorist organizations usually falls into the category of physical security weaknesses (areas where a terrorist group could successfully attack or attack with the least resistance) and movement of high-value assets, which includes personnel. It is during transit when people are at their most vulnerable. OPSEC measures can be crucial in mitigating risks to employees in transit. The security executive must prepare to protect critical information about the following:

- Departure times
- Arrival times
- Destinations
- Routes traveled
- Alternate routes
- Safe areas
- Types of vehicles used
- Names of passengers
- Names of support personnel (drivers, maintenance, and security)

Moreover, using low-profile and highly secured vehicles with known and trusted drivers, along with decoy vehicles, will help reduce the risk of a surprise attack.

Analysis of Threats and Vulnerabilities

Understanding who is interested in knowing more about your company and for what reasons is an essential component of an effective OPSEC program. From what or from whom is the security professional protecting the company? What are the likely methods they would use to obtain the information they seek? Generally, the security executive must plan for a reasonably assumed threat based on a threat analysis of the company or facility. Seldom will a specific threat be known. However, there are conditions under which a specific threat does become known. Planning for and implementation of controls should be accomplished accordingly. The following must be considered.

- *High-tech vulnerabilities:* Can technology (wireless audio and video capabilities) be used to exploit security controls and measures?
- *Official company communications:* What information is being released about the company, and what story does that information collectively tell?
- *Unofficial company communications:* Are employees sensitive to not revealing sensitive or critical company information to persons without a need to know?
- *Routine company activities:* What is revealed about the company to someone watching day-to-day operations?

Risks Assessments

Assessing risk and understanding risk does not eliminate risk—mitigating action is necessary to eliminate unacceptable risks and reduce the threat and vulnerability to acceptable risk. Assessing risk is the responsibility of the security executive, working with company risk managers. Accepting risk is the prerogative of the company's most senior executives, usually the chief executive officer, the chief operating officer, and chief financial officer, with input from the company security executive, often referred to as the chief security officer.

As stated in Chapter 5, in its simplest form risk can be described mathematically as

$$\text{Threat} \times \text{Vulnerability} \times \text{Impact on assets value}^{10} = \text{Risk}$$

or

$$T \times V \times I = R$$

In other words, the threat against an asset when considered in the context of the value of the asset and the vulnerability of the asset leads to an assessment of risk.

Indicators

Indicators are actions, nonactions (what is not being done—think of not picking up the newspaper in the driveway), and bits of information that can be assembled into a bigger and more revealing picture. Indicators are what those who want to learn more about your company look for. Being aware of what employees do and say is essential in order to understand what indicators are being presented for others to observe.

Countermeasures

Countermeasures are the security controls developed and implemented to help mitigate vulnerabilities discovered during a vulnerability and threat analysis and risk assessment. Countermeasures are designed to:

- Change existing practices or behaviors.
- Fortify existing controls.
- Cover whatever unauthorized persons should not see or be made aware of.
- Deflect the interest of others.

Essentially, countermeasures, when implemented to mitigate vulnerabilities, should enhance the company's overall security posture.

Assess Yourself for OPSEC Vulnerabilities

After completing a threat, vulnerability, and risk analysis, the security professional should consider assessing the effectiveness of newly implemented mitigating actions through testing. Essentially, testing is an attempt to target yourself, acting as if you were the adversary, and to see what you can learn. Any testing should be conducted in a controlled manner, coordinated with key stakeholders, and the methodology and results should be documented for future reference and analysis.

Hiring an outside security expert or company to conduct a vulnerability analysis of your operation is often a good idea. These experts generally approach the task with an open mind and no preconceived notions about security capabilities or vulnerabilities. Furthermore, many are experienced in conducting penetration testing and incident simulation. In assessing vulnerability against the threat of terror, testing is a valuable process and should be considered by every security executive. It is better to learn about weaknesses and vulnerabilities during a test than to learn about them during an actual event.

Lessons Learned

After all analysis is complete and corrective and improvement actions implemented, followed by well-defined and controlled testing, an after-action report should be prepared. The focus of an after-action report should be on how things worked. What was learned going through the complete process? What were the glaring failures? Were there many small failures? What can be done better in the future?

Recommendations for change and improvement should be part of any lessons-learned effort. More importantly, following up at a later date to ensure that all recommendations and changes were properly implemented is essential. All too often, the best-made plans for improving security processes are shelved and not implemented. Sometimes recommendations for improvement are not acted on, due to lack of funding, due to other priorities, or even for no reason at all. The consequences of this inaction can be deadly.

Security Awareness Training and Education

People are the key to operational security success. Employees must understand their responsibilities in terms of what they must not do (reveal information or actions) and what they must do to protect company assets, including themselves. All employees have primary responsibilities. Security is often viewed as additional duty that is less important than their primary duty. Changing this mindset, getting employees to understand the importance of good security practices as part of their primary responsibilities, is the challenge faced by the security executive. Depending on the company culture (existing individual employee security consciousness and support of the company security program) and the availability of resources, a security executive could find this to be anything from an easy task to an insurmountable effort.

Finally, when working to increase the security consciousness and situational awareness of employees, use techniques, material, and examples that are real. Exaggerated stories and unrealistic situations tend to breed skepticism. Be truthful and realistic and relate real-world experiences to the reality of your company operations.

Summary

Operational security (OPSEC) is a security process designed to augment existing security controls. When used properly, OPSEC adds an effective layer of security measures to the overall company security profile. OPSEC is designed to help the security executive mitigate the release of sensitive or critical information and activities, denying access to those who have no need to know. Preventing others from learning more about your company than they should know and using what they learn to their advantage or to your company's disadvantage is the goal of a good OPSEC program.

OPSEC Is a Five-Step Process, U.S. National Security Decision Directive (NSDD) 298, formalized OPSEC and described it as a five-step process:

- *Identification of the critical information to be protected*
- *Analysis of the threats*
- *Analysis of the vulnerabilities*
- *Assessment of the risks*
- *Application of the countermeasures*[11]

OPSEC Laws

> *The First Law of OPSEC: If you don't know the threat, how do you know what to protect? Although specific threats may vary from site to site or program to program, employees must be aware of the actual and postulated threats. In any given situation, there is likely to be more than one adversary, although each may be interested in different information.*
>
> *The Second Law of OPSEC: If you don't know what to protect, how do you know you are protecting it? The "what" is the critical and sensitive, or target, information that adversaries require to meet their objectives.*
>
> *The Third Law of OPSEC: If you are not protecting it (the critical and sensitive information), the adversary wins! OPSEC vulnerability assessments (referred to as "OPSEC Assessments"—OAs—or sometimes as "Surveys") are conducted to determine whether or not critical information is vulnerable to exploitation. An OA is a critical analysis of "what we do" and "how we do it" from the perspective of an adversary. Internal procedures and information sources are also reviewed to determine whether there is an inadvertent release of sensitive information.[12]*

Endnotes

[1] See: http://www.defendamerica.mil/cgi-bin/prfriendly.cgi?http://www.defendamerica.mil/articles/a021202b.html

[2] See: http://quote.bloomberg.com/apps/news?pid=10000087&sid=aiww9MKiNRio&refer=top_world_news#

[3] See: https://www.cia.gov/cia/reports/Ann_Rpt_2002/swtandhs.html

[4] http://www.defendamerica.mil/articles/a021202b.html

[5] See: http://www.scip.org/2_overview.php

[6] See: http://www.theglobeandmail.com/servlet/story/RTGAM.20070102.wdirtybomb0102/BNStory/National/home

[7] See: http://www.usatoday.com/money/industries/technology/2005-02-20-cyber-terror-usat_x.htm

[8] See: http://www.msnbc.msn.com/id/12523560/from/RSS/

[9] See: http://www.outpost-of-freedom.com/okc0601.htm and http://www.outpost-of-freedom.com/okcind.htm ("What Really Happened in Oklahoma City?")

[10] Andy Jones and Debi Ashenden, *Risk Management for Computer Security* (Boston: Elsevier Butterworth-Heinemann, 2005).

[11] http://www.defendamerica.mil/articles/a021202b.html

[12] http://www.defendamerica.mil/articles/a021202b.html

Coordinating and Planning with Antiterrorist Agencies

People constantly requesting government intervention are casting their problems at society. And, you know, there's no such thing as society. There are individual men and women and there are families. And no government can do anything except through people, and people must look after themselves first. It is our duty to look after ourselves and then, also, to look after our neighbors.
—Margaret Thatcher, interview published October 31, 1987

This chapter discusses the security executive's responsibilities as liaison to government counterterrorism agencies and provides a few important links to government agencies charged with emergency response and planning and combating terrorism and crime. These links can serve as a source of information for the security professional and as a means of making or establishing contact.

Within the United States, the United Kingdom, Australia, and Canada, many local, state, and federal or national government agencies have as their mission, in part or in total, the combating of terrorism. Some of these efforts are fully coordinated among many agencies; others are more isolated and disconnected. Corporate security executives must understand how these government agencies operate and what support they can or will provide their company. Furthermore, security professionals should understand what is expected of them by these agencies in order to ensure an effective counterterrorism working partnership.

Make no mistake about it, even though government agencies exist to help combat terrorism and make the nation-state they are charged with protecting safer, their focus is the protection of society at large and key elements of that society. In general, an individual business or corporation is not their priority. Government organizations charged with protecting against terrorism focus their support on critical components of society, such as the country's infrastructure for communications, transportation (air, land, and sea), health, medical, agriculture, water, energy, continuity of government, continuity of the nation's economy, and defense of the homeland. Some of these are owned and operated by corporations, whereas in some nation-states they have been nationalized.

As a security executive, it's easy to recognize that your company may only be a small part of any of the sectors just described. It's more difficult to recognize and accept that protecting your company assets is up to you and your company leadership.

Government organizations established to combat terrorism or provide any other form of security and protection support individual businesses through their effort to protect the country's infrastructures. They do not provide direct support to any business. The support provided to an individual company is indirect but essential. Very few businesses can sustain themselves, never mind grow or thrive, if a significant portion of the country's infrastructure is damaged or if the economic sector they are part of has been harmed.

Recognizing this, building relationships with government organizations charged with a protective and security mission, e.g., counterterrorism, can be valuable and should be done. At the very least, these government agencies may be able to provide guidance and support to business security executives trying to better understand the threat to the nation and the business sector within which they operate.

Contacting Government Agencies

Making contact with the various government agencies in most nation-states is relatively easy. Security executives can contact any of these organizations directly, seeking contact with industry liaison personnel. Most agencies are receptive to industry, particularly security executives seeking assistance or guidance in protecting against terrorism and for contingency planning and emergency preparedness.

Another approach to developing contacts and relationships with government agencies with a security and counterterrorism mission is through professional security associations. These associations generally have resources and utilize members to form committees focused on developing working relationships with law enforcement and government organizations.

Becoming a member of a local, national, or international professional security association will afford a security executive an avenue to developing important relationships and having access to useful resources. An example of such an organization is the American Society for Industrial Security (ASIS) International.[1] ASIS International has more than 34,000 members worldwide and is the largest international organization for professionals responsible for security. Many professional security associations will have individuals or committees focused on issues of terrorism and its impact on society and businesses. Making contact with these individuals or participating on committees is an excellent way to engage with other professionals dealing with terrorism and counterterrorism.

Useful Sources

National Resources—Serving Their Country

http://www.fbi.gov/terrorinfo/counterrorism/waronterrorhome.htm

This is the U.S. Federal Bureau of Investigation (FBI) website for counterterrorism. It provides links to useful counterterrorism-related information and information on how to contact the FBI. The FBI has field offices throughout the United States and liaison offices in many foreign countries and can be a useful source for business looking for guidance on counterterrorism issues.

http://www.dhs.gov/index.shtm

This is the U.S. Department of Homeland Security (DHS) website, with links to multiple resources for businesses focused on preparedness and critical infrastructure issues and support. The U.S. DHS focus is protecting the "homeland." An important part of that mission is counterterrorism. The DHS actively seeks out industry and business security professionals, offering guidance and assistance for those charged with protecting their organizations against terrorism. Contact information is provided on their website.

http://www.fema.gov/

This link is to the U.S. Federal Emergency Management Administration (FEMA). The site provides businesses information useful for contingency planning. Emergency and crisis management along with business recovery are primary areas covered. However, FEMA, as part of the U.S. Department of Homeland Security, does play a role in counterterrorism and can provide information and support to the private sector. Contact information is provided on their website.

http://www.state.gov/s/ct/rls/pgtrpt/

This link is to the U.S. Department of State website for patterns of global terrorism. Information on global terrorism is made available to site users. It is a helpful source for those researching and seeking to understand trends in terrorism activities. Contact information is provided at the site.

http://www.dfait-maeci.gc.ca/internationalcrime/terrorism-en.asp

This is a link to a Canadian website for foreign affairs and international trade, focused on international crime and terrorism. Links to Canadian international policy and information concern Canada's effort to prevent and respond to terrorist infiltration and attack are available. Furthermore, links to useful crime, terrorism, counterterrorism and security information and resources are available. For those interested, contact information is provided.

http://www.fco.gov.uk/servlet/Front?pagename=OpenMarket/Xcelerate/ShowPage&c=Page&cid=1007029394239

This is a link to the United Kingdom's Foreign and Commonwealth Office website for international terrorism. It provides useful information on terrorism, terrorist groups, and security.

http://www.pfe.gov.uk/

This is a link to the United Kingdom's website designed to assist those preparing for an emergency. Many types of emergencies are addressed, including guidance on the current risk of terrorism, how to counter international terrorism, and how to stay safe. Links to many other useful resources are available, ranging from guidelines on the risk of terrorism to travelers to security advice from the Metropolitan Police. There is a link for businesses, and contact information is provided.

http://www.mi5.gov.uk/

This is a link to the website of the United Kingdom's Security Service, offering security advice and threat-related information. Threats such as domestic and international terrorism along with proliferation of weapons of mass destruction and espionage are discussed. Security advice and guidelines for protecting assets are provided. The focus is on security planning and infrastructure protection. Contact information is provided.

*http://www.dpmc.gov.au/publications/protecting_australia/preparedness/
2_intelligence.htm*

This is a link to the Australian government's website focused on protecting Australia against terrorism. It includes links to sites with security and counterterrorism resources along with contact information.

*http://www.ag.gov.au/agd/WWW/NationalSecurity.nsf/Page/What_Governments_
are_doing_News_Room_Media_Statements_Media_Releases_2005_AG_visit_to_
strengthen_fight_against_terrorism_-_The_Hon_Philip_Ruddock_MP*

This link takes you to an Australian government national security website providing businesses information ranging from travel guidelines to contingency planning and critical infrastructure protection. The site also includes contact information.

International Resources—Serving a Multinational or International Community

http://www.interpol.int/

The Interpol website hosts a Public Safety and Terrorism page offering guidance to any interested person. Interpol can be contacted through the contact process they offer on their website.

Nongovernment Resources

http://www.terrorism.com/

This link is to the Terrorism Research Center, an independent institute dedicated to terrorism research, information warfare and security, critical infrastructure protection, homeland security, and other, related issues. It is a useful resource for the security professional seeking to better understand the threat of terrorism and contingency planning issues.

http://www.tkb.org/Home.jsp

This link is to the Memorial Institute for the Prevention of Terrorism (MIPT). It is a resource for research and analysis on global terrorist incidents, terrorist groups and leaders, and other terrorism-related issues. The site provides information for researchers, policymakers, emergency responders, and the general public.

Case Scenario

Assume a corporate security executive or chief security officer (CSO) has decided to establish a formal program for collecting terrorism-related information in order to support the corporation's effort to protect assets against the threat of terrorism. If you were this CSO, how would you go about developing such a program? One approach is the following.[2]

Collecting Information

As any good CSO knows, when it comes to getting information you are usually only as good as your sources. In government agencies at the local, state, and federal levels, not only is the use of sources practiced, it is usually encouraged. Law enforcement officers, counterterrorist specialists, and investigators often receive extensive training in handling sources. The use of sources in countering terrorism is vital, and reliable sources are second to none in helping to counter terrorism.

In the business world, one valuable source of information is employees. A CSO may be able to solicit support from employees in the corporation who have knowledge of information that could be potentially useful to the CSO in planning and preparing to protect the company. For example, some employees may spend time in different areas of the world, giving them an understanding of local history, culture, and activities that might be useful to a CSO as the company expands business into those areas. These employees may be native to the area or just very familiar with the area after living or working there for many years.

Sources

The word *sources* has a more "politically correct" connotation than the word *informants* or other, similar words one can think of to describe someone who provides information.

☐ ☐ ☐ ▬▬▬▬▬▬▬▬▬▬▬▬▬▬▬▬▬▬▬▬▬▬▬▬

There are two primary types of sources: overt and covert. Overt sources are people who openly provide information or generally any source of information that is available to the public. Covert sources are those people who provide information or other sources (spy satellites) whose identity is protected.

▬▬▬▬▬▬▬▬▬▬▬▬▬▬▬▬▬▬▬▬▬▬▬▬ ☐ ☐ ☐

Internal Sources

A corporation's internal sources must be overt sources. Those overt sources that would be of use should first be identified by their position. This is because no matter who is in that position, that person may have access to information that is beneficial to defending the corporate assets against terrorism.

The CSO would usually be meeting with them periodically to discuss matters of mutual concern. They also may be able to provide useful information. How? They may know of vulnerabilities in the asset protection defenses that make those assets more vulnerable to terrorist attacks. They also may have heard information of value to the CSO in the effort to protect assets, particularly in a high-risk environment.

☐ ☐ ☐ ▬▬▬▬▬▬▬▬▬▬▬▬▬▬▬▬▬▬▬▬▬▬▬▬

As your unit matures and you have a few more high-technology crime investigators, they should each be assigned specific organizations to visit regularly when they are not conducting investigations, inquiries, briefings, surveys, or the like.

▬▬▬▬▬▬▬▬▬▬▬▬▬▬▬▬▬▬▬▬▬▬▬▬ ☐ ☐ ☐

At the same time, the CSO must handle some overt sources personally because of their position. As the CSO receives information from other individuals who appear to be helpful and willing to assist at times, he or she would want to determine what type of information this person would have access to.

When someone does contact or has been contacted by the CSO and does not want his or her name used, for fear of reprisals, there should be a process to accommodate that. However, that accommodation should be coordinated with a member of the legal staff so that this protection can be properly handled. This process should be developed as one of the first coordination meetings held between the CSO and the manager of the legal department. In that way, the CSO would be able immediately to explain to the source exactly what protection can be ensured and under what circumstances.

In addition, the possibility of introducing the employee to a counterterrorism government agency representative should be discussed with the employee and the legal staff. The decision to assist a government agency must be based on the employee's willingness to be introduced to the government agency official. The CSO understands that once that has happened, the CSO will lose the employee's future information to the government agency, for that agency will undoubtedly classify that information as in the interest of national security and deny the CSO access to it.

External Sources

External sources could be anyone outside the corporation or anyone in the corporation who is not considered a corporate employee, e.g., a consultant or a subcontractor employee working in one of the corporate facilities.

The CSO should be very cautious in dealing with such sources. If they are overt sources, then there is less concern that someone may look on the CSO's activities as covertly recruiting external informants. If the source wants his or her identity protected, the CSO should be more cautious not to get tainted with accusations of source recruitment in violation of laws or regulations or becoming involved in government agency activities. Again, a process for handling these types of sources should have already been developed in coordination with the legal department staff.

"Carding" Sources

Those individuals who provide information useful to the CSO in the effort to understand the threat in different areas of the globe should be identified for future reference. For example, sources that may prove useful in helping the CSO understand local and regional potential threats when establishing operations in Third World countries (e.g., establishing a new mining operation in remote areas of Africa) should be recorded and then protected for future use. In the "old days," source information was kept on index cards. In the information age, this information is better kept in the unit's source database, where searches and queries can easily be conducted to find sources that have provided terrorist-related information in the past.

What follows is some of the basic information that should be placed in the database on a source.

- Name
- Employee number or other identification numbers
- Organization
- Address
- Telephone number
- Fax number
- E-mail address
- Any specific information that makes the person a good contact, for example, fluency in Arabic

- Time, date, and location of the first contact
- Purpose of the contact
- Results of the first contact
- Details of subsequent contacts
- Name of the security staff providing this input

The information can be expanded and include more details, such as Social Security number, date and place of birth, and home address. However, caution must be exercised to ensure that this information can be shown to be necessary in the event it becomes known to others outside the unit. Additionally, such information should have a short expiration date. If there isn't any contact with the source in a year, then the information should be deleted. However, such decisions are based on the culture and working environment within a business. It is a judgment call by the CSO.

The database should also have fields for input each time source contact is made and information is provided. The fields should include basically the same information as just noted, e.g., time, date, and place of contact, information provided, and what security staff member was contacted.

Classifying the Reliability of Sources and the Accuracy of Their Information

Sources come in all kinds, and each source has a motive for providing information and cooperating with investigators. A "track record" of source contacts maintained in the database provides that information; however, what is lacking is anything indicating the importance and validity of the information and the reliability of the source to provide reliable information.

Let's assume our CSO decided to include two fields in each database record that would assist in evaluating the source and the information provided by the source. The unit manager devised the following two fields:

- Reliability of source
- Reliability of source information

Each security staff member who had significant contact (when a source provided meaningful information) would be required to update the database with the information listed earlier but also "code the source and the information." The following codes were used:

- Source reliability:
  - Code 1: Always reliable
  - Code 2: Usually reliable
  - Code 3: Sometimes reliable
  - Code 4: Questionable reliability
  - Code 5: Has never been reliable
  - Code 6: Reliability unknown at this time

- Information provided by the source has proven to be:
  - Code A: Always accurate
  - Code B: Usually accurate
  - Code C: Sometimes accurate

○ Code D: Always of questionable accuracy
○ Code E: Never accurate
○ Code F: Of unknown accuracy at this time

By keeping the source database up to date, the CSO can have a ready source of reference to the source's reliability and be in a better position to judge the accuracy of the information the source is providing based on past information.

Caution must always be exercised when talking to sources. Continual questioning of their motives is necessary.

Such a database will be a good reference point for the CSO and the database should be queried prior to any interview with the individual to determine if that individual has previously provided information and whether that information was useful.

Networking

It is imperative that the CSO continually network with peers met at conferences and association meetings or in other professional settings. This is particularly important for a company CSO operating in unfamiliar areas with a high risk for terrorism. Some of the best information comes from other security professionals operating in high-risk areas and dealing with real problems. As they work to solve their problems, they gain valuable experience and information that most are quite willing to share with other professionals. Maintaining relationships with these professionals can be extremely valuable.

These individuals should also be identified in a database or just by placing their business cards in a file and categorizing them by their line of business, e.g., computer consultant, vendor, government employee.

In today's information environment, one can obtain a great deal of free information, advice, and guidance on an untold number of threats, particularly the threat of terror.

Most of these individuals will have e-mail addresses. Contacting them periodically via e-mail and telephone calls is a very cost-effective way to gather information and to keep abreast in your profession.

It is recommended that these individuals periodically be contacted to find out what's new. It is surprising how much relevant information can be gathered via this cost-effective method.

Liaison

According to the *Franklin Language Master Dictionary and Thesaurus*, the word *liaison* means "close bond; communication between groups." For the CSO, it means just that: communication between the CSO and the local, state, and federal counterterrorism agency staffs.

Such liaison is always in the best interest of the CSO's corporation as part of their involvement in the community. In addition, the sharing of information with law enforcement agencies on terrorism matters will be of mutual benefit to both groups.

□ □ □ ▬▬▬▬▬▬▬▬▬▬▬▬▬▬▬▬▬▬▬▬▬▬▬▬▬▬▬▬▬▬▬▬▬▬

> Membership and active support of your local high-technology crime investigation association will provide the opportunity to build a relationship of trust and support.

▬▬▬▬▬▬▬▬▬▬▬▬▬▬▬▬▬▬▬▬▬▬▬▬▬▬▬▬▬▬▬▬▬▬ □ □ □

As with other sources of information, the individuals with whom you come in contact should be entered into the database. Another advantage of such a database is that the source is not lost when an investigator leaves the unit.

Establishing a formal information-gathering program is a cost-effective way to assist in obtaining information to help protect corporate assets against the threat of terror. Prior to implementation, such a program should be discussed and approved by the corporate legal staff because such information collection processes are of a very sensitive nature.

Summary

Security executives will find value in developing and maintaining working relationships with government organizations focused on security, terrorism, counterterrorism, and emergency preparedness. This can be accomplished by contacting those organizations directly or by working through professional associations such as the American Society for Industrial Security International.

Endnotes

[1] See: http://www.asisonline.org/

[2] Some portions of this section were taken and partially modified from Butterworth-Heinemann's published book *High-Technology Crime Investigator's Handbook, Second Edition* (2006), coauthored by two of this book's authors and used here with permission.

□ □ □ **SECTION**
□ □ □ **III**
□ □ □

The Future World

FIGURE III-1 "The further backward you look, the further forward you can see." (Words of Winston Churchill as quoted in Ray Kurzeil, *The Age of Spiritual Machines,* New York: Viking Press, 1999.)

This section addresses the future: what the security professional and the business executive can expect and how they should prepare now to react to anticipated terrorists events. The future always brings uncertainty, but we can learn from the past and reasonably forecast future events.

Chapter 11: The Future Global Business Environment and Security Needs

This chapter addresses terrorist-related security issues associated with the continued globalization of business. Corporations continue to expand their markets and areas of operation. With that expansion, risks of terrorist attacks may be encountered. What those risks are and how a security professional should deal with them are addressed.

Chapter 12: The Future of International Terrorism

This chapter forecasts what international terrorism might look like in the near-term and long-term future. Can terrorism be prevented or even eliminated? Where might new instances of terrorism occur? Will we see more state-sponsored terrorism? Or will terrorism be the product of rogue individuals, groups, or organizations. What should our business successors expect and prepare for?

Chapter 13: The Successful Security Professional in Fighting Terrorism—Now and in the Future

This chapter discusses what the security professional must know and do in order to prepare properly to protect corporate interests from terrorists and other threats now and in the future.

Chapter 14: Closing Thoughts

This chapter briefly summarizes the entire book and presents some candid commentary from the authors.

11

The Future Global Business Environment and Security Needs

If you want to humble an empire it makes sense to maim its cathedrals. They are symbols of its faith, and when they crumple and burn, it tells us we are not so powerful and we can't be safe. The Twin Towers of the World Trade Center, planted at the base of Manhattan island with the Statue of Liberty as their sentry, and the Pentagon, a squat, concrete fort on the banks of the Potomac, are the sanctuaries of money and power that our enemies may imagine define us. But that assumes our faith rests on what we can buy and build, and that has never been America's true God.
—Nancy Gibbs, *Time* (Sept. 12, 2001) "Special Report: The Day of the Attack."

This chapter addresses the future global business environment and potential terrorist-related security issues associated with the continued globalization of business.

For those who have responsibility for the protection of corporate assets, this means protecting the assets from all threats—natural and man-made. Of course, the emphasis of this book is on the protection of those assets—information, facilities/equipment, and employees—from terrorist attacks.

In order to protect corporate assets from terrorists, it is vitally important that the security professional and those in business management understand the global business environment in which the corporation will do business and where the corporate assets are located and vulnerable to terrorist attacks.

Some may argue that *globalization* is another word for *internationalization*; others may argue that they are different terms. For our purposes, we use the meaning stated next. It is best to leave matters such as definitions to academicians, who live more in the theoretical world than in the real world—at least the real world of global trade and terrorism.

Globalization is the term used to describe the changes in societies and the world economy that result from dramatically increased international trade and cultural exchange. It describes the increase of trade and investing due to the falling of barriers and the interdependence of countries. In specifically economic contexts, the term refers almost exclusively to the effects of trade, particularly trade liberalization, or "free trade." ... More broadly, the term refers to the overall integration, and resulting increase in interdependence, among global actors (be they political, economic, or otherwise).[1]

The "globalization" of business has been progressing for centuries. Ever since the first European explorers sought out new worlds, their purpose was to "Christianize the heathens" and trade with them. Meanwhile, on the other side of the globe, Chinese and others were also exploring parts of the world and expanding their trading partners to those in the Middle East and Southeast Asia.

Economic globalization, the business of world trade and the "global marketplace," requires, and always has required, for the most part a stable environment. Yes, in times of crisis and conflict, arms trading does increase; however, that type of trade is very limited compared to other forms of trading, e.g., those goods sought by general consumers and other businesses. Trade on a global scale has been increasing for centuries, and it is expected to continue to increase, in some areas exponentially and more rapidly than in the past.

Since in order for trade to flourish, businesses need a relatively stable environment, when wars break out in a region, e.g., the two world wars of the 20th century, businesses suffer (except for manufacturing and arms trading, of course). The recent global terrorist trends have adversely affected businesses in areas where the terrorist are at their strongest, such as in the Middle East, followed predominantly by other Muslim areas of nation-states, e.g., Afghanistan, Indonesia, and the Philippines.

Of course, after the end of the two world wars, especially World War II, trade once again began to prosper, especially that between the nation-states of Europe and the United States as the United States implemented the Marshall Plan to help Europe rebuild. During the period, this did not occur in China because the Chinese communists seized control, which, of course, was in conflict with the ideas of democracy and private ownership of businesses of the Western world and, thus, not supported by the United States and most democratically free European nation-states. However, at the same time, noncommunist nation-states such as Japan, South Korea, Thailand, and Taiwan began their capitalistic trends of becoming successful global trading partners with nation-states around the world.

Whether or not terrorists realize that their attacks keep the Middle East nations from progressing into the future and becoming part of the global community (socially as well as the global economic-business world), this is in fact happening. After all, what business wants to invest in a nation hostile to them and the nation or nations they are from? What nation wants to accept such risks to their assets?

The terrorists are succeeding in fomenting hatred against those who do not think as they do, and at the same time they blame the non-Islamic states for the poverty conditions for which they, the terrorists, are in fact at least partly responsible. So the terrorists continue to find "new blood" from among the ignorant and unemployed masses to die for their cause without these new recruits even questioning the causes of their poverty and unemployment.

And what about the moderates and pro-business Muslims speaking out against these terrorists? It would be like speaking out against Hitler and the Nazis, with the results being intimidation, torture, imprisonment, and/or death to those who try to find middle ground as well as to their families.

In this the 21st century, we see that the improvements in relationships between nation-states such as the United States and China as well as improvements in communications and in transportation (the ability to ship goods around the world more efficiently, more cheaply, and more rapidly) that have led to increased and massive trade and also dependencies on that global trade. The Berlin Wall is gone, and a united Germany is a total democratic and capitalistic nation. The Soviet Union has been replaced by a Russian version of capitalism and even "Communist China" is now more of a socialist-capitalist nation than a communist one. The current trend is also one of an increasing number of nation-states becoming democratic. Thus the trend toward capitalism (and now global capitalism) continues and will do so for the foreseeable future. This trend into the future will drive more global trade, a trend that terrorists, of course, do not want to occur.

Globalization of Business

Corporations continue to expand their markets, facilities, and areas of operation around the world, many of which are supported by the host nation-states, who also benefit from such trades through:

- Increased employment of their citizens
- A rise in the standard of living
- More tax revenue
- Their citizens' ability to purchase cheaper goods

According to some, globalization is bad and contributes to the exploitation of the poor. Arguments can be made on both sides of this issue, but suffice it to say that globalization will not stop. Along with that expansion, increased risks from today's terrorists and their attack methodologies may be encountered for the foreseeable future, at least the next ten years or so.

□ □ □ ▮▮

"This is not a battle between the United States of America and terrorism. It is a battle between the free and democratic world and terrorism."
—*Tony Blair, British Prime Minister, after the terrorist attack on the United States on September 11, 2001*[2]

▮▮ □ □ □

What those risks are and how a security professional should deal with them will vary, depending on:

- The type of corporation
- Their locations worldwide
- Their owners
- Their products

Type of Corporation

The type of corporation does not appear to be a *primary* factor (although it seems to be somewhat of a factor) when terrorists consider whether or not to attack, with the possible exception of the petrochemical industry. That industry is under attack by eco-terrorists, who want to stop production for ecological reasons, and also by international and national terrorists, who perceive that attacks on fuel production and supply is a way of putting pressure on governments and also on the capitalist system. In the future this may change; however, it appears that this trend will continue because ownership, location, and the nation-state's involvement, real or perceived, are considered the primary factors.

Corporate Owners

The corporate owners are generally the stockholders, who may live in any part of the world. However, it seems their ownership is generally believed to be equated to their corporate headquarters' locations and other facilities and not the locations of the stockholders. Therefore, attacks against businesses are often based on their physical locations. Terrorists want them out of any nation-state that does not support the terrorists' goals. Being a Muslim-owned business is no protection, as we have seen not only in Afghanistan and Iraq but also in such Muslim nation-states as Indonesia, which are targeted also. People, e.g., corporate employees, are generally "soft" terrorist targets and also offer the most graphic displays of terrorist attacks when the news media show the blood and bodies of the attack victims.

□ □ □ ▬▬▬▬▬▬▬▬▬▬▬▬▬▬▬▬▬▬▬▬▬▬▬▬▬▬▬▬▬▬▬▬▬▬

The World Trade Center bombing was the February 26, 1993, attack in the garage of the New York City World Trade Center. A car bomb was planted by Islamist terrorists in the underground parking garage below Tower One. It killed six, injured over 1,000, and presaged the September 11, 2001, attacks on the same buildings.[3]

▬▬▬▬▬▬▬▬▬▬▬▬▬▬▬▬▬▬▬▬▬▬▬▬▬▬▬▬▬▬▬▬▬▬ □ □ □

Corporate Locations

If the corporations are those of the United States, Great Britain, or their allies in the "war on terror" and the drive to support democracy in the Middle Eastern nation-states, then, based only on that connection, they will be targeted for attacks and potential destruction and their employees, especially management, will be targeted for kidnappings and killings by terrorists, who may be viewed by their supporters as "revolutionaries" or "militants."

In other parts of the world, terrorists (considered "freedom fighters" by some) kidnap corporate executives, contractors, and other innocent people and demand a ransom not only to make their government look weak and powerless but also to get funding for their terrorist activities. Other terrorists would rather cut off the heads of their victims and display videos of such on Internet websites and in the global news media. Such tactics are expected to continue in the foreseeable future, making it imperative that employees receive training in avoiding being placed in vulnerable positions and what to do if captured by terrorists.

□ □ □ ▬▬▬▬▬▬▬▬▬▬▬▬▬▬▬▬▬▬▬▬▬▬▬▬▬▬▬▬▬▬▬▬▬

"9 oil workers abducted in Nigeria: LAGOS, Nigeria (Reuters)—Nigerian militants launched a string of attacks on the world's eighth-largest oil exporter on Saturday, abducting nine foreign workers from an offshore barge and attacking at least two other facilities."[4]

▬▬▬▬▬▬▬▬▬▬▬▬▬▬▬▬▬▬▬▬▬▬▬▬▬▬▬▬▬▬▬▬▬ □ □ □

With the "global terrorist networks" that exist in numerous countries around the world, it is not necessary for a corporation to be in the heart of the Middle East to be vulnerable to attack.

Although the people in the World Trade Center (WTC) in New York City were citizens from a multitude of nation-states who were employed by global corporations with offices there on September 11, 2001 (9/11), the terrorists are believed to have thought of the WTC (and the people in it) as United States' entities filled with Americans. They were reportedly attacked as a blow against the United States and not against the many nation-states' whose employees were also killed in that cowardly attack, including Muslims from Middle Eastern nation-states and other nation-states as well.

There were hundreds of corporations from more than 50 nation-states with employees working in the World Trade Center (excluding the United States), many of them either neutral and or even having sympathized with the terrorists. Today's terrorists do not discriminate and are more interested in mass killing "for effect," even if the victims are fellow Muslims. In the near future, the religious type of terrorist will continue to attack for maximum effect, regardless of the religious beliefs of their victims. In addition, these attacks will also be part of religious wars, even among Muslims who have different beliefs and goals. (*Note:* We concentrate on the Middle East because that region is the center of today's major terrorists, who are mostly Islamic extremists, although terrorist networks are found in many nation-states, for many reasons, some of which are local. For example, they are in Indonesia, Malaysia, Sudan, Thailand, Yemen, and many other countries, including in the United States and Great Britain. As discussed in Section I of this book, this has changed since the latter part of the 20th century, when the majority of groups identified by governments as terrorists were European based and supported by the Soviet Union and Cuba. The trend has shifted from politically based terrorists, e.g., supporting left-wing activities and communist activities, to religiously based terrorists.

In the future, today's terrorists will be joined by those in capitalistic nations where animal rights and ecology issues are prominent, e.g., polluting corporations, global warming issues; terrorist activities will increase if the nations and corporations do not do more to control the harmful effects on the earth caused by their policies and processes.

Corporate Products

The products manufactured by the corporations may also be a factor as to whether or not they continue as targets of terrorist attacks in the future. Furthermore, it is important to remember that the terrorists may not be international or Middle Eastern terrorists but domestic terrorists, such as those identified and responsible for what the U.S. government (e.g., FBI) considers a case of domestic terrorism (the attack on the federal building in Oklahoma City, Oklahoma, was carried out by U.S. citizens).

As we mentioned earlier, businesses—and global businesses maybe more so—require a stable environment in which to operate. The more chaos, the more difficult it is to do business successfully. This is one of the goals of the terrorists: to create an unstable environment and push foreign businesses out of their targeted nation-states and return the nation-state back to the Stone Age, as was the case in Afghanistan when the Taliban were in power. Also, some may continue to try to eliminate domestic businesses they believe violate their beliefs, e.g., selling video movies in Afghanistan, which is contrary to the strict fundamentalist way of looking at such things.

☐ ☐ ☐ ▬▬▬▬▬▬▬▬▬▬▬▬▬▬▬▬▬▬▬▬▬▬▬▬▬▬▬▬▬▬▬▬▬▬▬

"The only way to discover the limits of the possible is to go beyond them into the impossible."
—*Arthur C. Clarke (English physicist and science fiction writer, b. 1917),* Technology and the Future

▬▬▬▬▬▬▬▬▬▬▬▬▬▬▬▬▬▬▬▬▬▬▬▬▬▬▬▬▬▬▬▬▬▬▬ ☐ ☐ ☐

However, as businesses expand around the world, many will take more risks and begin operating in foreign nation-states that may not have a stable government and indeed may be the home of one or more terrorist cells. Businesses will take more risks as competition in the global marketplace continues to heat up and businesses continue to look for places with cheaper labor, cheaper raw materials, new markets, and favorable operating conditions. They need these in order to compete and offer products at lower prices based on lower operating costs. These favorable operating conditions may be given by a country's dictator, who also has in that country those classified as terrorists who are trying to change the government in power and rid their nation-state of a dictator. Remember, one person's terrorist may be another's freedom fighter.

☐ ☐ ☐ ▬▬▬▬▬▬▬▬▬▬▬▬▬▬▬▬▬▬▬▬▬▬▬▬▬▬▬▬▬▬▬▬▬▬▬

It is useful to distinguish economic, political, and cultural aspects of globalization, although all three aspects are closely intertwined. The other key aspect of globalization is changes in technology, particularly in transport and communications, which it is claimed are creating a global village.[5]

▬▬▬▬▬▬▬▬▬▬▬▬▬▬▬▬▬▬▬▬▬▬▬▬▬▬▬▬▬▬▬▬▬▬▬ ☐ ☐ ☐

As a security professional responsible for the protection of corporate assets, you will continue to find this type of environment for the foreseeable future. How you deal with those asset protection needs, e.g., defending them against terrorist attacks, will offer you some of your greatest challenges.

The High-Technology Factor

The globalization of business is being supported and even driven by continuing advancements in high technology (technology based on the microprocessor), and thus rapid and ever-expanding communications has also advanced the ability of terrorists to attack those they consider their enemy. Terrorists have been using the Internet, e-mail, cellular telephones, and the like to communicate with one another and also to spread their propaganda. They have become quite sophisticated in their use of these high-technology devices, including steganography and encryption.

□ □ □ ▬▬▬▬▬▬▬▬▬▬▬▬▬▬▬▬▬▬▬▬▬▬▬

As high technology becomes smaller, more powerful, and cheaper, terrorists will continue to take advantage of the current and future improvements in these devices.

▬▬▬▬▬▬▬▬▬▬▬▬▬▬▬▬▬▬▬▬▬▬▬ □ □ □

As technology improved, the sailing ships gave way to steamships and diesel engines, which increased their speed and size, and the industrialization of nation-states led to expanded and increased trade throughout the world. The advent of modern transportation has allowed today's criminals and terrorists to operate far beyond their home territories. Today they operate around the world, and as transportation and communications improve, they will acquire additional speed, sophistication, and ability to attack their targets.

□ □ □ ▬▬▬▬▬▬▬▬▬▬▬▬▬▬▬▬▬▬▬▬▬▬▬

"A laptop in every pot: A *New York Times* article is provoking an online debate over whether cell phones or laptops are truly the best way to bring the Internet to the world's poor. In-house Microsoft (Research) blogger Robert Scoble agrees with his boss, Bill Gates, that cell phones are the best way to make Internet access universal: When he travels overseas, he sees everyone reading their phones, not using laptops. David Rothman says he hopes that MIT's cheap-laptop experiment wins out, because it's easier to read on larger screens."[6]

▬▬▬▬▬▬▬▬▬▬▬▬▬▬▬▬▬▬▬▬▬▬▬ □ □ □

The dependence of corporations on high technology, which has left the most high-technology-advanced nation-states more vulnerable to attacks (and successful attacks at that) than the Third World nation-states, who have little in the way of high-technology infrastructure and therefore less reliance on it. This will also continue into the foreseeable future.

At the same time, however, some previously unaffected nation-states, e.g., those not vulnerable to high-technology or other forms of attack because they didn't have that high-technology-based infrastructure in place, are becoming more vulnerable to attacks from terrorists and others. For example, some nation-states have bypassed the installation of a telecommunications infrastructure based on telephone landlines and have gone directly to cellular technology for their internal communications needs. Therefore, this dependency will cause terrorists of the future to increasingly target the corporations and employees who make this infrastructure possible as well as use that technology in those nation-states as well.

□ □ □

"Intel: One billion transistors on tiny new chip: Company says it's on track to make fingernail-sized chips by the second half of 2007.... It had made the world's first microchip using tiny new manufacturing methods that promise to let the world's top chipmaker make more powerful, efficient processors. The fingernail-sized memory chip is etched with 1 billion transistors that are only 45 nanometers wide—about 1,000 times smaller than a red blood cell," said Mark Bohr, a leading Intel engineer. "It will pack about two times as many transistors per unit area and use less power. It will help future products and platforms deliver improved performance."[7]

□ □ □

Nanotechnology

According to many engineers, government and private scientists, and business leaders, nanotechnology is the future, a future in which humans will be able to do wondrous things. What is nanotechnology?

> *Nanotechnology is the understanding and control of matter at dimensions of roughly 1 to 100 nanometers, where unique phenomena enable novel applications. Encompassing nanoscale science, engineering, and technology, nanotechnology involves imaging, measuring, modeling, and manipulating matter at this length scale.... A nanometer is one-billionth of a meter; a sheet of paper is about 100,000 nanometers thick.*[8]

According to the United States' government:

> *The transition of nanotechnology research into manufactured products is limited today, but some products moved relatively quickly to the marketplace and already are having significant impact. For example, a new form of carbon—the nanotube—was discovered by Sumio Iijima in 1991. In 1995, it was recognized that carbon nanotubes were excellent sources of field-emitted electrons. By 2000, the "jumbotron lamp," a nanotube-based light source that uses these field-emitted electrons to bombard a phosphor, was available as a commercial product. (Jumbotron lamps light many athletic stadiums today.) By contrast, the period of time between the modeling of the semiconducting property of germanium in 1931 and the first commercial product (the transistor radio) was 23 years.*
>
> *The discovery of another nanoscale carbon form, C60, the fullerene (also called the buckyball) brought the Nobel Prize in chemistry in 1996 to Robert F. Curl, Jr., Sir Harold W. Kroto, and Richard E. Smalley. It also started an avalanche of research into not only the novel characteristics of C60, but also other nanoscale materials.*
>
> *Nanoscale science was enabled by advances in microscopy, most notably the electron, scanning tunneling, and atomic force microscopes, among others.*[9]

The United States and other modern nation-states as well as global businesses are racing to take advantage of what the future offers in products and services through the use of nanotechnology. One of the products being sought is nanoweapons.

□ □ □ ▬▬▬▬▬▬▬▬▬▬▬▬▬▬▬▬▬▬▬

Public Law 108-153; 108th Congress; an act: To authorize appropriations for nanoscience, nanoengineering, and nanotechnology research and for other purposes. Be it enacted by the Senate and House of the 21st-Century Nanotechnology Research and Development Act…. The President shall implement a National Nanotechnology Program. Through appropriate agencies, councils, and the National Nanotechnology Coordination Office established in section 3, the Program shall—

1. establish the goals, priorities, and metrics for evaluation for federal nanotechnology research, development, and other activities;
2. invest in federal research and development programs in nanotechnology and related sciences to achieve those goals; and
3. provide for interagency coordination of federal nanotechnology research, development, and other activities undertaken pursuant to the program.[10]

▬▬▬▬▬▬▬▬▬▬▬▬▬▬▬▬▬▬▬ □ □ □

Nanotechnology is here in its initial stages of research and development but is rapidly growing. We have all heard of its potential uses to clear blocked arteries, repair human cells, and the like. However, as a security professional responsible for assets protection, do you see any security issues? Of course nanotechnology devices may be embedded in an artificial fly or bee that can hover over a computer screen, with the embedded video recorder or live video transmitter capturing the information shown on the computer screen or capturing data flowing through computer networks, or one might sit in a room where sensitive discussions are taking place.

□ □ □ ▬▬▬▬▬▬▬▬▬▬▬▬▬▬▬▬▬▬▬

Controlling bioterrorism: John Steinbruner, University of Maryland arms control expert, has been calling for mandatory international oversight of inherently dangerous areas of biomedical research, specifically, an international body of scientists and public representatives to authorize such research…. [H]owever, … any effort to keep good science out of the hands of ill-intentioned people must be international to be effective. And both point to existing efforts to push a treaty making bioterrorism an international crime.[11]

▬▬▬▬▬▬▬▬▬▬▬▬▬▬▬▬▬▬▬ □ □ □

Let's take that one step further and, in the future, look at how the terrorists of the world might use such technology to destroy anything and anyone at the atomic level. Possible? Yes! Likely? If one has the knowledge and funding, this may well occur. Imagine buildings and people being "eaten away" by nanobots live on television. You can't see them and you can't stop them. Well, hopefully we can. But if security and asset protection follow today's trends into the future, then the funding of asset protection will always be after the fact and never ready when needed.

☐ ☐ ☐ ▬▬▬▬▬▬▬▬▬▬▬▬▬▬▬▬▬▬▬▬▬▬▬▬▬▬▬▬▬▬▬

Could the following be a future newspaper story? "It appeared that nanotechnology was used to develop an artificial bug that penetrated the high security of the New World Trade Center in New York City and released a plague virus that killed everyone within a 10-block area. A previous unknown terrorist group claimed credit for the attack."

▬▬▬▬▬▬▬▬▬▬▬▬▬▬▬▬▬▬▬▬▬▬▬▬▬▬▬▬▬▬▬ ☐ ☐ ☐

Add to all this the progress made in the area of biotechnology. Such advances will have broad appeal to humans, businesses who see massive profits, and terrorists. A bioweapon in the hands of future terrorists may be able to unleash devastating attacks whose death toll would make the plagues of the past seem minor. Remember that many of these terrorists welcome death. So what if they kill half the humans on earth, including themselves? To them it will be worth it.

This may sound more like science fiction than future science facts. However, many science fiction stories provided a look at the future. We recommend that you research this future high technology and determine for yourself if it offers not only great future benefits but also great threats. In the hands of terrorists who care nothing of culture, societies, people, or their environment, such as the world's great cities, the question is not whether they will use it, but when will they be able to do so? After all, we are talking about people often living under primitive conditions in caves and who readily will die for their cause. Do you think they really care what would happen to themselves or others once nanoweapons are unleashed?

Nanotechnology is rapidly approaching and the question is: Will we be able to defeat terrorism in the future to the point where such technology would not be used by individuals against their adversaries?

The security professional should also be researching to see where nanotechnology and related technologies of the future can be used to better protect corporate assets and not continually lag behind in the development of related security defenses. As Ray Kurzweil, noted author and inventor explains: We have a process that works rather well in controlling computer viruses. Shortly after a new computer virus is detected, it is reverse engineered and analyzed and an anti–computer virus program is developed and released to the world. We must be able to do the same thing for bioweapons, e.g., virus-based weapons. However, today's government agencies and their processes are too slow to react, often taking years to approve a "cure." In the future, waiting more than 24 hours, if that long, may not be possible if we are to save many lives.

☐ ☐ ☐ ▬▬▬▬▬▬▬▬▬▬▬▬▬▬▬▬▬▬▬▬▬▬▬▬▬▬▬▬▬▬▬

Who needs bioterrorists when we've got genetic engineers? But what caught the attention of the mainstream media was the report in January 2001 of how researchers in Australia "accidentally" created a deadly virus that killed all its victims in the course of manipulating a harmless virus. "Disaster in the making: An engineered mouse virus leaves us one step away from the ultimate bioweapon," was the headline in the *New Scientist* article. The editorial showed even less restraint: "The genie is out, biotech has just sprung a nasty surprise. Next time, it could be catastrophic."[12]

□ □ □

Expansion of the Global Marketplace and Its Areas of Operations

The global marketplace has expanded over the years from Europe to the Americas and Asia. It is expected that future expansions must consider Africa. Although many of its nation-states are rather unstable at this time, with the help of more modern nation-states and their global corporations, this should eventually change.

If you look at the terrorist attacks that have taken place in Africa, you can see that the terrorists are already there and ready to wreak havoc on the corporations of the world who dare enter their "domain" and try to change and improve the life of its citizens. Africa provides an excellent "test environment" where one can study the various factors involved:

- Tribal groups
- Democratic-minded people
- Corrupt dictators challenged by "freedom fighters" (or terrorists, depending on what side of the government you are on)
- Increased adoption of high-technology devices
- Wars among the African states and civil wars and the role terrorists play in those wars, e.g., Somalia
- Impact of modern nation-states in supporting their countries' businesses in the African nation-states
- Actions of terrorists to stop such modernization, except under their control

□ □ □

In 1999, Uganda became the first African nation to have more mobiles than traditional phones. Thirty other African nations followed by 2002.... [In] the megacity of Lagos, Nigeria, cell phones were one of the three largest industries there, neck and neck with religion and nutritional supplements.[13]

□ □ □

Africa is a continent worth studying to get some idea not only of what future corporate business will contend with vis-à-vis terrorists but also of the terrorist techniques that will be used there and then spread to other continents, and vice versa.

Future Global Corporations

What will future global corporations look like? They will continue to be dependent on and process-driven by high technology. This will increase their process efficiencies as well as allow them to expand into new markets and in fact create markets where none exist today. This dependency on high technology coupled with the products and locations will also make them more and more vulnerable to terrorists.

□ □ □ ▬▬▬

"The ability to learn faster than your competition may be the only sustainable competitive advantage."[14]
—*Arie de Geus*

▬▬▬▬▬▬▬▬▬▬▬▬▬▬▬▬▬▬▬▬▬▬▬▬▬▬▬▬▬▬▬▬▬▬▬▬▬▬▬ □ □ □

It would not be surprising if the competition increases to such an extent that competitors may, under the guise of terrorists, attack the networks and facilities of their competitors. After all, in the past some have used criminal tactics to steal information and proprietary processes and devices from their competitors, so why not use terrorist tactics to delay and stop their competitors' progress in gaining a competitive edge? How would one know the difference? That of course would be another challenge to add to the existing asset protection burden of the security professional.

Future global corporations will be more automated and take more advantage of high technology to use robotics and employ people all over the world working together electronically. So, as is the case for some today, employees, will be working out of local kiosks or their homes. Having such globally dispersed working environments may make it more difficult for terrorists to do serious harm to a globally operating corporation. As a result, individual employees working from their homes may be more vulnerable to kidnappings and attacks. In addition, don't be surprised to find terrorists as well operating from the homes of these employees if they decide to add cyberterrorist tactics and cyberterrorism to their terrorist repertoire.

□ □ □ ▬▬▬▬▬▬▬▬▬▬▬▬▬▬▬▬▬▬▬▬▬▬▬▬▬▬▬▬▬▬▬▬▬▬▬▬▬▬

An analysis of the history of technology shows that technological change is exponential, contrary to the commonsense "intuitive linear" view. So we won't experience 100 years of progress in the 21st century—it will be more like 20,000 years of progress (at today's rate). The "returns," such as chip speed and cost-effectiveness, also increase exponentially. There's even exponential growth in the rate of exponential growth. Within a few decades, machine intelligence will surpass human intelligence, leading to The Singularity—technological change so rapid and profound it represents a rupture in the fabric of human history. The implications include the merger of biological and nonbiological intelligence, immortal software-based humans, and ultrahigh levels of intelligence that expand outward in the universe at the speed of light.[15]

▬▬▬▬▬▬▬▬▬▬▬▬▬▬▬▬▬▬▬▬▬▬▬▬▬▬▬▬▬▬▬▬▬▬▬▬▬ □ □ □

Future Antiterrorist Protection Needs of Corporations

For at least 10 years, today's security professionals have been warning of a "Pearl Harbor" of the high-technology kind, i.e., total destruction of various portions of a nation-states' infrastructures. However, to date, terrorists have seen fit instead to make an impact on people, trying to arouse fear through kidnappings, car bombings, and decapitations. This is because terrorism is most effective when it receives the massive publicity that these types of atrocity engender. This trend is expected to continue in the future, and we may soon begin to see digital attacks becoming the preferred terrorist method, for one cannot discount the possibility that some terrorist groups will focus on the destruction of the infrastructures and economies of the modern nation-states that are their sworn enemies.

□ □ □ ▬▬▬▬▬▬▬▬▬▬▬▬▬▬▬▬▬▬▬▬▬▬▬▬▬▬▬▬▬▬▬▬▬

Information is now the same thing as a physical object. If you view an organism as so dangerous as to require P4 containment—the highest level, complete with air-locks, moon suits, double-door autoclaves, and liquid-waste sterilizers—then keep information about that organism under the same kinds of wraps.[16]

▬▬▬▬▬▬▬▬▬▬▬▬▬▬▬▬▬▬▬▬▬▬▬▬▬▬▬▬▬▬▬▬▬ □ □ □

We see the effect on today's modern nation-states' citizens when winter storms cut off electricity to thousands. Imagine that in the heart of some winter the computer networks that operate a modern nation-state's power grid go down for weeks. Will that create wide-spread panic, anxiety, and maybe worse? How will the citizens feel when they can no longer trust their financial institutions' calculations and be unable to use ATMs and the like?

Add to that the massive growth of identity theft, credit card fraud, etc. These are increasingly likely to be techniques used by terrorists as nations become better at tracing and controlling funds targeted for terrorist groups. Even terrorists groups like the Taliban need funding to support their activities.

Corporations that are responsible for these and other infrastructures have a serious duty to make them as resistant as possible to terrorist attacks. All corporations have the responsibility to protect their employees and to safeguard from terrorist attacks the corporate assets of their owners.

- As a security professional, do you think this is being accomplished adequately today?
- If not, why not?
- What responsibilities do you have to ensure that this is accomplished?
- What are you doing about it?
- What are you going to do about it?

All corporations should have sound plans to defend their assets against terrorist attacks, incorporate those plans into tomorrow's business plans, maintain those plans, and periodically test those plans. A combination of proactive and defensive methodologies is needed, with high-technology and sophisticated processes integrated into antiterrorist plans, policies, procedures, processes, and projects. The security professional must also see that such philosophies are integrated into all aspects of his or her corporation's business.

Case Study

As the chief security officer for XYZ Corporation, you were told by your boss that next year the corporation will be expanding its business, which includes the manufacturing of widgets, into a suburb in Iraq. You are told that since you have primary responsibility for leading the corporation's asset protection efforts, you must tell executive management what needs to be done to protect the corporate assets en route to and in Iraq at their new satellite location.

So now what do you do? No, you don't leave the corporation—you need the job and medical benefits, and it also pays well. The first step of course would be to contact those involved, probably a project team, who are responsible for successfully making this event happen. You should then become a member of that project team.

As a member of that project team, you should also consider the following:

- Develop and brief the team on an asset protection operational plan for moving the assets to Iraq, which includes equipment and people.
- Subsets of that plan should include:
  - Operational security plan
  - Transportation plan
  - Executive protection plan
  - Employee protection plan
  - Budget plan
- You must determine if a new building will be constructed or an existing building used. In either case, a facility physical security plan, including physical security survey, must be devised.
- Employees will be traveling to Iraq prior to the operation of the new facility; therefore, it is important that your planning include a travel security plan.
- Conduct research on Iraq, its culture, customs, society, and so on.
- Learn to speak the local language.
- Coordinate with your nation-state's government agencies to determine the threat environment.
- Coordinate through their support with the local authorities, e.g., local police, U.S. forces stationed in the area of the corporation's proposed facility.
- You must be actively involved in this project because it could mean life or death for corporate employees.

The foregoing is just a high-level outline as to what should be considered for implementation. Can you identify other major tasks to ensure that a successful facility is established there?

Summary

Corporations are increasingly operating in a global marketplace and as such are more susceptible to terrorist attacks anywhere in the world. Corporations will continue to expand their global operations, driven and supported by high technology. Although high technology is a crucial factor in lowering operating costs and increasing profits, it also makes corporate assets more vulnerable to terrorist attacks.

To date terrorists have used high technology for propaganda purposes, e.g., websites, and for communicating with each other via e-mail and cellular telephone. This trend is expected to continue, but many are expecting the day to come when the digital infrastructures of their sworn enemies are attacked. The "digital Pearl Harbor" may or may not create great fear among ordinary citizens, but it will be a devastating blow to the nation-states' economies if the right targets are successfully attacked.

Future corporations will continue their current trends and become more dispersed, with employees located around the world using the latest in high technology to conduct business.

The challenge for the security professional responsible for the protection of these valuable corporate assets is to prepare now to handle the future needs of corporate asset protection and to defend them against terrorist attack.

Endnotes

[1] See: http://en.wikipedia.org/wiki/Globalization

[2] See: http://koti.mbnet.fi/neptunia/terror1.htm

[3] See: http://en.wikipedia.org/wiki/World_Trade_Center_bombing

[4] See: http://us.cnn.com/2006/WORLD/africa/02/18/nigeria.oil.reut/index.html

[5] See: http://us.cnn.com/2006/WORLD/africa/02/18/nigeria.oil.reut/

[6] See: http://money.cnn.com/2006/01/30/technology/browser0130/index.htm?cnn=yes index.html

[7] See: http://money.cnn.com/2006/01/25/technology/intel_chip.reut/index.htm

[8] See: http://www.nano.gov/html/facts/whatIsNano.html

[9] See: http://www.nano.gov/html/facts/home_facts.html

[10] See: http://frwebgate.access.gpo.gov/cgi-bin/getdoc.cgi?dbname=108_cong_public_laws&docid=f:publ153.108

[11] See: http://www.kurzweilai.net/meme/frame.html?main=memelist.html?m=2%23682

[12] See: http://www.kurzweilai.net/meme/frame.html?main=memelist.html?m=2%23682

[13] See: Joel Garreau, *The Radical Revolution: The Promise and Peril of Enhancing Our Minds, Our Bodies—And What It Means to Be Human* (New York: Doubleday, 2004), p. 170.

[14] See Joel Garreau, *Radical Revolution*, p. 257.

[15] See: http://en.wikipedia.org/wiki/Law_of_Accelerating_Returns

[16] See Joel Garreau, *Radical Revolution*, p. 165.

12

The Future of International Terrorism

I am neither right-wing nor left-wing. Ideology doesn't interest me. The important thing is to be an international terrorist.[1]
—Mehmet Alo Agca

This chapter forecasts what international terrorism might look like in the near-term and long-term future.

Mehmet Alo Agca's philosophy of terrorism may not be that unusual these days. In the past, ideology played an important role in terrorism, especially in Europe and in the Americas. Today, such is not the case, except in a few instances, such as possibly those in Cuba and those in some South American and Central American nation-states and maybe a dictator or two in some African nation-states. Actually, as we have seen, in those areas it is not about communism or "power to the people" but about dictatorship and power, using the philosophy of communism as a cover to gain power and to dictate.

The times of "pseudo-communists" (dictators by another name) are over and have been for some time, and it is doubtful they will ever return. Perhaps one should never say never, but in this case it does seem to apply. However, those still around and others will continue to try to foment trouble for their adversaries by using terrorist tactics and supporting terrorism because it is still a valuable tactic for them.

Communism and its state-sponsored terrorist acts and those it supported will continue to decrease in the future.

Terrorism: The use of violence and intimidation in the pursuit of political aims.[2]

What Will Terrorism Look Like in the Future?

Here are some of the questions we would all like to have answered as we move into the future.

- Can terrorism be prevented or even eliminated?
- Where might new instances of terrorism occur?
- Will we once again see more state-sponsored terrorism?
- Will terrorism be more the product of rogue individuals, groups, and organizations?
- What methods will future terrorists employ?
- Will the cyberterrorists we've been expecting for years finally appear?
- What should our business and security successors expect and prepare for in order to foil terrorist attacks?

What follows are some possible answers to these questions.

Can Terrorism Be Prevented or Even Eliminated?

Yes, individual terrorist attacks can be prevented if we have good intelligence and good plans to eliminate the threat quickly. However, we do not believe they can ever be totally eliminated from the face of the earth. That is because it only takes one individual willing to die in the attack for it to be successful. Furthermore, as high technology becomes more sophisticated, attacks can be conducted with more success through the use of that technology. We see it already in the use of remote-controlled devices—an adaptation of high technology—to blow up people and things.

Where Might New Instances of Terrorism Occur?

New instances of terrorism will be seen as we have seen them in the past, which is where we least expect them to occur. The attacks will occur at those locations and against those interests and those of the allies wherever the "sworn enemy" of the terrorists has some influence or presence, as we have seen in the past, e.g., the bombing of a Western hotel in Jakarta.

Will We Once Again See More State-Sponsored Terrorism?

The answer is maybe. The key here is who is defining the terrorism. If two warring states in Africa use terrorist tactics, is it terrorism or just an act of war or the act of "freedom fighters"? The remnants of the communist countries, such as Cuba, may go on supporting terrorist tactics against capitalistic nation-states, but these will continue to decline as the "communist threat" declines. Since communists are atheists, the current religiously fanatical terrorists are in conflict with these "nonbelievers." After all, today's major terrorist groups want an Islamic-ruled world. However, as in politics, terrorism "makes for strange bedfellows." So there may be instances of such support. For example, will Cuba, contemporary Venezuela, or some other anti–United States or anti–Western nation-state allow today's and tomorrow's religiously based terrorists to reside and train in their countries?

A look at the past, when such nation-states as Lebanon, Libya, and Cuba were allegedly used to house and train terrorists who then committed terrorist acts in Europe and elsewhere, suggests it may happen again. After all, the saying "Your enemy is my enemy" still holds true in today's and tomorrow's world. What about China? China is an interesting nation-state and always has been. Although they have a communist form of government, it is unique to China as they struggle with having a communist form of government and a capitalistic economy. More than ever, they are "socialist-capitalists" more than communists. Furthermore, they have their own problems holding the country together with its large Muslim population as well as other minorities who would like to form their own nation-state. China will probably continue to fight terrorism internally and try to placate terrorists internationally, e.g., Iran, so that China does not become the target of terrorist attacks.

Today's Chinese communist government is not as interested in promoting communism and subverting the governments of nation-states as it once was. Economic competition has taken the place of communist ideology for the most part, and, as we mentioned before, capitalism and the global marketplace require stability.

China's goal of being *the* world leader is the same, but now it appears that they plan on dominating the globe economically more than politically. After all, economic domination does have political benefits, such as having China's trading partners influenced politically by China due to trade relations. So, unless there is some drastic changes in the Chinese government's leadership, terrorist actions, excluding those considered a part of information warfare, will not be supported by them, although some tactics against their own people are considered terrorist tactics.

Will Terrorism Be More the Product of Rogue Individuals, Groups, and Organizations?

Yes, the current trend suggests that nation-state–sponsored terrorism, which in the past had been mostly a communist state–sponsored terrorism, is fading, with a few exceptions (e.g., Iran, Syria). Furthermore, one has only to look at the changes taking place in the world to see that the growing influence of high technology (e.g., in communications such e-mail, websites, and the Internet in general) has led to individuals, groups, and organizations. Not only are these entities becoming more powerful, but they are communicating and working together around the world.[3]

One merely has to look at such groups as the World Trade Organization's (WTO's) protestors who show up wherever the WTO meets. Protestors, anarchists, and others can assemble a group anywhere from a few days to a few hours. The use of the cell phone, for example, has led to "swarming," where someone calls associates, who calls others, exponentially notifying all those with like opinions and goals to meet at a certain place at a certain time. Such "swarmings" are now becoming commonplace to gather for a party or a political demonstration and everything in between.

What Methods Will Future Terrorists Employ?

It is expected that future terrorists will continue to bomb places and people to create as much carnage for the television cameras as possible. However, it is expected that as the power of high technology increases, some terrorists will begin to use that technology not only to destroy corporations and nation-state networks but also to kill people, e.g., telemedicine or the disruption of elements of critical infrastructure such as water or power. Terrorists have become rather good at adapting various technological tools into terrorist tools and adapting to the circumstances they find themselves in and the sophistication of their targets' defenses. This is expected to continue and to get even more dangerous as their targets become more hardened and high-technology vulnerable and as that technology becomes smaller and more powerful.

Will the Cyberterrorists We've Been Expecting for Years Finally Appear?

This interesting question is difficult to answer. Yes, today's and tomorrow's terrorists are and have been students at universities and have been taught and trained in the use of high technology, everything from computer science to programming, network integrations, and the like. Some security experts are waiting for such attacks so that they can say, "I told you so!" Others fear such a day because the defenses are often so very inadequate to the challenges brought about by the use of terrorist tactics. If a terrorist group decides that it can get more support for its cause and/or create more fear in people through less human carnage, then they will turn to attacking corporate and nation-state infrastructures, at least to supplement their other tactics.

We have all seen the damage that a 14-year-old can do on the Internet. Imagine what a college-educated student of computer science can do. In time of a "cold" war or "hot" war, information warfare tactics that can be used by terrorists have occurred, and they will continue to occur. Are these the acts of terrorists or tactics of basic warfare? As we stated, it all depends on your definition of war and of terrorism and on which side of the conflict you are. Information warfare techniques have been used and continue to be used, e.g., Taiwan versus China. China may even consider Taiwan a "rogue, terrorist nation-state," and Taiwan may think that the tactics used by China are those of terrorists. As you can see, the answers are not always black and white (if they ever have been).

What Should Our Business and Security Successors Expect and Prepare for in Order to Foil Terrorist Attacks?

The corporate managers and chief security officers of today's and tomorrow's corporations should be prepared for physical, psychological, cyber-, and weapons-of-mass-destruction attacks. In order to defend against them, at a minimum, the plans, processes, policies, procedures, and operations identified in Section II of this book should be implemented and maintained.

Antiterrorist programs must be proactive, and thinking "out of the box" should be the rule and not the exception. Brainstorming sessions should be held often, leading to feasibility studies that lead to new processes, high-technology defenses, and the like that can be incorporated into the overall defenses of a corporation. Remember that the terrorists who will target your corporation are on a war footing, and you must be also. War by other means is still war. Also remember that not all businesses are targets, but all businesses are in the "war zone," which is global.

International Terrorism—Near Term and Long Term

Let's look at the future of terrorism from a near-term and a long-term point of view.

International Terrorism—Near Term

In the near term, based on current trends, religiously driven terrorism will continue to take precedent over other forms of terrorism. Using the definitions provided at the beginning of this book, terrorism has to do with political aims to one extent or another. Today's terrorism can be viewed that way because terrorists seek Islamic-supported and -driven nation-states. Thus, from that point of view it is political. On the other hand, today's terrorism has predominantly religious aims that embrace more than just their political goals. This will continue into the near future because they strive to make their religion their dominating goal over not only political aims but also social and cultural aims, encompassing every aspect of a human being's life.

As global intelligence networks couple with advances in more sophisticated high technology, the "war on terrorism" will continue to turn against the terrorists, who will continue to make the news with their attacks against humanity.

The key to winning this near-term war is whether or not the governments of the world's nation-states, including those in Africa, will have the intestinal fortitude (the guts) to wage this war as it should be waged. What is interesting is that the politics of terrorism affects those fighting terrorism more than it has influence over the terrorists. One can see how the French recently treated the riots throughout France as not those of terrorists but of poor youth (albeit Muslims) in need of work. Do those 2005 riots meet the definition of terrorism as cited earlier? You be the judge.

In the near term, today's acts of terrorism will become so much the norm that, unless it is of a 9/11 or comparable scale, the newspapers will move it from the front page to an inner page to become "oh, by the way" news of Iraq, Afghanistan, and the Middle East. Decreased reporting on terrorist acts in the future may also help mitigate the use of such tactics. After all, if no one knows about the attacks but those in the vicinity, the perpetrators are not getting their message across and "striking fear into the hearts of the infidels."

How the terrorist threat is treated will depend in large part on how the United States leads that effort. For example, under a more liberal administration, such as during the Clinton Administration, the terrorist attacks were for the most part considered a law enforcement responsibility, with a few military cruise missiles thrown in now and then. Under the George W. Bush Administration, terrorism is considered acts of war and is being fought primarily by military forces. How the United States will lead the fight against terrorists in the future may depend in large part on who is elected the next president of the United States.

For the foreseeable future, terrorists will be primarily international terrorists. However, these should not be confused with the terrorist activities of Afghanistan, Iraq, Saudi Arabia and the like, which have domestic terrorist aspects to them but are fought in large part by foreign terrorists. Today's and the near-tomorrow's terrorist groups will be made up of a combination of domestic and international terrorists. The mix will depend on their areas of operations, mutual goals, and opportunities. With today's high-technology capabilities of making fraudulent identity documents, coupled with the ease of fast travel to anywhere in the world, foreign terrorists will continue to be available to support domestic terrorists.

So, what some call a religious, global "holy war," or jihad (another Crusade), will continue. During this period, some state-sponsored terrorism will continue, but eventually it will decline in the Middle East (based on current trends). We have already seem the forming of some democratic process in the Middle East, e.g., Afghanistan, Pakistan, and Iraq elections and the beginning of elections in Egypt, Lebanon, and Palestine. If that trend continues without the outbreak of a civil war, e.g., in Iraq, then today's form of terrorism may more quickly be on its way out. It all depends.

The United States prevailed in all of these conflicts because we could spend our way out of danger. When a threat emerged, we bought time until we were mobilized and able to respond. But that strategy will no longer work.[4]

However, as the old saying goes, be careful what you wish for, because you may get it. The previous elections in Pakistan, at least in the terrorist stronghold of the northwest, succeeded in electing what the West would call Islamic extremists (Jihadists); the Hamas members elected in the Palestinian area are classified as terrorists by the West. This has shown that elections do not necessarily mean that democracy and moderates, as known in the West, will win.

What is of interest is that Western nation-states, especially the United States, believe that the United States' form of democracy is the will of all human beings. This has not been shown to be the case and in fact in the future may be even less so. Some of this may be due to a backlash against the current political powers in a given nation-state or a backlash against United States and Western influence and their social, religious (Christian and Jewish), and cultural influences and that of other nation-states.

It is expected that in many nation-states, the attitudes of the nation-states' voters will continue along those lines, especially in strong Muslim sectors of any particular nation-state. Furthermore, as democracies and elections are pushed by global democratic nation-states, the outcome may be for a more Islamic nation-state and may even cause their democratic form of government to be based on Islamic law; even the word *democracy* may mean something different than what the Western nation-states would like to see.

In the near term, this trend of pushing formerly nondemocratic nation-states, especially in the Middle East, to open up their countries to elections will show a trend of nation-states that are not as secular as some would want them to be.

The terrible thing about terrorism is that ultimately it destroys those who practice it. Slowly but surely, as they try to extinguish life in others, the light within them dies.[5]
—*Terry Waite (b. 1939), British religious adviser, hostage in Lebanon*

International Terrorism—Long Term

Terrorists are generally bitter and full of hatred. That can only last so long. The longer one is in the "terrorist business," the more it wears one down. After a while, if they are not dead or in jail, they slowly fade away. A person can only hate so much for so long before just getting tired of it all. Is that just an outside looking in? Yes, but, at the same time, look at the terrorists of the heyday of European terrorism, the time of the Baader Meinhof gang, the Red Brigade. Where are they now? Jailed, "retired," or dead. They began their era of terror in the early 1960s but actually didn't get into full swing until the 1970s and 1980s. By the 1990s, they were pretty much gone.

Any power must be an enemy of mankind which enslaves the individual by terror or force, whether it arises under a fascist government or communist flag. All that is valuable in human society depends upon the opportunity for development accorded to the individual.
—*Albert Einstein*

Can we expect the same from the Islamic fundamentalists? Many think not and say they are a different breed. Yes, they are, because, unlike other historical terrorists, these folks don't mind dying for their cause. Of course, that does not include the likes of those who let others die for the cause while they stay cozy in their caves and hide from actual fighting. It would seem that some terrorists and their proud families don't get it. They die for the cause while their leaders are either "too valuable as a terrorist asset" or not dumb enough to die for their cause.

No bastard ever won a war by dying for his country. He won it by making the other poor dumb bastard die for his country.[6]
—*George S. Patton Jr.*

As the oil-dependent global powers, such as the United States, the European nation-states, India, and China, begin a more aggressive search for alternative and more cost-competitive fuels such as solar, wind, nuclear, and clean-burning coal, the need for oil will begin to decline. As the need for and availability of oil declines, these nation-states' concerns and political emphasis on Middle Eastern nation-states will decline. As these nation-states begin to withdraw their military and even some of their Western influence from these countries, some of the terrorists' concerns and attacks will lessen but not stop entirely. After all, without the use of intimidation and violence, what have most of these terrorists to love or die for? This is their life, and many know no other lifestyle. So they will continue their attacks in the name of whatever but in the future will be relegated to being ordinary criminals and bandits, as are many of them today, under the guise of being terrorists.

Increased Terrorist Risk for Global and Nation-State Corporations

Terrorist attacks against corporations are expected to continue, at least in the near future. These attacks will be carried out primarily by those involved in the religiously driven international terrorists' crusades against foreigners and continue to be primarily attacks of opportunity and waged indiscriminately against corporations and their employees regardless of the type of corporations or who the employees are—from CEO to janitor and everyone in between, including fellow Muslims working for the foreign corporations.

As we have seen from the 9/11 attacks and those of Jakarta hotels, Bali businesses owned and operated by Muslims, the religiously based terrorist attacks against businesses have not been singled out because of the type of business or even ownership, but because that's where groups of foreigners from their enemies' nation-states congregated. They rationalize the killings by saying that if they killed fellow Muslims, oh well, that is what they get for collaborating with those foreigners!

In the longer term, we will see more targeted attacks against specific businesses, depending on their business. These will be carried out by other types of terrorist groups, such as eco-terrorists, and animal rights groups. We have already seen indications of this where they singled out sport utility vehicle (SUV) parking lots and animal research facilities, such as that at the University of Washington in the United States.

So, as some types of terrorist groups begin to subside, others will emerge. The more the world's corporations increase their presence in the global marketplace and expand to new marketplaces with increased global competition from other corporations, the more they will be vulnerable to terrorist attacks and even "sucked in" to the domestic terrorist attacks and conflicts of civil wars and the like in various nation-states.[7]

Who Will Future Terrorists Be?

Based on current trends, future terrorists will continue to be primarily globally connected groups, some foreign state-sponsored and some sponsored solely by special-interest groups. The current trend of international terrorism will be the norm, with just a few solely domestic terrorist activities.

Due to high technology, the world is now globally connected in such a way that many of the like-minded can share not only their views by means of today's communications and modern transportation systems, they can support each other by various methods. Therefore, even what a nation-state may classify as a domestic terrorist group will be sponsored in some way (e.g., funding, equipment, weapons) by foreigners. Thus, there will be fewer and fewer terrorists who can be called domestic terrorists or domestic terrorist groups.

Future Religious Terrorists

Religiously based terrorists, primarily those classified as Islamic extremists, will continue but in a decreasing role. They will not go away completely but simply decline as their recruitment pool begins to dry up. This can occur only when those who they want to recruit can live in a stable environment, receive an education, and find jobs so that they can live above the poverty line of their nation-state. Until then, they will be easy prey as recruits for terrorists. After all, they have nothing to lose because they have nothing at all!

Remember, the goal of many Islamic extremist terrorist organizations is to create Islamic nation-states. As thousands continue to migrate to European nation-states and vote in their religious candidates, they will increasingly become a powerful force, with the goal of coming to power and, in a decade or two, taking over some European nation-states. When that occurs, can democracy continue? Or will those in power eliminate it altogether? Unless European nations wake up and take action soon, this will occur.

It is ironic that the freedoms offered today's Muslims in Western nation-states are being used to subvert those same nation-states in the name of democracy!

The leaders of these groups will for the most part continue to be educated individuals. One may wonder why individuals with a good education and money become terrorists. That would make an interesting psychological study. Their motivation may vary from hatred of their rich parents making them want to do something to hurt them, or it may be contrary to their beliefs. Today's and tomorrow's terrorist leaders practice terrorism for several reasons.

- Some want their religious beliefs, which they consider the right way of life as directed by God, to be the law of the land—of the world.
- Some become terrorist leaders for power or may even be sincere, using religion, ecology, or animal abuse as their justification.
- Others become terrorist leaders to rid their nation-state, their region of the world, or even the entire world of what they think are cultures and societies that are an affront to God or to their society and culture or both.
- They want their nation-state to be self-ruled and not ruled by what they think are nation-states who rule them as a colony, e.g., the IRA in Northern Ireland or the Basque separatists in Spain.
- They want to end the reign of what they perceive as corrupt, family-run governments.

There may be other reasons but these are the primary ones.

Future Environmental Terrorists

Besides the religious terrorists who dominate the world today, there is a growing number of individuals and groups who have been classified as environmental terrorists. This is predominantly in the Western and more developed and democratic nation-states, such as the United States, Canada, and some European nation-states.

The FBI defines eco-terrorism as the "use or threatened use of violence of a criminal nature against innocent victims or property by an environmentally oriented, subnational group for environmental-political reasons, or aimed at an audience beyond the target, often of a symbolic nature."[8]

These groups operate primarily as domestic terrorists but are supported by others around the world who hold similar views. As we discussed earlier, the outside support is there, and it is expected that as the Western nation-states continue to "exploit" natural resources around the globe, animals for experiments, and so on, they will continue to be attacked, and those attacks will increase in the future.

One of the nonreligious terrorist groups identified by some government agencies is the Earth Liberation Front (ELF), whose website states[9]:

> *The Earth Liberation Front ("ELF") is an underground movement with no leadership, membership or official spokesperson.*
>
> - *There is no ELF structure; "it" is nonhierarchical and there is no centralized organization or leadership.*
> - *There is no "membership" in the Earth Liberation Front.*
> - *Any individuals who committed arson or any other illegal acts under the ELF name are individuals who choose to do so under the banner of ELF and do so only driven by their personal conscience.*

Unlike other terrorist groups, ELF claims not to have a structure, although there may be like-minded individuals who consider themselves ELF members who meet and form their own subgroup or cell.

Earlier we talked about the "swarming" made available by today's high technology, e.g., cell phones. Such devices may offer help for future terrorist groups such as ELF to find "targets of opportunity" where ELF "members" may meet to attack a given target on short notice. This makes them almost impossible to predict or to take preemptive action against because you are effectively dealing with the whim of the initiator.

Their website has articles related to their cause, as the following headlines indicate:

- Vilified as "Terrorists," Eco-activists Face New Offensive by Business
- FBI Arrests 3 Suspected ELF Members in Placer Co.: Alleged Plot to Blow Up Cell Towers and Power Plants
- VANCOUVER, British Columbia—A court on Thursday ordered the extradition of suspected eco-terrorist Tre Arrow, one of the FBI's most-wanted fugitives, to face firebombing charges in the United States.

A formal group that some in business may consider an eco-terrorist group is Greenpeace International. According to their website:

> *Greenpeace exists because this fragile earth deserves a voice. It needs solutions. It needs change. It needs action. Greenpeace is a nonprofit organization, with a presence in 40 countries across Europe, the Americas, Asia, and the Pacific. To maintain its independence, Greenpeace does not accept donations from governments or corporations but relies on contributions from individual supporters and foundation grants. As a global organization, Greenpeace focuses on the most crucial worldwide threats to our planet's biodiversity and environment.[10]*

"The violent tactics of groups like Animal Liberation Front and Earth Liberation Front are well documented, and ALF itself was named as a terror organization by the Department of Homeland Security in January of this year [2005]. That these groups, along with Greenpeace (with their propensity for illegally boarding cargo ships), would come under law enforcement scrutiny is hardly surprising. In fact, one would be worried if they didn't warrant some scrutiny, given the tactics many of them use."[11]

Another in the "family of modern terrorist groups is the controversial animal rights group People for the Ethical Treatment of Animals (PETA). They believe that

> *animals have rights and deserve to have their best interests taken into consideration, regardless of whether they are useful to humans. Like you, they are capable of suffering and have an interest in leading their own lives; therefore, they are not ours to use—for food, clothing, entertainment, experimentation, or any other reason.*[12]

The FBI's top domestic terrorism official, James Jarboe, identified the Animal Liberation Front (ALF) and the related Earth Liberation Front (ELF) as America's most active domestic terrorist organizations. The FBI estimates that ALF and/or ELF have committed more than 600 criminal acts in the United States since 1996, resulting in damages in excess of $43 million.[13]

Anarchists of the Future as Terrorists?

Anarchy is the "state of disorder due to absence or nonrecognition of authority; absence of government and absolute freedom of the individual, regarded as a political ideal."[14]

Nation-states, especially those that are more advanced, may consider anarchists terrorists. These range from those who always seem to show up at WTO meetings wherever they take place in the world to domestic anarchists against any form of not only government but sometimes even businesses.

Anarchism is the belief that no government is just and that no government is therefore exactly what we ought to strive for.[15]

While it is obvious that they will always be in conflict with any type of authority, e.g., local, state, provincial, national, or federal government or the like, to some they may be today's and tomorrow's freedom fighters because they fight to free all peoples from the "tyranny" of governments and all authorities.

The interesting thing about the nonreligious terrorists is that they are for the most part people who reside in modern nation-states that lack any massive need to concentrate on such things as food, water, and shelter. In these modern nation-states, there is always someplace to get a free meal and free shelter for the night. In the less developed nation-states, people do not have the time for such causes because they have a difficult enough time finding food and shelter. They have no time or inclination to worry about protecting animals—many which they would gladly eat!

In the future, as more and more nation-states progress to the point where its citizens have sufficient food, shelter, employment, and expendable income, we shall see an increase in what may be called the "yuppie terrorists"—those with enough food, shelter, clothing, healthcare services, and the like as well as idle time to join such altruistic causes.

Trade Unions of the Future to Use Terrorist Tactics?

The drive to lower costs in order to be competitive in the global marketplace means that the current trend to gain the maximum efficiencies and productivity out of the corporate employees, coupled with the drive to cut employee benefits and lay off more and more employees as efficiency gains are made, may assist in driving the continual decline in trade unions and their power.

In addition, the use of high technology to monitor workers, invade their privacy, and dictate their lifestyle, e.g., "We don't hire smokers," may cause some union leaders to become more radical in their methods, as was considered the case by many when unions were first trying to form and when they were dominated and supported in some nation-states by the communist governments. Remember "Workers of the World Unite!"?

When workers have had enough and see no end to the decline of jobs, their working conditions, and subsequently their lifestyle, they may rationalize the need to become more active in demanding their "employee rights." Corporations will of course say that it is not their fault because they must compete in the global marketplace and must lower costs to do so. They will state that they may be eliminating jobs, lowering benefits, and so on but are trying to retain as many employees as possible. They will say that if they do not do so, the corporation will go into bankruptcy, be sold, or cease to exist, and nobody wins in that case. Do we see a conflict here?

What is considered exorbitant buyout executive management packages and pay may provide the terrorist spark of the future when the employees have had enough. These may include executive management kidnappings, arson, and other tactics used by today's and tomorrow's terrorist groups.

Freedom Fighters of the Future, or Future Global High-Technology Terrorists?

As we alluded to earlier, those who are in power and want to maintain the status quo consider those who want that power or at least want to remove the existing power as defined by those in charge as terrorists. If you recall, when Ronald Reagan was president of the United States, his administration supported and called those fighting to overthrow the Nicaraguan government "freedom fighters," while the Nicaraguan government considered them terrorists.

□ □ □ ▄▄▄

This battle of definitions of primarily domestically dominated terrorist groups will continue for the foreseeable future and maybe for as long as there are governments or even a world government. After all, there will always be someone who wants the power to rule that others may have.

▄▄▄ □ □ □

In the future, will hackers become the modern-day terrorists? Or are they the 21st-century freedom fighters? Because high technology continues to grow and to dominate and drive our way of life, let's discuss what some may call the 21st-century cyberterrorists, the "hacker." Let's look at it from one person's point of view.

Most of the security and law enforcement people view hackers as the archenemy of the 20th and 21st centuries. This view is also supported by the news media. In their interest to sell, sell, sell, the news media have made the name *hacker* synonymous with anything from juvenile delinquents and terrorists to mass murderers and even linked them to the information age equivalent of the nuclear bomb in their ability to destroy the information-based world as we know it. New laws have been written in countries around the world to support the investigation, apprehension, prosecution, and incarceration of these "vicious and violent" threats to societies and even to humankind itself!

□ □ □ ▄▄▄

The definition of the term *hacker* and the goal of the hacker—basically a computer enthusiast whose goal is learning all he or she can about computers and making them the most efficient machines possible to support humankind and our search for knowledge—has sadly been manipulated, modified, destroyed, erased, and/or deleted.

▄▄▄ □ □ □

Let's separate the hackers from the basic criminals that defraud users and damage and otherwise destroy systems and information for "fun" and without a meaningful purpose, such as the drive-by shooters of our large U.S. cities. To understand this, let's examine what is happening today and the trends that forecast tomorrow. There are miscreants, juvenile delinquents, and "wannabe's" out there causing us some grief. The folks changing websites are like the writers of graffiti on the walls and highways of our cities. The only difference is that the guys with the paint can't afford a computer, only spray paint. Others are destroying computer-based information, modifying it, and denying access to the systems that store, process, and transmit that information. This is wrong and we are not denying that. However, let's put this in perspective. Do they deserve 5–10 years in prison for this, in the company of murderers, rapists, and child pornographers? If you are in law enforcement or security, you might say, "Yes. If they can't do the time, they shouldn't do the crime." That would be not only sad but unprofessional as well.

At the risk of rehashing old news, the Mitnick case was an example of the criminal justice system gone awry. Mitnick may have been a pain in the ass, but he was no Capone or a terrorist, although he was treated as if he was that dangerous—yes, in what he *could* have done if he had wanted to but not in what he actually did. He was an embarrassment to the government agencies whose political and public relations egos were damaged while he was on the loose—like so many other hackers now being investigated and charged by our nation-states. These employees of the nation-state with their high tech and millions of dollars couldn't even find the guy, so when he was found, it was get-even time. This is mentioned only as an example of what millions of federal dollars cannot accomplish and also what power the federal government can bring to bear on an individual. It is only the beginning if one looks at the trends.

□ □ □ ▬▬▬▬▬▬▬▬▬▬▬▬▬▬▬▬▬▬▬▬▬▬▬▬▬▬▬▬

Maybe the people we should be putting in jail and charging with malfeasance, failure to apply due diligence, and apathy are the managers responsible for that information and the information systems.

▬▬▬▬▬▬▬▬▬▬▬▬▬▬▬▬▬▬▬▬▬▬▬▬▬▬▬▬ □ □ □

As stockholders in these companies, we want our assets protected! Many of these folks are not even adding the basic protection most of us have been recommending for decades! Maybe they deserve to be attacked just for that.

How about the Pentagon computers? These people are responsible for the *defense—the national security—of our nation*, and they struggle to protect that information from—forgive my use of the term here—hackers! That being the case, how well are we protected from the real threats to these systems from organized crime, intelligence agents of other nations, and terrorists? What must the priorities of the future be?

We also have the United States and other "civilized, information-based nations" using these threats as an excuse to gain more power, more control over our lives. The U.S. Secretary of Defense, who was allegedly quoted a year or so ago, said that if Americans want more security they will have to give up some of their freedoms. Wait! It gets worse. Look at Intel's Pentium III chip that could allegedly provide government agents and others the chip serial numbers of a user's computer without his or her knowledge, thus allow monitoring, tracing, and tapping of the user's communications. Do we have a conflict between individual rights and government's need for information to combat crime and terrorism? Will this continue to be a contentious issue? Can we reach a resolution? Must freedoms be challenged and even limited?

Products are being developed and used that require more and more of our personal identification—no—more of who we are, what we do, how we think: fingerprint required before cashing a check, genetic records of (so far) convicts only; and the beat goes on. The Oklahoma City bombing occurs and the government tries to use the opportunity to ram through a new antiterrorist law, which if it had passed in its original form would have meant less freedom for all of us, and still does. Why? Couldn't the bombers be charged with murder? Why do we need new, freedom-limiting laws to prosecute murderers? Does it matter whether they get the death penalty or life in prison for murder or for antiterrorist conduct?

The reason being used by government agencies for more power and control is the protection of the information infrastructure of the nation. Wait a minute! Isn't most if not all of that privately owned? Look at Russian's SORM, "alleged" Chinese attacks against a U.S. website devoted to the outlawed Falun Gong sect. If so, then have the Chinese attacked the United States? If so, was it an act of war? a terrorist act? Look also at other Asian nations' attempts at spying on Internet users, monitoring and controlling the Internet and their citizens' use of it, and again the beat goes on.

In the United States, the Clinton administration planned to create a government-wide security network of "electronic obstacles complete with monitors and analyzers to watch for potentially suspicious activity on federal computer systems." Who will define "potentially suspicious activity"? Add to that a former U.S. attorney general who pressured other nations to restrict, curb, and/or otherwise control encryption products. The government's desire to access information that may have intelligence value in the fight against terrorism and crime easily crosses the line of individual privacy rights. The quest to protect our security continues to challenge individual freedoms.

Add to all this the fact that in the United States, according to the FBI, major crimes are down and the trend is for fewer major crimes in the future. At the same time, the federal government's discretionary budget is decreasing. That means that federal agencies such as the FBI, NSA, CIA, and DIA must all fight for the same dollar. So they are all out there looking for new missions and new money to support their efforts and organizations.

Will the limited resources be applied in the right areas? Will monies be spent to combat the hacker threat as part of the terrorist threat—at a time when foreign nations' intelligence efforts continue to seek, through illicit means, our economic, technical, and—in an ever-more dangerous game—nuclear secrets? We are witnessing a period when the Russian bear is coming out of hibernation; real terrorists are gaining new weapons technologies and seeking to attack the interests of the free world in the old-fashioned way—by blowing it up!

National governments, especially the military elements, are gearing up for more war on terror and also information warfare in the 21st century. They are employing people with "clean" backgrounds and putting them in a bureaucracy with policies, procedures, etc. These are the "good hackers," also known as the information warriors of the future. Is this a useful strategy? Are there risks associated with this strategy?

As stated earlier, the U.S. President Ronald Reagan once called the Nicaraguan rebels "freedom fighters" while their government called them criminals and terrorists. The same holds true throughout the world. Those in power want to keep it and make the rules. Those that are left out of the governmental process want their voices to be heard—thus the conflict. As the nation-state begins to have less importance, its employees will fight to keep their power and conflicts will arise at the expense of personal liberties. Will these be tomorrow's freedom fighters or terrorists? The global hacker community, although often misguided as to worthwhile objectives in its attacks, is at least beginning to establish better communication lines among themselves.

The hackers of the world are using the Internet to communicate and to attack systems on a global scale. Many of the attacks are aimed at totalitarian governments, government agencies, and political parties or against the slaughter of animals for their fur, all of which can be considered politically motivated attacks. These are the worst kind and the most feared by nation-states. The attacks mounted by global hackers, based on a "call to arms" by hackers, against the government of Indonesia's websites is an example of what they can do and, more importantly, what is yet to come.

When growing up, these hackers were probably never given a coloring book and praised for coloring within the lines. These people, the really good ones, were given a set of crayons and a blank sheet of paper by their parents and told to draw something using their imagination. These are folks who, when attacking systems, write code on the fly, using new and imaginative ways to penetrate systems.

☐ ☐ ☐ ▬▬▬▬▬▬▬▬▬▬▬▬▬▬▬▬▬▬▬▬▬▬▬▬▬▬▬▬▬▬

The global hackers must rise above the level of juvenile delinquency and begin to go back to the true hacker mentality. They must also be the ones to help lead the defenses and lead the fight against tomorrow's terrorists, especially tomorrow's cyberterrorists and others.

▬▬▬▬▬▬▬▬▬▬▬▬▬▬▬▬▬▬▬▬▬▬▬▬▬▬▬▬▬▬ ☐ ☐ ☐

These hacker freedom fighters may be the ones we will need in the 21st century to protect our freedoms on a global scale. We won't be able to rely on our governments or on the military's info-warriors, for they will be protecting the nation-state and the status-quo—and it won't be the first time that has happened!

A final thought: We should have a global hacker appreciation day dedicated to all the hackers, phreakers, crackers, nuts, weirdos, and associated other human beings who surf, spam, use, misuse, and abuse the global information infrastructure. Because of their crazy personalities, criminal conduct, and all-around blatant disregard for rules, laws, and government controls, they have kept millions of people employed, made all our lives more interesting, our work more challenging, and our information security market—and world economies—growing. Furthermore, they will be the ones in the future to defend nation-states and corporations against cyberterrorist attacks from domestic and international groups.

Case Study

As the chief security officer (CSO) for a global corporation sponsoring experimentation on animals to research new cures for human diseases, you have been notified that a United Nations report has accused your corporation of the subjugation and abuse of employees working for the corporation in an African country. In addition, in the same week in which the report was released, there has been a contamination of the groundwater at your U.S. facility.

You fear that such news sent around the world will in fact cause some terrorist groups to single out your corporation for attack. What action, if any, would you take as the CSO responsible for the protection of these corporate assets worldwide from terrorist groups?

☐ ☐ ☐ ▬▬▬▬▬▬▬▬▬▬▬▬▬▬▬▬▬▬▬▬▬▬▬▬▬▬▬▬▬▬▬▬

One option always available is to do nothing, i.e., business as usual. After all, you are not aware of any specific threats against the corporation and you do have contingency emergency and disaster recovery plans in place in the event of some disaster, emergency, or other incident. If one occurs, you just activate the applicable plan already in place.

▬▬▬▬▬▬▬▬▬▬▬▬▬▬▬▬▬▬▬▬▬▬▬▬▬▬▬▬▬▬▬▬ ☐ ☐ ☐

This is a logical, cost-effective approach and does not call for an "alarmist" attitude or approach to what may be a nonexistent threat. However, to err on the side of caution, you have your security representatives at all global locations contact their liaison representatives in the police agencies at the local and nation-state levels to determine if they are aware of any new terrorist threats against one of the corporate locations.

You also contact the local FBI office in the United States responsible for the area where you reside, to ask them if they know of any types of threats against your corporation in particular or against your type of corporation or business in general. They reply about the general terrorist threats and probably add that some information may not be generally available to you because it is controlled information.

You decide to take advantage of the FBI agent's offer to provide a threat briefing to your staff and executive management. However, the information shared is not specific enough to help.

Not having enough information to confirm or discount a potential attack and recognizing that your company continues to receive negative publicity in areas where there are known organizations with a history of acting against your company, you may need to take a more proactive approach. You start by establishing a heightened security status throughout company global operations and specifically in the African nation-state and at the corporate headquarters. You implement that phase of the antiterrorist plan you have developed and maintained. Part of that plan includes the daily reading and analysis of the websites of those groups known to employ terrorist tactics against corporations they consider their adversary and potential target. For your corporation these would include all aggressive human rights websites as well as the websites of those classified as eco-terrorists and animal rights activists. You include Internet and other media searches for the name of your corporation linked with the words *action, terrorism,* and *terror.*

You take this approach because your corporation, formerly very low-key, now has been thrust onto the world news stage. Such identification, no matter how much the corporate relations staff tries to put a positive spin on it, now may make you an active terrorist target.

In addition, being an active target gives these terrorists the opportunity for better-than-normal publicity and the news limelight by attacking your corporation at one or more locations using the excuses offered by the news media reporting on your corporation. Many readers or watchers of the news will agree with the terrorist attacks and think the corporation deserves it after what the corporation and its management have done to their African employees and to the earth and animals.

"Global Trends 2015" Terrorism-Related Excerpts

The following items are terrorism-related items quoted directly from the National Intelligence Council's report "Global Trends 2015: A Dialogue About the Future with Nongovernmental Experts" (December 2000).

Transnational Terrorism (p. 50)

States with poor governance, ethnic, cultural, or religious tensions, weak economies, and porous borders will be prime breeding grounds for terrorism. In such states, domestic groups will challenge the entrenched government and transnational networks seeking safe havens.

At the same time, the trend away from state-supported political terrorism and toward more diverse, free-wheeling transnational networks—enabled by information technology—will continue. Some of the states that actively sponsor terrorism or terrorist groups today may decrease or even cease their support by 2015 as a result of regime changes, rapprochement with neighbors, or the conclusion that terrorism has become counterproductive. But weak states also could drift toward cooperation with terrorists, creating de facto new state supporters.

Between now and 2015, terrorist tactics will become increasingly sophisticated and designed to achieve mass casualties. We expect the trend toward greater lethality in terrorist attacks to continue.

Reacting to U.S. Military Superiority (p. 56)

Experts agree that the United States, with its decisive edge in both information and weapons technology, will remain the dominant military power during the next 15 years. Further bolstering the strong position of the United States are its unparalleled economic power, its university system, and its investment in research and development—half of the total spent annually by the advanced industrial world. Many potential adversaries, as reflected in doctrinal writings and statements, see U.S. military concepts, together with technology, as giving the United States the ability to expand its lead in conventional war-fighting capabilities.

This perception among present and potential adversaries will continue to generate the pursuit of asymmetric capabilities against U.S. forces and interests abroad as well as the territory of the United States. These U.S. opponents—state and such nonstate actors as drug lords, terrorists, and foreign insurgents—will not want to engage the U.S. military on its terms. Instead they will choose political and military strategies designed to dissuade the United States from using force or, if the United States does use force, to exhaust American will, circumvent or minimize U.S. strengths, and exploit perceived U.S. weaknesses. Asymmetric challenges can arise across the spectrum of conflict that will confront U.S. forces in a theater of operations *or on U.S. soil.*

Threats to Critical Infrastructure

Some potential adversaries will seek ways to threaten the U.S. homeland. The U.S. national infrastructure—communications, transportation, financial transactions, energy networks—is vulnerable to disruption by physical and electronic attack because of its interdependent nature and by cyberattacks because of the dependence on computer networks. Foreign governments and groups will seek to exploit such vulnerabilities using conventional munitions, information operations, and even weapons of mass destruction.

Terrorism

Much of the terrorism noted earlier will be directed at the United States and its overseas interests. Most anti-U.S. terrorism will be based on perceived ethnic, religious, or cultural grievances. Terrorist groups will continue to find ways to attack U.S. military and diplomatic facilities abroad. Such attacks are likely to expand increasingly to include U.S. companies and American citizens. Middle East– and Southwest Asian–based terrorists are the most likely to threaten the United States.[16]

Case Study

Your CEO has directed you to provide input to the corporate long-term business plan to include future terrorist threats against the corporation and a plan to mitigate them. How would you go about doing that? One approach would be the following.

- Identify general terrorist threats and attacks of the past and identify and project trends into the future.
- Identify all specific attacks against corporations in your industry, analyze them, and identify lessons learned.
- Identify and analyze all specific terrorist threats, attacks, and trends against your corporation on a global basis.
- Search government websites for information related to terrorist trends and all other useful information.
- Contact the law enforcement, security, and intelligence agencies in every nation where you have facilities or any point of presence and get their input and views on terrorism and specifically tactics, types of terrorist groups, goals, etc.
- Based on all your research, conduct a global risk analysis relative to the foregoing incorporating the specific risks by each corporate office or point of presence.
- Incorporate all the foregoing into an antiterrorist report for the CEO that includes an outline of your corporation's antiterrorist program.

By establishing the foregoing as a project plan and tasks, you can begin to look at terrorist trends that might impact the corporate assets in the future, allowing, don't forget, for the unknown factors and the worst-case scenario.

Summary

On the more optimistic side, as the old saying goes, "This too shall pass." The future of terrorism will continue to evolve as our global environment evolves. The terrorist threats will ebb and flow, increase and decrease based on the state of the countries involved, their allies, and their governments as well as on how fast their modernization progresses.

The left-wing-oriented political terrorists of old have faded as "religiously driven" terrorists have increased. As nation-states progress and modernize, providing the basic necessities and more for its citizens, and as oil-driven nation-states have less interest in those countries producing oil, other forms of terrorism will increase as today's religious zealots decline in the use of their terrorist tactics.

We will see an increase in the use of terrorist tactics by animal rights groups, save-the-earth terrorists, and the like as nation-states become more modern, high-technology devices and methods increase, and as their citizens become more prosperous, with more "recreational" time available to them.

Another type of group that may emerge as a terrorist group in the future is the union group. Such a group will employ terrorist tactics as employees are laid off and benefits slowly decline due to their high costs and the corporations strive to lower overhead costs to compete better in the global marketplace, which will continue to expand and be increasingly more competitive.

The terrorists called freedom fighters by some will probably maintain their current level, but they may even decline in the future as more democracies are created around the world.

Endnotes

[1] The Pope's attempted assassin, as quoted in Claire Sterling, *The Terror Network* (New York: Berkley Books, 1981), p. 297.

[2] New Oxford Electronic Dictionary by SHARP.

[3] For an excellent discussion on the power of individuals and groups, see James Dale Davidson and Lord William Moog-Rees, *The Sovereign Individual* (New York: Touchstone, 1997).

[4] From Caspar Weinberger and Peter Schweizer, *The Next War* (Washington, C: Regnery, 1996), p. xvii.

[5] See: http://home.att.net/~quotesexchange/terrorism.html

[6] See: http://www.military-quotes.com/Patton.htm

[7] See: http://www.usemb.se/terror/rpt2003/rpt2003.pdf

[8] Quoted from the *Whidbey News-Times* newspaper, Oak Harbor, Washington, Vol. 115, No. 10, January 18, 2006, p. 1

[9] See: http://www.earthliberationfront.com/

[10] See: http://www.greenpeace.org/international/

[11] See: http://www.inthebullpen.com/archives/2005/12/20/nytaclu-fbi-monitors-eco-terror-ist-groups/

[12] See: http://www.peta.org/

[13] See: http://www.furcommission.com/news/newsF04k.htm

[14] New Oxford American Dictionary, electronic version by SHARP.

[15] See: http://www.sniggle.net/anarchism.php

[16] See: https://www.cia.gov/terrorism/global_trends_2015.html

The Successful Security Professional in Fighting Terrorism—Now and in the Future

A good plan executed today is better than a perfect plan executed at some indefinite point in the future.[1]
—George S. Patton Jr.

This chapter discusses what the security professional must know and do in order to prepare properly to protect corporate interests and assets from terrorists now and in the future.

The role of the security professional in today's business or corporate world offers many serious challenges, none as serious or important as the challenge of defending your corporation successfully against the threat of terrorist attacks. Much of the security professional's future antiterrorist activities can be handled effectively and efficiently as part of a corporation's overall asset protection program. In fact, some antiterrorist tasks are redundant with that of an overall asset protection program. What a security professional in today's and tomorrow's global corporate environment must do as a leader in the protection of corporate assets, such as people, facilities/equipment, and information, will in many ways be based on defending those assets against future terrorist threats.

In preparation for ensuring that you can provide the best antiterrorist protection and general threat mitigation to corporate assets, there are certain things you must know and do, now and in the future, in order to become the best security professional. A major step in that process is establishing and managing an effective protection program that incorporates protective measures designed to combat the threat of terrorism and tailored to your business needs and operations. This includes taking advantage of the advice offered in Section II of this book.

Let's break down what is needed what you should know and what you should do into three topics:

- Education
- Experience
- Knowledge

What you should do for the corporation of course is to provide the baseline of a sound protection profile, including measures to protect against potential acts of terror, as was discussed in Section II of this book. In this chapter, we discuss what you personally should do as part of your career development as a security professional and not necessarily as a corporate security professional.

What You Should Know

One of the basic needs of a security professional is a good education. There are several types of "education," and this includes a formal education through colleges, universities, seminars, conferences, technical schools, and the like. There is also the "education"—the learning—you get out of just living, which we call experience.

Education

The formal education you receive might be a high-quality education or maybe one not as good as you could have received. Many place stock in certain colleges that are well known and have a good reputation, such as Cambridge and Oxford in the United Kingdom and Harvard and the Massachusetts Institute of Technology (MIT) in the United States. However, what is truly important is not where you go to school (although better schools open more job opportunities) but what you learned while there. After all, one goes to school to learn, right? No, not necessarily.

In today's world, a college degree is almost a necessity in order to be invited to interview for a position in a corporation. Of course, that depends on the job. For the position of a security professional, a college degree is becoming mandatory, to compare favorably with all the college-educated "others" against whom you are competing. Ironically, you have a better chance at that corporate security position with a bachelor of arts degree in, say, basket weaving than with just a high school diploma.

The higher in the corporate security professional career path you go, the more education required, in particular an education that includes business fundamentals, since many security professionals end up working in business and must understand how businesses work and how business professionals think and act. Many security professionals have degrees in a variety of majors, from business to a general arts and everything in between. Some who end up in the security profession get their degree in criminal justice. Over the last several years we have seen an increase in the number of colleges and universities offering majors in security management and security-related majors. This is an excellent trend, as long as it continues within the context of operating in a business environment and includes training and education in common business areas, which will probably continue.

The important thing is to get an education, at the very least an advanced general education. Other degrees (bachelor of science or bachelor of arts) may also be beneficial.

- *Social science*: This is basically the study of societies and social relationships. It provides awareness of and knowledge concerning how people and societies act and react. Since security is first and foremost a social profession, that is, dealing with people, social science offers a good baseline for a security professional.
- *Psychology*: This is the scientific study of the human mind and its functions, how behavior is affected in a given environment, and the attitudes of a person or group. Obviously, this knowledge would be very helpful to a security professional, that is, knowing how people think and how they react under given situations.

- *Business*: A degree in business with a major in some subfield such as economics or finance would be very helpful to a corporate security professional because that is the environment in which a security professional will be working.
- *Computer science*: With today's corporations being so dependent on high technology, a good understanding of that technology and its uses and how it operates would be a very constructive degree. After all, one of today's most important corporate assets is its information and the systems that store, display, process, and transmit that information. Furthermore, asset protection needs are quickly being filled by advanced technological devices—all based on the computer and its microprocessors of course.
- *Technology*: Advances in technology will aid the security professional to become more technologically savvy. That is, the security professional who best understands technology (and there are many technologies but information technology may be the most useful for the security professional to understand) will be positioned best for understanding the type and nature of problems the future security professional and security executive will face.

There are of course many other college or university majors that a security professional could receive a degree in. The foregoing are some of the most advantageous for the security professional in developing a career in the security profession, other than that of a security major of course.

However, in today's competitive world, a bachelor's degree is no longer enough. A master of art or master of science degree is essential to having an enhanced knowledge base and for providing that competitive edge for a higher-level security professional position in a corporation. So what would be the best graduate degree major? That depends on what your major was for your bachelor's degree.

Ideally, a person who wants a career and advancement in the security profession will have a bachelor's degree in security or other major, as just discussed. If so, the most logical step is for a security professional to receive a master of business administration (MBA) degree with a major in international business. Is this surprising? Think about it. You will be working in a corporate or business world where your corporation will be operating globally and competing in a global market. It is vitally important that you understand that world in order to provide the professional security services and support required for the corporation to defend itself against competitors and, of course, the terrorist who may threaten your corporation's assets.

Many of today's universities, at least in the United States; as well as conferences held in the United States and other nations are beginning to spend more time discussing terrorism, intelligence gathering, and the like.[2] Even the techniques gained through the experience of competitive intelligence gathering (visit SCIP.org) can be used to gather information about terrorists and their threats to your corporation.

Learning a Foreign Language

At the same time, you should consider a minor in a foreign language. Assuming you are a native English speaker, the primary language for today's business world and especially for tomorrow's world will also include Mandarin Chinese. Other possibilities include Spanish, if your corporation resides in the United States and does a great deal of business with Mexican and Central and South America.

When choosing a foreign language, look at the global business environment and choose a secondary language or two based on what languages are spoken the most in the global marketplace. Besides Chinese and Spanish, it may be French, Japanese, and/or German.

In today's and tomorrow's world, preoccupied with terrorism and antiterrorism measures, you should consider a Middle Eastern language if you want to become more of an expert in antiterrorism, e.g., Arabic (spoken by more than 150 million people round the world) or even Farsi (Persian language of Iran).

The important thing is to be able to converse in a major language (other than your native language) that is also used throughout the world by the most people in the most businesses or used mostly by terrorists. Although Arabic may not be a major language in today's or tomorrow's business world, it could prove the most useful in understanding some terrorist groups as well as in supporting the building of businesses in the Middle East after the terrorist threats hopefully subside in the future. After all, the Middle East has a rich history and culture, which are now being overshadowed by terrorism, and opportunities will arise once the terrorist threats are mitigated.

Technical Schools

Technical schools offer not only language classes but also classes in various types of computer science–related certifications and degrees. These schools specialize in various concentrations needed in today's business world. They offer the opportunity to enhance your knowledge base and to make you a more effective security professional.

As a security professional, especially one unfamiliar with terrorism or terrorist threats, you should take advantage of today's conferences, workshops, and courses on the topic. If you think your corporation is not at risk and you are unprepared to defend the corporate assets against terrorist attacks (and thus do not consider such education of value), then if you are wrong, corporate employees could die. Fighting terrorism is very serious. Those who ignore it may pay a very high price in the future.

Experience

As the old saying goes, "Experience is the best teacher." While this may be true, it is sometimes a difficult way to learn and to gain that necessary knowledge. However, the more experience you can get in all aspects of security and asset protection, the better position you will be in to defend those corporate assets against terrorism.

Your most important areas of experience in order to mitigate the threat of terrorist attacks successfully are, in no particular order of priority:

- Risk management, which includes threat assessments, vulnerability studies, and analyses relative to terrorism in general and terrorist groups in particular
- Physical protection against terrorist attacks: facilities engineering and designing against car bombs and "people bombs"
- Application of high-technology devices to security needs
- Liaison and an excellent working rapport with government officials (foreign and domestic, wherever corporate assets are located) involved in antiterrorist functions
- Cost-effective use of security resources, e.g., budgeting and analyses

The longer one works in the profession, the more experience gained. Furthermore, in today's and tomorrow's global working environment, it is imperative that security professionals begin to focus more on the protection of corporate assets against terrorist threats. Yes, threats posed by other criminals, such as thieves and fraudsters, are still important. However, looking at one's corporation's locales, ownership, goods produced, and the like will help the security professional determine how much emphasis to place on the terrorist threats specific to the corporation and on the general threats to employees and area facilities.

Knowledge

Looking at today's and tomorrows risks from terrorism as discussed in this book provides a direction as to what knowledge you as a security professional should have and maintain currency in. After all, you must know not only the enemies but also the environment in which you and they operate as well as how to defeat them by mitigating the risk of their attacking the corporate assets successfully.

□ □ □ ▬▬▬▬▬▬▬▬▬▬▬▬▬▬▬▬▬▬▬▬▬▬▬▬▬▬

The means by which enlightened rulers and sagacious generals moved and conquered others, that their achievements surpassed the masses, was advanced knowledge. Advanced knowledge cannot be gained from ghosts and spirits, inferred from phenomena, or projected from the measures of Heaven, but must be gained from men, for it is the knowledge of the enemy's true situation.[3]
—*Sun-tzu*

▬▬▬▬▬▬▬▬▬▬▬▬▬▬▬▬▬▬▬▬▬▬▬▬▬▬ □ □ □

So, as it relates to terrorism, what must a security professional know to tip the balance in his or her favor? The security professional should be able to identify and have a good working knowledge relative to:

- Today's specific terrorist groups that pose a threat to the corporation
- Tomorrow's potential terrorist groups
- Their current and potential future methods of operations
- The historical and current cultural, societal, and other background information on the identified terrorists and terrorist groups that can assist in gaining a better understanding of how they think and act
- The historical and current culture, history, society, and language of the areas where the corporation has a presence
- The history of past attacks, e.g., who, how, where, when, why, and what
- Risks posed to your corporation on a global basis but broken down into more specifics for each physical and logical location of the corporate assets
- How to establish an effective antiterrorist program
- How to test that program proactively and modify it accordingly using cost-effective and efficient methodologies and processes

This knowledge is always a work in progress because it is never-ending, and your knowledge base must always be kept current. So you must continue to read, study, and analyze as much as you can about terrorism and terrorist activities because they will be with us for the foreseeable future.

□ □ □

When there is a civil war where your people are working, one physical security metric rises above all others: keeping all your employees alive.[4]

—*John Hedly, head of group security for Nestle in Vevy, Switzerland*

□ □ □

Killing terrorists is the function of the military and law enforcement professionals. However, as a corporate security professional, you cannot rely on any government agency to protect your corporation all the time. You are responsible for defending the corporate assets against all threats, and that includes terrorist threats. This does not mean that you try to start a corporate antiterrorist SWAT team. However, it may be a consideration in nation-states where you cannot rely on the local military or law enforcement to support you with professional help in a timely manner. You may think this is extreme, but never discount any antiterrorist tasks out of hand. All options should be considered. Also consider the feasibility of subcontracting or outsourcing some of your antiterrorist tasks, e.g., extracting corporate employees from hazardous areas in a time of terrorist attacks.

Since we are already in what some call "a state of war" against terrorism—you may not think so but the terrorists certainly do—you must learn some important lessons about warfare. The classic book previously quoted, *The Art of War,* by Sun-tzu, is a good place to start. In addition you must begin now to meet future terrorist threats. In order to do so, and as a minimum, the corporate security professional should understand the following:

- Future global working environment
- Future high-technology advances and potential due to the "curve" and "singularity" and what nanotechnology may offer in terms of increased terrorist threats and defenses[5]
- Future plans and objectives of the corporation
- The philosophy of the OODA Loop[6] and how to use it to help defend against terrorism
- Basic defensive and offensive tactics of war
- Identify and learn about potential future terrorists and their potential methods of operation, some of them identified in this book

It is also your responsibility, as alluded to in Section II, to plan, prepare, and maintain the best state-of-the-art antiterrorist program consistent with the threats, vulnerabilities, and risks your corporation faces.

□ □ □

Never tell people how to do things. Tell them what to do and they will surprise you with their ingenuity.[7]

—*George S. Patton Jr.*

□ □ □

Security Professionalism and Terrorism

As part of being a security professional, you should also be involved in security- and antiterrorist-related associations and attend related seminars and conferences in order to assist in maintaining currency on this topic. This also gives you the opportunity to share information with other corporate security professionals and related terrorist experts. Once you have gained considerable experience, you may even consider giving something back by lecturing on corporate security and terrorism, based on your education, experience, and knowledge gained over the years. Furthermore, as you gain knowledge and progress up the career ladder, you should mentor less experienced security professionals so that they can assist in defending corporate assets against terrorism.

Case Study

You are updating your career development plan and have noted a weakness in the field of terrorism and antiterrorist defenses. You decide to increase your knowledge, education, and expertise in that area in the coming year. How should you begin to do that?

One approach would be to do the following.

- Set up a project plan using this chapter's topics of education, experience, knowledge, language skills, etc., to establish antiterrorism plan categories.
- Determine what antiterrorism information you should know, what experiences you should have, and so forth.
- Determine your antiterrorism skills and skill level.
- Identify your antiterrorism weaknesses.
- Identify those courses, skills, and the like that will eliminate your current weaknesses.
- Establish a list of tasks and a timetable for eliminating the weaknesses in your antiterrorist education, experience, and knowledge.
- Coordinate with your supervisor to gain support and budget to complete your project plan successfully, making a case for doing so based on establishing and managing a corporate antiterrorism program for the corporation.
- Implement the plan.

Summary

As a security professional, now is the time to begin a formal process to prepare yourself to be in a position to provide the best protection profile, including antiterrorism defenses for your corporation. That is done by understanding:

- The world in which we live
- Your corporation's global marketplace and locations
- Corporate future plans
- Future high-technology devices and equipment and their impact on defending against terrorism
- Current and future terrorist groups and their methods of attack
- The importance of gaining the best education, experience, and knowledge to help you develop and implement the best and most cost-effective antiterrorism plan consistent with the identified risk

Endnotes

[1] See: http://www.military-quotes.com/Patton.htm

[2] For example, entering the terms *universities* and *terrorism courses* into a popular search engine led to 4.5 million hits!

[3] From, Sun-tzu, *The Art of War*, new translation by Ralph D. Sawyer (New York: Barnes & Noble Books, 1994), pp. 229–233.

[4] Quoted from CSOONLINE.COM, "Where the Metrics Are," February 2005 issue.

[5] If these terms are unfamiliar to you, search the Internet for websites and books that address them.

[6] As with the terms *curve* and *singularity*, research this term and learn how to use this philosophy.

[7] See: http://www.military-quotes.com/Patton.htm

Closing Thoughts

All attempts to destroy democracy by terrorism will fail. It must be business as usual.[1]
—Margaret Thatcher

This chapter briefly summarizes the entire book and presents some candid commentary from the authors. It culminates our discussion about corporate security and terrorism. Hopefully we have provided a basic foundation on which to expand your knowledge of terrorism, some ideas as to how to defend against terrorist threats, and how to establish and manage a corporate antiterrorism program.

- Section I of this book gave some insight as to the history and identification of threats of terrorism so that you know what you are defending against.
- Section II explained what you should do to provide a basic foundation for establishing and managing a corporate protection program that incorporates methods to protect against terrorist threats. Essentially, the authors have attempted to give you the necessary tools to build an effective antiterrorism program to protect corporate assets from terrorist threats.
- Section III gave some ideas about what the future may hold based on the past and current trends vis-à-vis a global working environment and what future terrorist threats may be, as well as what a security professional should begin doing now to be prepared for future terrorists.

As we stated in the Preface, there are those who believe that terrorism is directed solely at governments and that government agencies and their military personnel are to defend against terrorism. This is a misconception. One just has to look at the 9/11 attacks, where terrorists went through the airports operated by corporations, through their non-governmental security systems, boarded commercial aircraft, and crashed them into corporately owned buildings housing corporate employees. Then of course there are the attacks in Indonesia (e.g., Jakarta hotel and Bali restaurants) and the London subway system.

Hear No Evil, See No Evil, Do No Evil

Over the years, the kidnappings and killings of numerous personnel throughout the world involved company employees, and other company assets were and still are targets for terrorists. They are the "soft targets," in contrast to fortified military bases and government buildings.

▢ ▢ ▢ ██

Justice without force is powerless; force without justice is tyrannical.
—*Blaise Pascal*

██ ▢ ▢ ▢

There are some security professionals whose corporate employees or facilities have not been attacked by terrorists. Consequently, they may be living with a false sense of security—a very dangerous mindset for a security professional under any circumstances. After all, they don't operate in hostile environments and don't make products that hurt people, animals, or the environment—they aren't political or religious and don't even allow smoking in their facilities and—oh, by the way—they also recycle trash! So terrorists don't hate them, or do they? Maybe not, maybe it's just a case of being in the wrong place at the wrong time, like thousands on the subways and trains or in the office buildings and restaurants of what was thought to be peaceful places.

Some security professionals and corporate management have as yet not gotten the message that the terrorist threat is real and that one day they or other corporate assets may be the target or part of the "collateral damage" of a terrorist attack. This is not paranoia but just "playing the odds"—also known as making objective risk management decisions.

▢ ▢ ▢ ██

When elephants fight, it is the grass that suffers.[2]
—*African proverb*

██ ▢ ▢ ▢

There are many around the world, even in the United States, who do not consider terrorism that great a threat, and, if a threat, it is certainly not a "war on terror" as stated by the current administration of U.S. President George W. Bush and many of his allies.

Some in the news media consider the current environment as being caused by some nation-states' actions, e.g., the United States. Regardless of the cause, terrorism is a global threat and must be dealt with. Failure to do so could lead to dire consequences. As security professionals, the old adage "Better safe than sorry" comes to mind and may be worthy of consideration, if for no other reason than to reduce the likelihood of becoming a victim of a terrorist event. Keep in mind the importance of contingency planning and doing so in accordance with solid risk management principals.

After an attack occurs, we once again see the folly of our ways when we apply security based only on defending against thieves, hackers, embezzlers, and the like. We also once again see how naïve we continue to be when it comes to defending against such attacks.

▢ ▢ ▢ ██

Well, one can argue semantics. But know this: The threat is real, gaining in sophistication, with new players joining and some leaving, and they want to inflict as much death and destruction as they possibly can—even if they die in the process!

██ ▢ ▢ ▢

Then of course throughout the world the politics of it all gets in the way and impedes our abilities to fight terrorism successfully on a global basis. North Korea and Iran and probably some other hostile two-bit nation-states will eventually have their nuclear weapons and conjure up reasons to use them. Even if they don't use them, they may sell the technology or actual devices to other terrorists.

We may scorn the ideal and beliefs of rogue nations with nuclear capabilities and terrorist organizations threatening global security. But make no mistake, they are prepared and willing to act, as evidenced by many recent past events. That is what makes them more dangerous than the "good ol' terrorists of the past," who were much more predictable and—as unusual as this may sound—much less violent and threatening.

Islamic Terrorists—Profiling, Racism, and Prejudices

Most nation-states, at least those with a democratic form of government, deplore singling out people or groups of people because of race, religion, or other factors that distinguish them from others. We expect and in fact demand that all people be treated equally. That is a basic foundation of a democratic form of government and is a quandary for antiterrorist professionals because, at the same time, it is difficult to escape the fact that today's terrorists, especially those we consider international or foreign terrorists, are Muslim extremists.

This is a fact, and it presents a dilemma to democratic forms of government. Can this profile be used to target potential terrorist threats officially? Officially, no, but is that logical? That is a double-edged sword. For example, if that profile were used exclusively, some other terrorists, albeit maybe Muslim, might get through the screening process, e.g., females. On the other hand, searching 90-year-old ladies at airport entry points may be taking the equality equation a bit too far, wasting valuable and limited antiterrorist resources.

As with the development and implementation of all security measures, we must achieve a balance based on understanding and managing risks. We must not waste valuable resources in fighting terrorism. Security professionals often have a bad reputation for making stupid, knee-jerk decisions. For example, the decision to keep metal forks and use plastic knives with airline food could be considered simple but foolish.

Another example: After 9/11, military personnel were stationed at the ends of major bridges, e.g., the Golden Gate Bridge in San Francisco. What was the purpose of that? Essentially, this was a public relations act. In a larger context it is impossible, and the public would not tolerate stopping each car and searching it before it went onto the Golden Gate Bridge. So a van full of explosives drives onto the bridge and stops, and the terrorist pushes a button and blows up the van and the bridge span. That cannot be stopped. Again, the case for understanding and managing risk must prevail over nonsensical "feel good" actions.

If modern terrorists want to live after committing an act of terror, then they use methods to protect themselves, making it harder for them to achieve their goals successfully. If they are willing to die, they become more of a threat and difficult to stop. Extremists make the job of those involved in security, protection of assets, counterterrorism, and law enforcement much more difficult today than it has ever been.

☐ ☐ ☐ ▬▬▬▬▬▬▬▬▬▬▬▬▬▬▬▬▬▬▬▬▬▬▬▬▬▬

The bottom line is this: If someone is willing to die while committing a terrorist act, it is almost impossible to stop that person from being successful!

▬▬▬▬▬▬▬▬▬▬▬▬▬▬▬▬▬▬▬▬▬▬▬▬▬▬ ☐ ☐ ☐

The current groups of Islamic extremist terrorists are not like those of old. There are other terrorists (nonreligious) of course, and we discussed them, but they are usually more localized and pose less of a risk of massive life and property destruction. Furthermore, they seem to want to live!

So what does this have to do with corporate security and terrorism? Think about such examples when you begin to implement an antiterrorist program. It should be logical and based on the threat and the associated risks, just as you would develop any other type of asset protection program—based on the related risks and costs.

Ridding the World of Terrorism

Is that possible—to rid the world of this threat? Probably not, but it is perhaps a worthy goal nonetheless. At least by focusing on this problem we can deal it a rather massive blow. One way to succeed may be to better organize nation-states in strong opposition to terrorism, albeit state-sponsored or independent groups, to fight terrorism in a much more committed way, that is, all nations using diplomatic, political, and military measures to their fullest extent.

Terrorists respect strength and power, and they continue to laugh at the weak resolve of Western nation-states and use that weakness to their advantage, e.g., Islamic extremist leaders preaching hatred in mosques in Western nations under the guise of freedom of speech.

Aggressive offenses will make the world's corporate assets much safer. However, to do so we must rely on the military prowess and political will of nation-states. As we have often seen, this is not so easily accomplished, even when such nation-states are themselves attacked. So the corporate assets throughout the world will continue to be potential targets of terrorists. As a corporate security professional, you have the lead in the effort to safeguard corporate assets! Don't wait for others to do it, for it may not get done.

Are We in a Religious War?

Today's terrorists are different, and some believe we are in the middle of another "Great Crusade." Many don't like to compare today's "Crusade" to the past crusades involving Christians and Muslims, but many of today's terrorists liken it to those days. If they perceive it to be that, then for all practical purposes it is that type of war.

☐ ☐ ☐ ▬▬▬▬▬▬▬▬▬▬▬▬▬▬▬▬▬▬▬▬▬▬▬▬▬▬

The terrorists practice a fringe form of Islamic extremism that has been rejected by Muslim scholars and the vast majority of Muslim clerics—a fringe movement that perverts the peaceful teachings of Islam. The terrorists' directive commands them

to kill Christians and Jews, to kill all Americans, and make no distinction among military and civilians, including women and children. This group and its leader—a person named Osama bin Laden—are linked to many other organizations in different countries, including the Egyptian Islamic Jihad and the Islamic Movement of Uzbekistan. There are thousands of these terrorists in more than 60 countries. They are recruited from their own nations and neighborhoods and brought to camps in places like Afghanistan, where they are trained in the tactics of terror. They are sent back to their homes or sent to hide in countries around the world to plot evil and destruction.
—*George W. Bush, President of the United States of America*

How much you as a security professional can do about it is of course dependent on the potential terrorist threats to your corporate assets and how much risk corporate management is willing to take to defend those assets. One thing is certain: Even if you take no additional safeguards, you should at least have conducted an objective risk assessment specific to the possible terrorist threats at all corporate locations worldwide and briefed executive management on the results, recommended action accordingly, and let them make the final decision.

In peace. As a wise man, he should make suitable preparation for war.[3]
—*Horace*

The threat of terror is different than other threats to corporate. It is not about someone stealing information or property, embezzling money, or not following company policies and procedures, thereby putting the company at risk. No, this should be taken much more seriously. Terrorist attacks if successful will accomplish three things:

- They will kill people—and they will try to kill as many as they can.
- They will destroy company property—and they will destroy as much as they can.
- They may destroy enough to eliminate the business or at least send it into bankruptcy.

The basic question to you is this: Can you and corporate management take the chance that "It can't happen here" or "It can't happen to me"?

Intelligence Collection and Coordination between Government Agencies and Corporations

What has been happening for many years is a lack of cooperation between agencies responsible for fighting crime and terror. With the realization of the need to change and the value of cooperation, we are seeing a change. Since 9/11, there has been both a national and international effort to improve this condition. However, progress is slow. Some believe it is getting better; others say nothing has changed.

The bottom line is this: If you as a corporate security professional want federal agency intelligence on the threat to your corporation or other vital antiterrorist information, the best you can do is to cultivate a personal relationship with one or more members of a federal agency that is in a position to provide you that information through an informal process. Therefore, it is vital for you to cultivate your own sources, such as some intelligence agents.

As a corporate security professional, aside from forming information-sharing and communication channels with counterterrorism federal agents, you have a responsibility to collect and develop your own information/intelligence through other sources. This includes using the largest source of information—the Internet.

Also keep in mind that the thrust of the government agencies, e.g., the federal government, is to help local governments prepare to react to terrorist attacks. It is difficult to find a federal government agency whose purpose is to assist corporations to prepare to defend against terrorist threats. Basically, you are on your own.

☐ ☐ ☐ ▬▬▬▬▬▬▬▬▬▬▬▬▬▬▬▬▬▬▬▬▬▬▬▬▬▬▬▬▬▬▬

> If you rely on any government agency (other than maybe the reactive fire department and medical services), you are building an antiterrorist program on false hopes and maybe even false promises.[4]

▬▬▬▬▬▬▬▬▬▬▬▬▬▬▬▬▬▬▬▬▬▬▬▬▬▬▬▬▬▬▬ ☐ ☐ ☐

Also remember that it is vitally important that your personnel security program provide screening for potential terrorists based on the current and any future terrorist profiles. This is a touchy area to be sure but, realistically, one that will help mitigate security risks.

Is this going too far? That depends on how much you consider terrorism a threat to your corporate resources and how aggressive you want to be in defending those assets against terrorists.

Local Law Enforcement Fighting Terrorism and the Impact on Your Corporation

Fighting terrorism, which includes defending the homeland against terrorist attacks, requires the combined efforts of the nation-state's citizens, businesses, and law enforcement at all levels of government. One of the results of the 9/11 attacks against the United States was the creation of the Homeland Security Department (HSD). More than 20 federal government agencies were integrated into it. As with any bureaucracy, the HSD has continued to broaden its role and now encompasses more than ever before:

> *Before 9/11, we had 47 agencies, congressional committees, and presidential commissions that could and did interfere with, exert control over, and generally waste the time of the agencies that were trying to fight terrorism. Once the horror of 9/11 was fully realized, our government went into action—and*

made itself bigger, more complicated, and a hell of a lot slower to move.
Within one short year, there were 57 agencies, committees, and commissions
that would do the work that 47 had been doing. Unbelievable![5]

The problem of combating terrorism and protecting people and assets against acts of terror is not simple. Based on the preceding quote, it is clear that a corporation must rely first on itself to protect and defend the corporate assets directly. Furthermore, the first government responders to any incident of terror will come from the local emergency response agencies, such as the health, fire, and safety services. These organizations are wonderful entities with great intentions and capabilities to serve. Dealing with large-scale acts of terror taxes them greatly.

□ □ □ ▬▬▬▬▬▬▬▬▬▬▬▬▬▬▬▬▬

WASHINGTON—U.S. Newswire. The nation's current homeland security strategy, by failing to sufficiently incorporate the advice, expertise, or consent of state, tribal, and local public safety organizations, is fundamentally flawed, according to a new report released … by the International Association of Chiefs of Police (IACP).

▬▬▬▬▬▬▬▬▬▬▬▬▬▬▬▬▬ □ □ □

Federal and state governments are better positioned to respond to large-scale events; however, their focus is mostly on critical infrastructure and the health and welfare of citizens, not on the protection of business assets.

As a corporate security professional, you must attempt to understand this new terrorist-filled world in which we live, work, and play and how it may adversely affect the company you support.

Summary

- Terrorism will continue on a global scale for the foreseeable future.
- Targets will continue to be soft targets, such as corporate assets (e.g., people, facilities).
- Those willing to die for their cause are difficult to stop.
- Although they are difficult to stop, you can minimize the risks of their successful attacks.
- In protecting your corporate assets from a successful terrorist attack, you cannot rely on any proactive assistance from anyone, e.g., federal agencies.
- As a corporate security professional, it is up to you to provide an antiterrorist program for your corporation that mitigates all logical risks to corporate assets.

Endnotes

[1] See: http://home.att.net/ quotesexchange/terrorism.html
[2] See: http://www.quoteland.com/topic.asp?CATEGORY_ID=152
[3] See: http://www.quoteland.com/topic.asp?CATEGORY_ID=152

[4] Some help is available in the form of training. See: http://transit-safety.volpe.dot.gov/ Training/Courses/CourseDesc/security.asp

[5] Excerpt from Colonel David Hunt, U.S. Army (Ret.), *They Just Don't Get It: How Washington Is Still Compromising Your Safety and What You Can Do About It* (New York: Crown Forum, 2005), p. 98.

Appendix A
Terrorism Definitions and Concerns

Definitions

United States—FBI Definition

Terrorism is the unlawful use of force or violence against persons or property to intimidate or coerce a government, the civilian population, or any segment thereof, in furtherance of political or social objectives.

United States—CIA Definition

International terrorism is terrorism conducted with the support of foreign governments or organizations and/or directed against foreign nations, institutions, or governments.

United States—Definition of the Departments of State and Defense

Terrorism is premeditated, politically motivated violence perpetrated against a noncombatant target by subnational groups or clandestine state agents, usually intended to influence an audience. International terrorism is terrorism involving the citizens or territory of more than one country.

What Is a Terrorist?

- Don't confuse terrorists with the "normal" criminals.
- A terrorist is one who causes intense fear; one who controls, dominates, or coerces through the use of terror.

Concerns

Why Use Terrorist Methods?

- When those in power do not listen
- When there is no redress of grievances
- When individuals or groups oppose current policy
- When no other recourse is available
- When a government wants to expand its territory
- When a government wants to influence another country's government

What Is a Terrorist Act?

- What is the difference between terrorist and freedom fighter?
- Does "moral rightness" excuse violent acts?
- Does the cause justify the means?
- When the government in office says it's a terrorist act?

Results of Terrorist Actions

- Increase in security
- Governments restrict freedoms
- Awareness of grievances by the population
- Death, damage, and destruction
- Governments listen
- Possible social or political changes

Terrorist Technology Threat Environment

- More reliability on information to run businesses and governments
- Larger concentration on information that can be accessed
- Security as add-on to technology—more weaknesses
- Destruction of automated information can cripple a government, business, and the economy
- Information that can be stolen and theft is not known
- Computers operating at low frequencies
- Electronic circuits vulnerable to interference
- A gun that transmits a high-energy beam (e.g., radio wave, microwave) can disable computer systems
- Techno-terrorism
- Causing more disruption
- Promotes cause with less negative public image
- Can be used by more terrorists with less funding

Techno-Terrorist: Some Possibilities?

- Using a computer, could penetrate a control tower computer system and send false signals to aircraft, causing them to collide in midair or crash into the ground
- Using fraudulent credit cards to finance their operations
- Penetrating a financial computer system to divert millions of dollars to finance their activities
- Bleaching $1 bills and using a color copier to reproduce them as $100 bills and flood the market with them to destabilize the dollar
- Using cloned cellular phones and computers over the Internet to communicate with encryption to protect their transmissions
- Using virus and worm programs to shut down vital government and business computer systems
- Changing hospital records, causing patients to die because of an overdose of medicine or the wrong medicine
- Penetrating a government computer, e.g., IRS, which begins issuing checks to all citizens
- Destroying critical government computer systems that process tax returns
- Penetrating computerized train-routing systems, causing passenger trains to collide
- Taking over telecommunications links or shutting them down
- Taking over satellite links to broadcast their messages over televisions and radios

Appendix B
Recommended Readings and References

Davidson, James Dale, and Mogg-Rees, Lord William, *The Sovereign Individual: Mastering the Transition to the Information Age*. New York: Touchtone, 1997.

Ezeldin, General Ahmed Galal, *Terrorism and Political Violence: An Egyptian Perspective*. Chicago: University of Illinois at Chicago, 1987. (Translation). Originally published: Cairo: Dar El Houriah for Journalism, Publishing, and Printing, 1985.

Faridi, F. R. (editor), *Islamic Principles of Business Organization and Management*. Kuala Lumpur: S. Abdul Majeed and Co., 1997.

Flood, Susan (editor), *International Terrorism: Policy Implications*. Chicago: University of Illinois at Chicago, 1991.

Friedman, Thomas L., *The World Is Flat: A Brief History of the Twenty-First Century*. New York: Farrar, Straus, and Giroux, 2005.

Garreau, Joel, *The Radical Revolution: The Promise and Peril of Enhancing Our Minds, Our Bodies—And What It Means to Be Human*. New York: Doubleday, 2004.

Holms, John Pynchon, with Burke, Tom, *Terrorism: The Complete Book of Terrorist Groups, Their Deadly Weapons, Their Innocent Targets, and Their Terrible Crimes*. New York: Windsor, 1994.

Hunt, Colonel David. *They Just Don't Get It: How Washington Is Still Compromising Your Safety—And What You Can Do About It*. New York: Crown Forum, 2005.

Jacobs, Harold (editor), *Weatherman*. New York: Ramparts Press, 1970.

Jones, Andy, and Ashenden, Debi, *Risk Management for Computer Security*. Oxford, UK: Elsevier Butterworth-Heinemann, 2005.

Kovacich, Gerald L., and Halibozek, Edward P., *The Managers Handbook for Corporate Security*. Boston: Butterworth-Heinemann, 2003.

Kurzweil, Ray, *The Age of Spiritual Machines*. New York: Viking, 1999.

Rivers, Gayle, *The War Against Terrorists: How to Win It*. New York: Charter Books, 1986.

Sterling, Claire, *The Terror Network*. New York: Berkley Books, 1981.

Toffler, Alvin, and Toffler, Heidi. *War and Antiwar: Survival at the Dawn of the 21st Century*. New York: Little Brown, 1993.

Weinberger, Caspar, and Schweizer, Peter. *The Next War*. Washington, D.C., Regnery, 1996.

Appendix C
Information Warfare and Terrorism—Some Thoughts

The attacks on the World Trade Center, the Pentagon, Spain, and the United Kingdom's transit systems, hotels, and restaurants, car bombs, and the like, though extreme, were conventional terrorist attacks. However, some of the retaliatory action that took place in the following days and weeks occurred in cyberspace. The outcome of these actions must be judged by the results. However, the attacks were hopefully also a wakeup call to information systems security (InfoSec) professionals and others.

Information warfare attacks and defenses related to terrorism are being implemented. The following are just a few of the information warfare–related examples of such activities that occurred within just a few days of 9/11.

- *Hacker Defaces Thousands of Sites in WTC Protest*: A hacker defaced thousands of websites and rerouted traffic to the attacker's website. Part of the message included: "Fluffi Bunni Goes Jihad" and "We're Coming for you Oslahmamama."
- The Chaos Computer Club, a German hacker group, ironically condemned the "use of the Internet as a battleground" and thought "communication networks are essential for contributing to international understanding."
- *Crackers Prepare Retaliation for Terrorist Attack*: The "Dispatchers" stated that they have disabled ISPs in Palestine and have as a goal destroying ISPs in Afghanistan. They claim to have over 1,000 computers under their control. They are allegedly joined by crackers in the United States, the UK, Russia, Brazil, Mexico, China, Australia, Canada, India, Egypt, Germany, Holland, and Denmark.
- *Jewish Group Seeks Crackdown on "Terrorists" Online*: B'nai B'rith in Canada is allegedly urging law enforcement officials to "crack down" on websites that help in the promotion of Islamic terrorists.
- *Senate OKs Use of Carnivore Against Terrorism*: The U.S. Senate has approved the use of the FBI software program "Carnivore" for e-mail surveillance during their investigations of terrorism.
- *Lawmaker Wants Cybersecurity in Antiterrorism Plans*: A U.S. congressional body proposes that the Director of Homeland Security address electronic attacks as part of U.S. plan to combat terrorism.
- *Taliban Threatens U.N. Techies*: They threaten to kill U.N. workers using computers and communications equipment inside Afghanistan.

There are many threats to information, networks, and information infrastructures that we depend on in our information-based world. Increasingly in the present environment, one of the most dangerous out there is terrorists. We already have seen that they care little for their own lives or their innocent victims. So do you think they would have any concern about destroying your networks and the information infrastructures we all depend on, whether it be the primary target or just in the line of fire? You must first understand terrorism and then begin an aggressive, proactive defensive posture to protect the networks and information that you are responsible for defending. Remember, no one and no systems are immune to attacks.

Terrorist Information Warfare Tactics

As we have noted, the purpose of any act of terrorism is to terrorize the target audience. The motivation of a terrorist is to undermine the effectiveness of a government by whatever means it chooses. This includes attacking nongovernment facilities and networks, as we have seen. It is worth remembering that a terrorist in one country is a freedom fighter in another and, as a result, that there is no stereotype. When you take into account the different cultures around the world and the differing political regimes that exist, it is easy to understand that a wide variety of actions may be terrorist actions when carried out for political means.

Let us first address a term that is in current and widespread use: cyberterrorism. While it can be accepted that this term can be used to convey a general meaning, it is not possible to accept the current use of the term to be anything more. The definition of terrorism that was adopted by the "gateway model" in the United Nations in the spring of 1995 is as follows.

> A terrorist *is any person who, acting independent of the specific recognition of a country, or as a single person, or as part of a group not recognized as an official part of division of a nation, acts to destroy or to injure civilians or destroy or damage property belonging to civilians or to governments in order to effect some political goal.*

> Terrorism *is the act of destroying or injuring civilian lives or the act of destroying or damaging civilian or government property without the expressly chartered permission of a specific government, thus, by individuals or groups acting independently or governments on their own accord and belief, in the attempt to effect some political goal.*

> All *war crimes will be considered acts of terrorism.*

> Attacks on *military installations, bases, and personnel will not be considered acts of terrorism but, instead, acts by freedom fighters that are to be considered a declaration of war towards the organized government.*

Given current events it is noteworthy that a very different definition was offered at the Fifth Islamic Summit that was convened to discuss the subject of international terrorism under the auspices of the UN:

> Terrorism *is an act carried out to achieve an inhuman and corrupt* (mufsid) *objective, and involving threat to security of any kind, and violation of rights acknowledged by religion and mankind.*

It is notable that in the main body of this definition, there is no reference to the nation-state, something that, in the West, would be fundamental to any understanding of terrorism. The author then goes on to make a number of additional points to clarify the definition, the most significant of which are:

    a. *We have used the term* human *instead of* international *for the sake of wider consensus, official or otherwise, so as to emphasize the general human character of the statement.*
    b. *We have referred to various types of terrorism with the phrase "security of any kind."*
    c. *We have mentioned the two criteria, i.e., religious and human, first to be consistent with our belief and then to generalize the criterion.*

This totally different approach to the issue of terrorism is significant and a clear reminder to the nation-states that consider themselves to be Western that not all cultures view the issue in the same manner as Americans.

Even given these diverse views of the meaning of terrorism, there is an underlying trend of physical destruction and of the actions being of such a magnitude and type as to cause "terror" to the people. This does not fit well within the "cyber" environment because there is no direct physical destruction (other than 0s and 1s), and without the effect of the bullet, or the blast, or the carnage of the bomb, the "terrorization" of the people is difficult in our current state of technological advancement. It is more likely that as our cultural values change and we become more highly dependent on technology than we currently are, the cyberterrorist in the true sense will come into being. For example, today and more so into the future, as we increase our proliferation and dependence on telemedicine, a terrorist may:

- Attack a computer system, shutting off life support to patients.
- Change their dosages of medicine, killing them in the process.
- Manipulate blood bank information, causing the wrong blood type to be given to patients and resulting in numerous deaths.

What Do They Want to Achieve?

Let us first look at what a terrorist will want to achieve through the use of the Internet. This may be one thing or multiple things. The terrorist organization may wish to use the medium for the transmission of communications between individuals and groups within the organization. Look at the potential:

- The terrorist has been offered all of the facilities that the Cold War spy always dreamed of. It is possible to be anonymous on the Internet, with "pay for use" mobile phones and free Internet accounts.

- In many cases, no attempts are made by the service providers to ascertain that the details provided by a customer are real and actually relate to the user.
- Once the user is online, there are a number of ways in which a user can further disguise his or her identity.
- Anonymous remailers and browsers can disguise the identity of the user.
- High-grade encryption is freely available that law enforcement cannot yet break, and (particularly in the West) civil liberty groups want to ensure that this situation remains so. The desire of civil liberty organizations to maintain the privacy of messages on the Internet actually has nothing to do with terrorists— they have the liberty and privacy of the individual at heart, but the terrorist is just one of the winners of the pressure that they seek to exert.

A well-reported example of such terrorist use of the Internet is the activity of Osama Bin Laden, who is reported to have employed steganography (the ability to hide data in other files or the slack space on a disk) to pass messages over the Internet. It was reported that Bin Laden was "hiding maps and photographs of terrorist targets and posting instructions for terrorist activities on sports chat rooms, pornographic bulletin boards, and other websites." According to another report, couriers for Bin Laden who have been intercepted have been found to be carrying encrypted floppy disks. Other references to the use of the Internet by Bin Laden describe a new form of the Cold War "dead-letter box," which was a predetermined place where one agent deposited information to be collected by another agent. A June 2001 report indicated that Bin Laden was suspected of using encryption for his messages for at least five years.

According to reporter Jack Kelley, the former FBI director Louis Freeh stated that "Uncrackable encryption is allowing terrorists—Hamas, Hezbollah, Al-Qaeda (another name for Bin Laden's organization), and others—to communicate about their criminal intentions without fear of outside intrusion." Kelley also reported that according to other unnamed officials Bin Laden's organization uses money from Muslim sympathizers to purchase computers from stores or by mail, after which easy-to-use encryption programs are downloaded from the Internet. As evidence, they site the case of Wadih El Hage, one of the suspects in the 1998 bombing of two U.S. embassies in Africa, who is reported to have sent encrypted e-mails under a number of aliases, including "Norman" and "Abdus Sabbur" to associates of Al Qaeda.

Also cited as evidence is the case of Ramzi Yousef, the man convicted of masterminding the World Trade Center bombing in 1993, who is reported to have used encryption to hide details of the plot to destroy 11 U.S. airlines. The computer was found in his Manila apartment in 1995 and passed to U.S. officials who cracked the encryption and foiled the plot. The same report goes on to say that two of the files took more than a year to crack. This is in itself revealing because it gives some indication of the level of effort that government and law enforcement agencies are prepared to invest in their efforts to bring to justice this type of criminal as well as the level of effort and sophistication being used by terrorists.

It is clear that Osama Bin Laden is also skilled in the use of the media to promote the aims and aura of the organization. This is evident from his use of the press to provide interviews. He is a well-educated and, through his family, a wealthy man. He has a good understanding of the way in which the media can be used to influence public opinion and has used the media to promote his philosophy.

Tactics

Having identified some of the types of effects that terrorists might want to use the Internet to achieve, let us now examine the tactics and tools they would employ to realize their aims. In the case of Osama Bin Laden, he is apparently communicating via the Internet using steganography and encryption. By dealing with the two issues separately for the purposes of describing the tactics, we in no way mean to imply that steganography and encryption do not go together, in fact, quite the reverse is true. If you are paranoid and you want to make sure your messages get through undetected and in a condition that is unreadable to anyone that should guess their presence, then the combination of techniques is a powerful one.

The tactics described next are used by cyberterrorists (those who use cyberspace) and techno-terrorists (those who use technology but not in cyberspace) to commit their acts of terror.

Data Hiding

The term that is commonly applied to the hiding of data is *steganography*. The word, derived from Greek, literally means "covered writing." The concept covers a vast array of methods of secret communications that conceal the very existence of the message. In real terms, steganography is the technique of taking one piece of information and hiding it within another. Computer files, whether images, sound recordings, text and work processing files, or even the medium of the disk itself all contain unused areas where data can be stored. Steganography takes advantage of these areas, replacing them with the information one wishes to hide. The files can then be exchanged, with no indication of the additional information that is stored within. A selected image, perhaps of a pop star, could itself contain another image or a letter or map. A sound recording of a short dialogue could contain the same information. In an almost-strange twist in the use of steganography, law enforcement, the entertainment industry, and the software industry have all started to experiment with steganography to place hidden identifiers or trademarks in images, music, and software. This technique is referred to as *digital watermarking*.

How does it work? Well, the idea is simple. You want to hide one set of data inside another, but the way to achieve this will vary depending on the type of material in which you are trying to hide your data. If you are hiding your data in the unused parts of a disk, then you are not, primarily, constrained by the size of the data, because you can break it into a number of sections that can be hidden in the space. Storage space on disks is divided into "clusters," which in Microsoft DOS and Windows file systems are of a fixed size. When data is stored to the disk, even if it requires less storage than the cluster size, an entire cluster is reserved for the file. The unused space from the end of the file to the end of the cluster is called the *slack space*. For DOS and older Windows systems that use a 16-bit file allocation table (FAT), this results in very large cluster sizes for large partitions. As an example, if the partition on the disk was of a 2-Gb size, then each cluster would be 32 Kb. If the file being stored on the disk required only 8 Kb, the entire 32-Kb storage space would be allocated, resulting in 24 Kb of slack space in the cluster. In later versions of the Microsoft Windows operating system, this problem was resolved (or at least reduced) by the use of a 32-bit FAT that supported cluster sizes of as small as 4 Kb, even for very large partitions.

Tools to enable you to do this are available on the Internet for free. Examples of this type of tool include the following.

- *S-Mail:* This is a steganographic program that will run under all versions of DOS and Windows. The system uses strong encryption and compression to hide data in EXE and DLL files. (Yes, it is possible to hide files within full working programs; after all, that is what a virus does.) The software has a pleasant user interface and has functions in place to reduce the probability of its hiding scheme being detected by pattern or ID string scanners (tools that can identify the use of steganographic techniques).
- *Camouflage:* This is a Windows-based program that allows you to hide files by scrambling them and then attaching them to the end of the file of your choice. The camouflaged file then appears and behaves like a normal file and can be stored or e-mailed without attracting attention. The software will work for most file types and includes password protection.
- *Steganography Tools 4:* This software encrypts the data with one of the following: IDEA, MPJ2, DES, 3DES, and NSEA in CBC, ECB, CFB, OFB, and PCBC modes. The data is then hidden inside either graphics (by modifying the least significant bit of BMP files), digital audio (WAV files), or unused sectors of floppy disks.

If you are attempting to hide data in files, no matter what the type, then you have two options.

- You can hide your material to the file by adding to the data that is already there and thus increase the size of the file.
- You can replace some of the data that is already in the file with the information you want to hide and retain the same file length but have a slightly reduced quality in the original representation.

To explain this in more detail, if you are using an image file to hide data, the normal method is to use the "least significant bit" of each information element as a place to store hidden data. In doing this, the changes to the image are so subtle as to be undetectable to the naked eye. But the changes are significant enough for steganographic software to be able to hide relatively large quantities of information in the image and also for the software to recognize a pattern within the image that it can use to reveal hidden material.

It would not be unrealistic to hide the contents of this section in a relatively small image.

Here are some other methods that can be used to hide data in other types of files.

- Programs such as Snow, which can conceal messages in ASCII text by appending white spaces to the end of lines. Conventional text normally has 80 columns of information to the page. When we save a text file of information that we have created on a computer screen, we do not use all 80 of the columns—if the word at the end of the line falls short of the 80th column, then we get a carriage return character after the last letter. If it is the last line of a paragraph, then there may be a considerable number of unused columns in the row. The Snow program fills in all of these unused spaces and uses the least significant bit of each of the bytes to hold an element of the hidden message.

- Software such as wbStego lets you hide data in bitmaps, text files, HTML files, and PDF files. The data is encrypted before it is embedded in the carrier file.
- If you want to hide messages in music and sound files (MP3), then software such as MP3Stego will hide information in these files during the compression process. The data is compressed, encrypted, and then hidden in the MP3 bit stream. Although MP3Stego was written with steganographic applications in mind, again there is the potential for it to be used for the good of the music and movie industries by allowing them to embed a copyright symbol or watermark in the data stream. If an opponent discovers your message in an MP3 stream and wishes to remove it, that individual can uncompress the bit stream and recompress it, which will delete the hidden information. The data hiding takes place at the heart of the encoding process, namely in the *inner loop*. The inner loop determines the quantity of the input data and increases the process step size until the data can be coded with the available number of bits. Another loop checks that the distortions introduced by the process do not exceed the predefined threshold.
- The Linux enthusiast can use programs such as StegFS, a steganographic file system for Linux. Not only does it encrypt data, it also hides it so that it cannot, given current detection techniques, be proven to be there.

This plethora of software choices and encoding schema gives the terrorist a wide set of options to suit the chosen method of communication. If the selected method of covering the communications is through a newsgroup that exchanges music, then an MP3 encoder is most sensible; after all, if the other users of the newsgroup have the same taste in music as the sender and recipient of the message, there is no problem—they can download the file, play it, enjoy it, and yet be totally unaware of the hidden content. If the chosen method of communication involves image sharing, then, again, the images can be posted in public, with anyone able to view the images but only those aware of the additional content likely to use tools to extract it.

On the plus side, it is increasingly possible to detect the use of steganography. Software is now becoming available that will identify the use of an increasing range of steganographic packages.

One example of a tool that can detect the use of steganography is the Steganography Detection and Recovery Toolkit (S-DART), which was sponsored by the U.S. Air Force Research Laboratories and commissioned by WetStone Technologies, Inc. The aim of this kit was to develop algorithms and techniques for the detection of steganography in digital image files, audio files, and text messages. The aim of the project was to develop a set of statistical tests that could detect the use of steganography and also identify the underlying method employed to hide the data.

Another tool is Stegdetect, an automated tool for detecting steganographic content in images. It is capable of detecting a number of the different steganographic methods used to embed hidden information in JPEG images. Currently, the methods that can be detected by this software package are jsteg, jphide for Unix and Windows, invisible secrets, and outguess 01.3b.

While these tools are still limited in the range of data-hiding techniques they can detect, this will increase rapidly. However, as with viruses and most other forms of malicious code on the Internet, the detection tools will always lag behind the tools that provide the capability.

Cryptography

If you are a terrorist and you want to communicate using the Internet, you are probably not going to risk your life or your liberty should people be unable to recognize the use of steganography on its own. Because steganographic software is not interested in the type of material it is incorporating into the carrier file, it will hide an encrypted message just as happily as it will hide a clear text message.

An encryption program scrambles information in a controlled manner through the use of a cryptographic key. In the past, you sent a message encrypted with a particular key to someone and they had to be in possession of the same key to decrypt the message. This is known as *symmetrical cryptography*. This, unfortunately, meant that you had to communicate the key to the person to whom you were sending the message.

This was achievable for governments that have the infrastructure to distribute the cryptographic keys in a secure manner; however, this type of approach is just not realistic for the general public to consider. It is only in recent years that the technology has increasingly been found in the public domain. Perhaps the best known of the publicly available high-grade encryption systems is Pretty Good Privacy (PGP), the system developed by Phil Zimmerman. As a result of the prominence that PGP has achieved, our discussion concentrates on this system.

PGP is a public-key encryption software package that was initially intended for the protection of electronic mail. PGP was published domestically in the United States as a freeware offering in 1991 and was quickly adopted all over the world, with the result that it has become the de facto worldwide standard for encryption of e-mail.

The author of the software was under investigation for about three years by authorities (the U.S. Customs Service) who were investigating a possible breach in the arms control relating to the export of weapons, which includes high-grade encryption. It is one of the nonsensical facts of the age of technology that it was considered an offense to export the software package that incorporated the encryption algorithm, but there seemed to be no problem with leaving the country with the algorithm printed on a T-shirt. The investigation was finally closed in January 1996 without Zimmerman's being indicted.

It is interesting that in at least one interview, Zimmerman stated, as part of the rationale for the development of PGP, that the software was now used all over the world, particularly in Central America and Burma, by the government in exile from Tibet and by human rights groups and human rights activists who were documenting the atrocities of death squads and keeping track of human rights abuses. He went on to state that he had been told by these groups that if the governments involved were to gain access to the information that had been encrypted, all of the individuals involved would be tortured and killed.

Propaganda

Another reason that a terrorist organization may use the Internet is to spread the organization's message and further their cause. For this, the Internet is an outstanding tool. It is the most widely used, uncontrolled medium that has international reach. The number of organizations that have exploited this reach and lack of censorship is huge. Some of the better examples are the Provisional Irish Republican Army (PIRA), the Euskadi Ta Askatasuna (ETA), the Mexican Zapatistas, and the Chechen rebels.

The PIRA has a well-founded presence on the Internet through the auspices of its political wing, Sinn Fein, and publications with a strong online presence, such as An

Phoblact. Websites that support the aspirations and the "cause" of the PIRA can be found in a number of countries. Some good examples are the Sinn Fein home page and Sinn Fein Online. Other informative sites can be found at the Irish Republican Network and the Trinity Sinn Fein website. In addition to the large number of sites that provide information on the IRA, other sites provide a different perspective on the conflict in Northern Ireland, with some of them providing a more balanced view than others, although undoubtedly that statement in itself demonstrates a prejudice because other people would take a different view of the balance of reporting on the sites. The conflict in Northern Ireland is one of the longest-running "terrorist" actions that has taken place in the English-speaking world and, not surprisingly, attracts a lot of comment and debate and presence on the web. While the PIRA is the best known of the groups that represent one side of the conflict, a large number of other groups claim to be active in the province. The main ones are:

- Continuity Irish Republican Army
- Combined Loyalist Military Command
- Irish National Liberation Army
- Irish People's Liberation Organization
- Irish Republican Army
- Loyalist Volunteer Force
- Real Irish Republican Army
- Ulster Defense Association
- Ulster Freedom Fighters

The majority of these also have, to a greater or lesser degree, a web presence. Some of the more notable of these are:

- The Irish People's Liberation Organization, which represents another view of the republican perspective
- The Ulster Loyalist web page, which represents a loyalist view
- The Ulster Volunteer Force (UVF) presence with the UVF page of the Loyalist Network.

In addition to all of these many partisan views of the situation, there are a number of sites that attempt to provide a "neutral" view of the situation. Examples of these can be found at Rich Geib's Universe or the Irish Republican Army Information Site. Other sites that provide insight into the attitudes of and toward the various parties in the province can be found at Vincent Morley's flags web page and a unionist Mural Art from Belfast page.

An example of a terrorist site from another part of Europe is the case of the Euskadi Ta Askatasuna (ETA). This violent terrorist group, which lays claim to a portion of northern Spain and southern France, has its own web presence to present the case for its grievances, to explain culture and history, to justify its actions, and to seek support. As with other, similar groups, it has its supporters and detractors, both of which use the web to try to influence the opinion of their readers.

In the case of supporters of ETA and the Basque state, which they themselves refer to as "Euskal Herria," the primary web pages are the Euskal Herria Journal, which promotes itself as a Basque journal and puts forward the aims and expectations of the group that it represents, and the Basque Red Net, which puts forward a very well-developed argument based on the culture and history of the area.

A view of ETA from the Spanish government can be seen at the Ministry of the Interior page on the terrorist group, which has the title "ETA—Murder as Argument." This web page is produced in three languages (Spanish, French, and English) to enable the widest reasonable readership of the arguments presented. One French view of the issues can be seen at the website of the Mediapaul Project.

In an example from Central America, the Zapatista rebels in the Chiapas region of Mexico have become one of the most successful examples of the use of information systems and communications by a hugely outnumbered and outresourced group of activists. The Zapatistas used the Internet to outmaneuver the Mexican government and to bring world pressure to bear on a situation that was entirely internal to Mexico. The use of the Internet gained the Zapatistas support not only from throughout Mexico but also from the rest of the world. It will also now be used as a template for actions in other parts of the world, and the implications of the Zapatista rebellion will have an effect on other confrontations with contemporary capitalist economic and political policies.

The surge of support for what Europeans and North Americans see as a very parochial action in a Central American republic came when a report written for Chase Emerging Markets clients by Riordan Roett was apparently leaked to Silverstein and Cockburn's *Counterpunch* newsletter. The report was found to call for the Mexican government to "eliminate" the Zapatistas in order to demonstrate its command over the internal situation in Mexico. When this news and the report were posted on the web, there was a worldwide reaction against the Mexican government, America, and the American bank that had commissioned the report.

Part of the response to this news was an increase in the hacking of Mexican government websites. In addition, the Electronic Disturbance Theater (EDT) released what they referred to as a digital translation of the Zapatista Air Force Action, which they called the Zapatista tribal port scan. This was carried out to commemorate a nonelectronic act that involved, on January 3, 2000, the Zapatista Air Force's "bombarding" of the Mexican Army federal barracks with hundreds of paper airplanes on each of which was written a message for the soldiers monitoring the border.

Despite the fact that the action in the Chiapas region has effectively been under way since 1994, there is still support and online action such as that by the EDT in 2001.

In the former Soviet Union, the situation with regard to the ongoing conflict in Chechnya is one that the media is now starting to class as an "information war." The Chechen separatists are represented on the Internet primarily by two sites, one from the Chechen Republic of Ichkeria and the other from Kavkaz-Tsentr. The Ichkeria site is seldom updated, but the Kavkaz-Tsentr is reported as an example of a professional approach to information war. This site is kept up-to-date with daily reports on Chechen military successes against Russian forces as well as more light-hearted items and the events that surround Chechnya.

According to numerous reports from organizations, including the BBC, Moscow is applying the same tactics that it observed NATO using in the former Republic of Yugoslavia to try to win the information war in Chechnya. In the previous Chechen war, which started in 1994, the then-fledgling commercial station NTV showed graphic pictures from both sides of the conflict. Now, however, the Russian broadcasters and press are much more selective in the reporting of the fighting.

The Kavkaz-Tsentr site has repeatedly been targeted by hacker attacks since at least 1999. The hackers have defaced the website with anti-Chechen images and slogans and have redirected traffic intended for the site to a Russian Information Center site. However the site has normally managed to restore normal operations within 24 hours.

Vigilantes and the Reaction to the World Trade Center and Pentagon Attacks

This discussion has been included here because the case that will be highlighted shows the dangers of "vigilantes" and people who, for the best of intentions, take actions for which they have not researched the background information. The action in question was reported by Brian McWilliam of *Newsbytes* on September 27, 2001, who revealed that members of a coalition of vigilante hackers had mistakenly defaced a website of an organization that had offices in the World Trade Center. The hacker group, called the Dispatchers, attacked the website of the Special Risks Terrorism Team, which in fact was owned by the Aon Corporation. The other sites that were attacked by this group were both in Iran, which of course is not in Afghanistan and is in fact hostile to the Taliban regime and Osama Bin Laden. One can understand the anger and the frustration and the desire to strike out in the aftermath of the attacks, but this type of action, by uninformed and unrepresentative individuals does much to damage relationships with countries and organizations that have not (at least in recent years) caused any offense and are in fact sympathetic to the cause.

Denial of Service

When a terrorist organization cannot achieve its objective by its normal means, the bullet and the bomb, it has the potential to use the Internet and the connectivity of the systems on which we now rely so heavily to achieve the desired impact. There are a number of advantages and disadvantages to this approach, but being unable to use the normal techniques allows another vector of attack to be utilized that has the advantages of being both untraceable to the source and nonlethal.

When compared to the average activity of a hacker, who has a limited capability in terms of equipment and sustainability, the terrorist will normally have a greater depth of resources and of motivation. An action taken by a believer in support of a cause will have a much higher motivation to succeed than the whim of an idle mind or simple curiosity.

What Is a Denial-of-Service Attack?

A denial-of-service attack is characterized by an attempt by an attacker or attackers to prevent legitimate users of a service from accessing that service. Types of denial-of-service attacks that may be seen include:

- Network flooding, resulting in the prevention of legitimate network traffic
- Attempts to disrupt connections between two machines, which results in the prevention of access to a service
- Attempts to prevent a particular individual from accessing a service
- Attempts to disrupt service to or from a specific system or person

Not all disruptions to service, even those that result from malicious activity, are necessarily denial-of-service attacks. Other types of attack may include a denial of service as a component, but the denial of service itself may be part of a larger attack.

The unauthorized use of resources may also result in a denial of service. For example, an intruder might make use of your anonymous ftp area as a location to store illegal copies of software, using up disk space, using CPU time, and generating network traffic that consumes bandwidth.

The Impact

Denial-of-service attacks can disable either the computer or the network. This can neutralize the effectiveness of your organization. Denial-of-service attacks can be carried out with limited resources against large, sophisticated, or complex sites. This type of attack may be an *asymmetric attack*, that is, an attack where a less capable adversary takes on an enemy with superior resources or capabilities. For example, an attacker using an old PC and a slow modem might be able to attack and overcome a much faster and more sophisticated computer or network.

Types of Attack

Denial-of-service attacks can manifest themselves in a number of forms and be targeted at a range of services. There are primarily three types of such attacks:

- *Destruction or alteration of configuration information for a system or network*: An incorrectly configured computer may not operate in the intended way or operate at all. An intruder may be able to alter or destroy the configuration information and prevent the user from accessing his or her computer or network. For example, if an intruder can change information in your routers, the network may not work effectively or at all. If an intruder is able to change the registry settings on a Windows NT machine, the system may cease to operate or certain functions may be unavailable.
- *Consumption of precious resources*: Computers and networks need certain facilities and resources in order to operate effectively. This includes network bandwidth, disk space, CPU time, applications, data structures, network connectivity, and environmental resources such as power and air conditioning.
- *Physical destruction or modification of network elements*: The primary problem with this type of attack is physical security. In order to protect against this type of attack, it is necessary to defend against any unauthorized direct access to the elements of your system, whether they be the computers, routers, network elements, or power and air conditioning supplies or any other components that are critical to the network. Physical security is one of the main defenses used in protecting against a number of different types of attacks in addition to denial of service.

Denial-of-service attacks are normally targeted against the network elements. The technique normally employed in an attack is to prevent the host from communicating across the network. One example is the "SYN flood" attack. In this type of attack, the attacker initiates the process of establishing a connection to the victim's machine, in a way that prevents the completion of the connection sequence. During this process, the machine that is the target of the attack has reserved one of a limited number of data structures required to complete the impending connection. The result is that legitimate connections cannot be achieved while the victim machine is waiting to complete bogus "half-open" connections.

This type of attack does not depend on the attacker's being able to consume your network bandwidth. By this method, the intruder is engaging and keeping busy the kernel data structures involved in establishing a network connection. The effect is that an attacker can execute an effective attack against a system on a very fast network with very limited resources.

According to a report posted on May 23, 2001, the Computer Emergency Response Team/Coordination Center (CERT/CC), one of the most important reporting centers for Internet security problems, was offline for a number of periods during Tuesday and Wednesday as a result of a distributed denial-of-service attack.

The CERT/CC posted a notice on its website on Tuesday saying that the site had been under attack since 11:30 a.m. EST that day and that, as a result, at frequent intervals either it was unavailable or access to the site was very slow. The CERT/CC is a government-funded computer security research and development (R&D) center based at Carnegie Mellon University. The site monitors Internet security issues, such as hacking, vulnerabilities, and viruses, and issues warnings about such issues and incidents.

According to the report, the organization was still be able to conduct its business and had not lost any data. The center issues warnings and sends alerts through e-mail. News of the attack on CERT/CC came on the day after researchers at the University of California at San Diego issued a report stating that over 4,000 DoS attacks take place every week.

A distributed denial-of-service attack, such as the one experienced by the CERT/CC, comes when an attacker has gained control of a number of PCs, referred to as *zombies*, and uses them simultaneously to attack the victim.

According to an unclassified document published November 10 by the NIPC, technologies such as Internet relay chat (IRC), web-based bulletin boards, and free e-mail accounts enable extremist groups to adopt a structure that has become known as *leaderless resistance*. Some extremist groups have adopted the leaderless resistance model, in part to "limit damage from penetration by authorities" that are seeking information about impending attacks.

According to the report, which was prepared by NIPC cyberterrorism experts, "An extremist organization whose members get guidance from e-mails or by visiting a secure website can operate in a coordinated fashion without its members ever having to meet face to face."

In addition to providing a means of secure communications, the range and diversity of Internet technologies also provide extremists with the means to deliver a "steady stream of propaganda" intended to influence public opinion and also as a means of recruitment.

The increasing technical competency of extremists also enables them to launch more serious attacks on the network infrastructure of a nation-state that go beyond e-mail bombing and web page defacements, according to the NIPC.

According to a separate article on international terrorism by a professor at Georgetown University, the leaderless resistance strategy is believed to have been originally identified in 1962 by Col. Ulius Amos, an anti-Communist activist, and this approach was advocated, in 1992, by a neo-Nazi activist, Louis Beam.

Lessons Learned

There are many lessons for the InfoSec professional to learn from the September 11, 2001, attacks on the World Trade Center. The lessons are based on the lack of security and defenses indicated by the successful attacks, e.g., airport security, aircraft security. As an InfoSec professional, it is clear that some of the most basic processes that can assist in making your networks and information more secure from all those who threaten them are ignored, including the following.

- Users are often allowed access without pre-employment background checks; after they no longer need access, their IDs and passwords remain on the system.
- InfoSec personnel are often overworked and otherwise too busy to follow up periodically to determine if the accesses are still required. They rely on the users (or company management) to "turn themselves in" when they no longer need access or leave the company or government agency.
- Physical access to facilities and IT devices—e.g., desktop computers networked to local area networks, the Internet, intranets—is weak or nonexistent.
- Often InfoSec responsibilities are given to employees as an "additional job," with little or no training, e.g., a records clerk in a hospital making almost minimum wage.
- Employees are not checked as they carry removable media out of the facility; sometimes they are not even checked and the authority verified when carrying hardware out of the facility.
- Networks and computer devices are poorly secured.
- InfoSec budget is kept to a minimum in order to save money or spend it on other, "higher priorities."
- And, of course, the constant spreading of computer viruses.

   What we can learn from this horrendous tragedy is at least the following.

- Prior to access to IT devices that store, transmit, or process sensitive information, a background check of an individual must be conducted, and accesses must be verified and validated on a regular basis.
- Physical security of facilities should be hardened.
- One must aggressively follow up where there are vulnerabilities or where personnel are not complying with the InfoSec policies, procedures, and processes.
- Profiling of users must be done to determine their normal work habits; those operating outside the norm must be aggressively investigated.
- InfoSec is important and must accordingly have sufficient budget to do a proper job.
- InfoSec staff should be highly trained, certified, and paid accordingly.
- InfoSec professionals must always be alert to potential attacks and be in a position to defend successfully against those attacks and plan for the unexpected.
- A current and often-tested emergency/disaster recovery/contingency plan must be in place, and all applicable personnel must be trained in what to do in the event of various incidents.

- InfoSec professionals must understand, especially in the United States, that the world has drastically changed and is a more dangerous and inhospitable place—we are at war. Get on an InfoSec "war footing."

Also remember that:

- A second Pearl Harbor has occurred, and the warnings of a coming electronic Pearl Harbor may not be far off, and you may be a victim.
- You've seen what global terrorists can do to the world financial community through their attack on the World Trade Center. Imagine what they could do by means of "electronic bombing" of the world's financial computer networks.

The increased threat of global terrorism is real, and sooner or later they will use cyber-space weapons, and your systems may be one of their targets. They already are computer literate and somewhat sophisticated in the use of computers. Don't let your information and networks become an easy target for cyberterrorists and techno-terrorists.

Authors

This appendix was written by Andy Jones, Business Manager, Secure e-Business, QinetiQ (formerly known as DERA/MOD), Malvern, UK; and Dr. Gerald L. Kovacich, ShockwaveWriters.com. It contains excerpts from their book *Introduction to Global Information Warfare*, written with Lt. Col. Perry Luzwick and Information Warfare and Information Assurance specialist, U.S. Dept. of Defense retired and Information Assurance Manager, Northrop Grumman Corporation, published by Auerbach Publishers in March 2002. Attack information was taken from the infowar.com website archives for the month of September 2001.

- Definition of *terrorism* adopted by the gateway model, United Nations, Spring, 1995.
- http://www.inlink.com/~civitas/mun/res9596/terror.htm
- *Al-Tawhid, A Quarterly Journal of Islamic Thought and Culture* article: "Towards a Definition of Terrorism" by Ayatollah Muhammad 'Ali Tashkiri.
- *Bin Laden: Steganography Master?* by Declan McCullagh, Feb. 7. 2001.
- *Bin Laden's name raised again—A primer on America's intelligence archenemies,* by Robert Windrem.
- "Terrorist Instructions Hidden Online," *USA Today*, by Jack Kelly, June 19, 2001.
- "Terror Groups Hide Behind Web Encryption," *USA Today*, by Jack Kelley, June 19, 2001.
- Webopedia definition from: http://webopedia.internet.com/TERM/S/slack_space.html
- StegFS homepage can now be found at: http://www.mcdonald.org.uk/StegFS/
- Air Force Research Laboratories, http://www.afrl.af.mil/if.html
- Sinn Fein website: http://www.sinnfein.ie/
- Sinn Fein Online http://www.geocities.com/sinnfeinonline/

- http://www.geocities.com/diarmidlogan/
- http://www.csc.tcd.ie/~sinnfein/
- http://www.irsm.org/irsp/
- http://www.ulsterloyalist.co.uk/welcome.htm
- http://www.houstonpk.freeserve.co.uk/uvfpg.htm
- Rich Geib's Universe: http://www.rjgeib.com/thoughts/terrorist/response1.html
- Irish Republican Army information site: http://www.geocities.com/CapitolHill/Congress/2435/120.
- Vincent Morley's Flag web page: http://www.fotw.stm.it/flags/gb-ulste.html
- Unionist Murals from Belfast: http://www.geocities.com/Heartland/Meadows/7985/mural.html
- *The Basque Journal*: http://free.freespeech.org/ehj/html/freta.html
- *Basque Red Net*: http://www.basque-red.net/cas/enlaces/e-eh/mlnv.htm
- Spanish Ministry of the Interior web page: http://www.mir.es/oris/infoeta/indexin.htm
- http://www.ac-versailles.fr/etabliss/plapie/MediaBasque2001.html#ancre45175
- Electronic Disturbance Theater website: http://www.thing.net/rdom/ecd/ecd.html
- Kavkaz Tsentr website: www.kavkaz.org
- "Hacking Vigilantes Deface WTC Victim's Site," by Brian McWilliam, *Newsbytes*, Sept. 17, 2001.
- "CERT goes down to DoS attacks," by Sam Costello, IDG News Service, May 23, 2001.
- The NIPC publication is available at: http://www.nipc.gov/publications/highlights/2001/highlight-01-10.pdf

Appendix D
Letter Bomb Checklists

Watch Out For:
- Small packets bearing an unusual postmark
- Small packets with no return address
- Any small books arriving

Do Not:
- Move any strange or suspicious letters or packets
- Drop the letter in water
- Try to open the envelope with a paper knife or letter opener

Do:
- Isolate it
- Evacuate the room and alert the staff
- Call corporate security
- Call the police

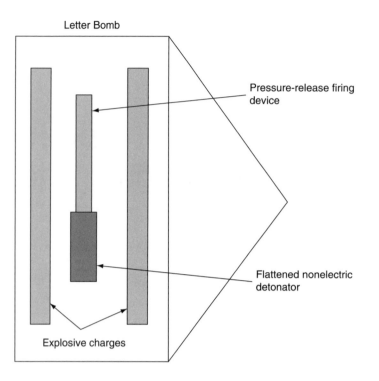

Letter Bomb

Pressure-release firing device

Flattened nonelectric detonator

Explosive charges

FIGURE D-1 Structure of a typical letter bomb.

Letter Bomb

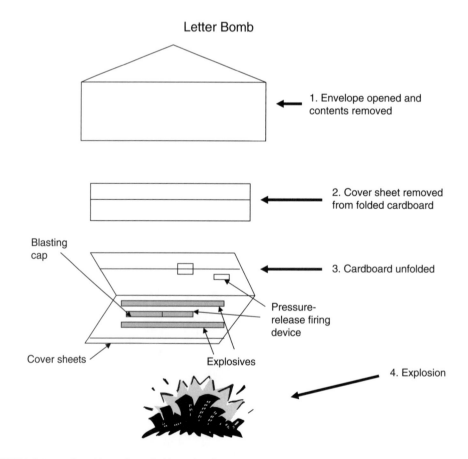

1. Envelope opened and contents removed

2. Cover sheet removed from folded cardboard

3. Cardboard unfolded

Blasting cap

Pressure-release firing device

Cover sheets

Explosives

4. Explosion

FIGURE D-2 Internal workings of a typical letter bomb.

Index

About the Authors

Edward Halibozek: Mr. Halibozek has been employed by a Fortune 100 company for more than 20 years and is currently the Vice President of Corporate Security. He is currently a member of the Board of Directors for the Chief Special Agents Association in Los Angeles California and a member of the American Society for Industrial Security. Mr. Halibozek served four years (1997–2000) as an industry member on the National Industrial Security Program Policy Advisory Committee (NISPPAC). He holds a bachelor of science degree and master of science degree in criminal justice from California State University, Long Beach. He also earned an MBA from Pepperdine University, Malibu, California. Mr. Halibozek is the coauthor of three books, all for Elsevier's Butterworth-Heinemann.

Dr. Andy Jones: During a full military career Andy Jones directed both intelligence and security operations and briefed the results at the highest level and was awarded the MBE for his service in Northern Ireland. After 25 years of service with the British Army's Intelligence Corps, he became a business manager and a researcher and analyst in the area of information warfare and computer crime at a defense research establishment. In 2002, on completion of a paper on a method for the metrication of the threats to information systems, he left the defense environment to take up a post as a principal lecturer at the University of Glamorgan in the subjects of network security and computer crime and as a researcher on the threats to information systems and computer forensics. At the university he developed and managed a well-equipped computer forensics laboratory and took the lead on a number of computer investigations and data recovery tasks. He holds a PhD in the area of threats to information systems and is a member of MENSA. In January 2005 he joined the Security Research Centre at British Telecommunications, where he is currently the head of security technology research. Dr. Jones is the coauthor of three books, two of which are published by Elsevier's Butterworth-Heinemann.

Dr. Gerald L. Kovacich: Dr. Kovacich received his undergraduate degree in Asian history and politics from the University of Maryland, his graduate degrees in public administration and telecommunications management from Northern Colorado University and Golden Gate University, as well as a doctorate in criminology from August Vollmer University. Prior to his retirement as a security professional, he was a Certified Fraud Examiner (CFE), a Certified Protection Professional (CPP), and a Certified Information Systems Security Professional (CISSP). Dr. Kovacich has over 40 years of experience in counterintelligence/counterespionage, security, asset protection, criminal and civil investigations, antifraud operations, information warfare, and information systems security experience for the U.S. government as a special agent and as a manager for several international technology-based corporations. He is an international lecturer and consultant on these topics as well as the author or coauthor of 14 other security-related books, 11 of which are with Elsevier's Butterworth-Heinemann. Dr. Kovacich continues to write and conduct research relative to these topics.